Building Outdoor Furniture
Third Edition

Percy W. Blandford

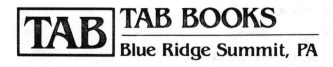

TAB BOOKS
Blue Ridge Summit, PA

THIRD EDITION
FIRST PRINTING

© 1992 by **TAB Books**.
Earlier editions © 1983 and 1988 by **TAB Books**.
TAB Books is a division of McGraw-Hill, Inc.

Library of Congress Cataloging-in-Publication Data

Blandford, Percy W.
   Building outdoor furniture / by Percy W. Blandford.—3rd ed.
     p.   cm.
   Rev. ed. of: Designing and building outdoor furniture, with 57
projects. 2nd ed. 1988.
   Includes index.
   ISBN 0-8306-4044-4 (p)
   1. Outdoor furniture—Design and construction. I. Blandford,
Percy W. Designing and building outdoor furniture, with 57
projects. II. Title.
TT197.5.09B58 1992
684.1'8—dc20   92-769
                                     CIP

TAB Books offers software for sale. For information and a catalog, please contact
TAB Software Department, Blue Ridge Summit, PA 17294-0850.

Acquisition Editor: Kimberly Tabor
Book Editor: Steve Moro
Director of Production: Katherine G. Brown
Book Design: Jaclyn J. Boone
Cover Design and Illustration: Graphics Plus, Hanover, PA   HT3

Contents

Introduction

If the climate where you live allows you to spend time outdoors for worthwhile periods, you need furniture intended for use in the open air. You can make all the furniture you need, and construct it to fit your needs. Each will be an individual product of which you can be proud, as it differs from quantity-produced pieces.

The greatest need is for seating, of which there can be a great variety. This is followed by tables, but there are many other items you can make for yard, patio, deck or garden. Making outdoor furniture has much in common with making indoor furniture. It tends to be more substantial, and construction is simpler. Solid wood features almost exclusively, but much indoor furniture makes great use of manufactured boards. You can make much outdoor furniture with hand tools only, but power tools have some advantages, including taking some of the labor out of the work.

You can make some outdoor furniture by merely nailing or screwing, but cutting and gluing joints is more satisfying. While comparatively crude construction would suffice for some things, using cut and fitted joints for most furniture will produce things to be proud of that can be expected to last a long time.

In the following pages the early chapters provide some basic information on design and techniques; then the remainder of the book is made up of instructions on projects. There are chapters to provide groupings, but aspects of some furniture could be appropriate to more than one chapter, so if you want to learn about a particular type of furniture, look through the whole book. Several designs could be adaptable to other sizes and uses, so you can treat this as an ideas book as well as instructions on specific projects.

For each project you should find adequate drawings and instructions. Read through and relate instructions to drawings. As you progress, try to always visualize the move after the next. In that way, you can ensure doing whatever is needed as it is required. All sizes are in inches, unless stated otherwise. In the Materials Lists, widths and thicknesses are finished sizes, but most lengths are full to allow for trimming and cutting joints. In most projects wood of near sizes would be acceptable, providing you allow for the differences in marking out and cutting joints.

This third edition contains 12 all new projects, and a selection of favorites from the popular first edition.

1
Design

Furniture for outdoor use serves many of the same purposes as furniture for use indoors but presents several special considerations as well. It might occasionally be possible to use indoor furniture outdoors, but you will soon discover that it is not the best for the purpose. Outdoor furniture tends to get rough treatment. Quality indoor furniture would suffer if used very much outdoors. Indoor furniture is not usually designed to withstand dampness and dirt. Excessive sunlight will damage its finish. This is particularly true for any upholstery. The finish put on indoor furniture will not always stand up to outdoor conditions, and the glue used might soon deteriorate.

Outdoor furniture should be specially designed. There might be a few items that you could take indoors for use, but it is better to regard open air as outdoor furniture's normal environment. That does not mean outdoor furniture should be massive and crude. Some of it fits that description, but other items qualify as fine specimens of cabinetwork as much as indoor furniture. Outdoor furniture does not have to be uncomfortable. Some of it can be simple and rather basic, but if its proportions are right, it will give all the comfort you need. Attached upholstery cannot be used on furniture that will have to stay outside in rain, but much can be done with cushions that can be taken indoors.

Sizes and Proportions

No matter how much skill is lavished on a piece of furniture, it is wasted if a chair is too high to allow your feet to reach the ground, or a table is too high or low to be used when you are seated. Sizes and proportions have to be right. Fortunately, most of us are of average size; a furniture size that is right for the majority will suit us. One advantage of making your own furniture is that you can alter sizes to suit individuals. If you have someone very tall or very short in the family, you can alter the dimensions to afford them the same comfort that the average person gets with average equipment.

For sitting upright, make the support around 16 inches from the floor. Reduce this to as low as 12 inches, or go up an inch or so; the height is about right when your thighs are horizontal. For something like fishing or tending a camp fire—where you have to lean forward or reach the ground—the height can come down to perhaps 10 inches, but that is not the height you want to sit at for long periods. Allow for the thickness of a cushion, if one is to be used, but remember, it is the compressed thickness that counts. Even quite a thick cushion goes down to about 1 inch under body weight.

If you are to sit upright for eating or working at a table, the seat should be big enough. At the front it can be 16 inches wide or more, and about the same back to front, but it could be an inch or two narrower at the rear (FIG. 1-1A). If you measure one of your indoor chairs, the proportions will be found to be much the same.

It is possible to manage with a smaller seat, but you will not want to sit on it too long. Stools should have tops no more than 10×6 inches. This is particularly true if they are intended to fold very compactly. Such a support could be valued as an alternative to standing or sitting on the ground, but it is a compromise (FIG. 1-1B).

With a rigid seat, allow for some padding. If it is a slung seat, made of canvas or other flexible material, the important height is near the point of greatest sag (FIG. 1-1C). The sling must support you under and around those two bits of hard bone in your posterior. It is surprising how little area of seat is needed.

In an upright position, most people want support for their backs if they are to sit for long. Stools or other backless seats are unsuitable for long use. Consider a chair back reaching high enough to support your shoulder blades, but for most outdoor furniture, support at the small of your back is sufficient. This means having the top about 15 inches above the seat (FIG. 1-1D). Then you have to consider its angle. A level seat and an upright back would not be comfortable. It is the angle of the part that fits into your back that counts. The arrangement of its support is not so important, providing that it is clear of your back. The part you rest against needs to slope back slightly; 10 degrees past vertical is about right (FIG. 1-1E).

With that sort of upright chair there will be a matching table. For a comfortable working or eating height, it will be somewhere between 27 inches and 30 inches from the floor (FIG. 1-1F). This will be just below the level of your elbows, when sitting, so you can reach comfortably over the table.

Consider some variations. If you make small folding stools and want a folding table to use with them, make it low to match their heights. Bring it down to as low as 20 inches (particularly if compactness of folding is important).

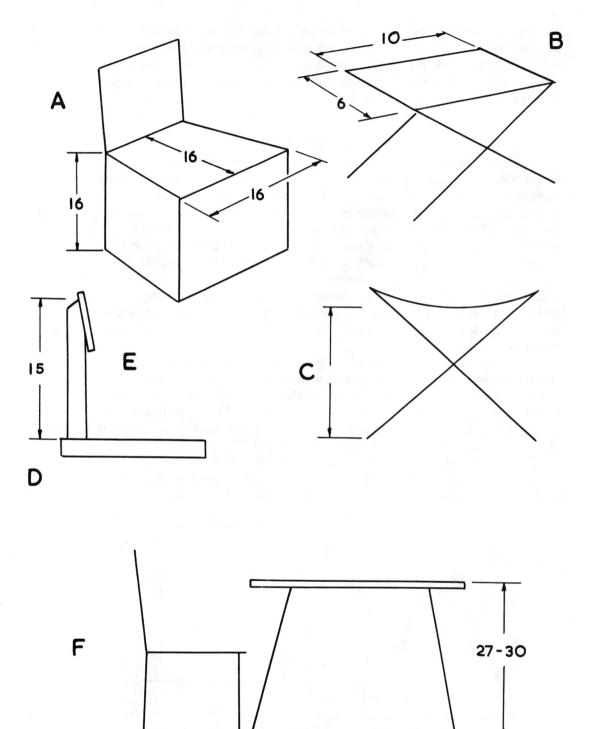

Fig. 1-1. Suggested average dimensions for various types of furniture.

The table area will be determined by your needs, but it should not be too small in relation to the height if it is to be freestanding; otherwise it will be unstable. If it is to be attached to the ground, that problem does not arise. For a freestanding table, particularly of lightweight construction, make its top sizes no less than the table height. In other words, the minimum size occupies a cube.

Lounging Seats

Much sitting in the open air can be described as lounging. If you do not want to sit at a table, the requirements of seating are very different. You do not need to sit so high, and you will want to lean back. It is the angle of your thighs that is crucial for comfort. The front edge can be nearly as high as for an upright seat, but your thighs slope back. How much of a slope depends on the degree of lounging. Back to front can be up to about 20 inches (or more) if cushions are to be included. Ideally, the slope of the back of the chair should be adjustable. In the most upright position, the back should be 10 degrees or so more than a right angle to the seat (FIG. 1-2A). Further angular positions can be set back, depending on how near a horizontal position you want to reach, but 45 degrees past perpendicular to the seat is a reasonable limit (FIG. 1-2B). With a fixed back, settle for a compromise position.

Lounging chairs exist without arms, but if you want to lean back and read or sew there is an advantage in having a chair with arms. The area contained in the arms and back needs to be large enough to allow body movement. If someone wants to curl up with their legs under them, there should be room. In any case, you do not want anything like a form-fitting chair. A seat of 20 inches square is about right, but it could be a few inches wider (FIG. 1-2C).

Usually the seat is parallel, but it could be slightly narrower at the back. The arms can be about 10 inches above the seat and can be slightly nearer it at the back (FIG. 1-2D). Many chairs have seat and arms parallel in the side view. The

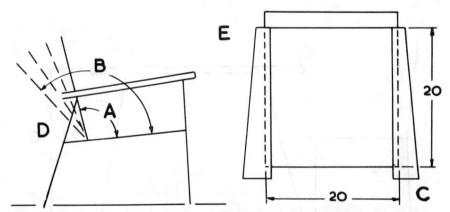

Fig. 1-2. An armchair can have different back angles and the legs can slope to give stability. The seat of an armchair is usually bigger than for a chair without arms.

arms should not restrict the seat, so they are usually parallel with it on their inner edges. They can taper back on the outer edges; this is largely for the sake of appearance (FIG. 1-2E).

Benches

Wider seats for two or three people have much in common with arm chairs or lounging seats, but they are usually arranged rather more upright. They are not as upright as chairs for use with tables—unless that is their purpose. The seat height is comparatively low, 14 inches to 16 inches, and deeper back to front than some chairs (probably 18 inches to 20 inches). The back is given a comfortable slope, and it can go higher than a simple chair (FIG. 1-3A).

Comfort in a seat can be increased by giving it a curve. Some plastics are molded almost to figure form, but it is impractical to make a double curvature in wood. Instead, curve it back to front, usually made up with laths (FIG. 1-3B). Back supports are usually made of slats straight across (FIG. 1-3C). Shoulders accept straight support where a posterior is better fitted with a curve. Curve it across a back if slats are vertical on hollowed supports (FIG. 1-3D).

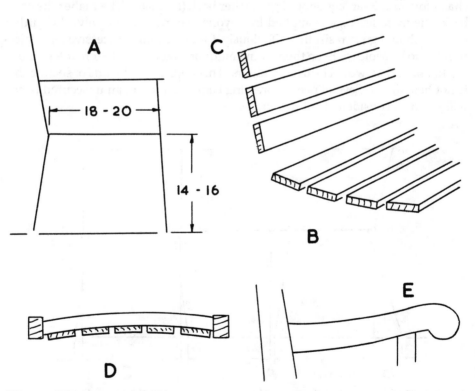

Fig. 1-3. The general sizes of a chair can be developed to allow for a curved seat, a slat back, and curves in the back and arms.

Arms do not have to be straight. Some shaping in the side view improves appearance; it actually conforms better to your arm resting with the elbow in the hollow and your wrists and hands over the curve. Shaping depends on the available equipment for cutting curves in fairly thick wood (FIG. 1-3E).

Stability

A chair, table, lounger, or other piece of furniture that will not stand steadily could be just an inconvenience or a definite danger. The design must be stable. If you are making things that will be attached to the ground, that takes care of stability—as far as falling over is concerned—but the structure could still be so fragile that it collapses.

On the whole, supports of anything should cover at least the same floor area as the top. Unfortunately, users of furniture do not just sit with their weight thrusting downward. Design furniture for hard use. Leaning back heavily in a chair is usual. Tilting a seat on two legs is common. Leaning or sitting on a table must be expected.

Examination of chairs in your home will show stability. Front legs need not be quite as far forward as the front of the seat (FIG. 1-4A). People do not tend to tilt chairs forward. Rear legs should go further back (FIG. 1-4B). The higher the chair back, the more leverage is applied by anyone leaning back heavily; the further the legs should go to resist this. Obviously, there are limits; excessive leg projection has to be avoided. Even then, some outdoor chairs have their rear legs much further back than would be usual indoors. This applies to all kinds of seating that is not held down. Several people pressing back together on an unsecured bench will put on a considerable tilting strain.

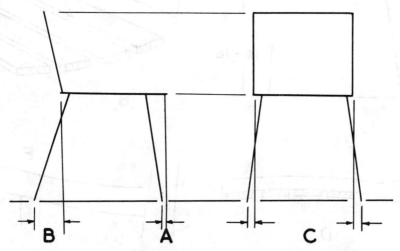

Fig. 1-4. The seat of a chair is arranged for convenience, but the legs splay outward to give stability in use.

When viewed from the front, there is less need for a great spread of legs because there is less tendency for a user to put on sideways loads. Nevertheless, it helps to have the spread of feet greater than the seat (FIG. 1-4C). This is particularly true if the seat is not very wide. A broad-arm chair is more stable because of its width.

Table supports should spread to come under the corners of the top, or very near that, whether there are separate corner legs, slab ends, or some other means of support. Much depends on size. A large tabletop will be tolerant of feet further in from the corners than would a small table that needs all the spread for stability that can be given.

Weight affects rigidity and stability. A massively constructed piece of furniture gains stability by its sheer weight, if it is of reasonable proportion. Examples are picnic tables with bench seats included alongside (all supported on heavy crossed legs). Some almost require a crane to move them.

Rigidity

Rigidity is the resistance of a structure to unintentionally fold or collapse. Stability is the resistance to tipping over. They are related, but rigidity is more the consideration of producing a structure where the parts provide mutual support, without necessarily being heavy—unless that is a requirement.

Resistance to deflection comes from triangulating. On a three-sided frame with loose joints (FIG. 1-5A), you cannot push it out of shape. If you have four pieces similarly joined, you can alter the shape easily (FIG. 1-5B). If you make the shape into two triangles by adding a diagonal, its shape cannot be altered (FIG. 1-5C). This is the principle that governs keeping structures in shape. It also applies to standing on uneven ground. A tripod will stand without wobbling. Four or more legs will not always stand firm with equal load on all legs. Tables and chairs do not lend themselves to three-legged construction, but three-legged stools are possibilities and a round table tabletop can have three legs.

Light frames can be held in shape with diagonal braces. A pair of legs can have one brace straight across near the feet and a diagonal above that (FIG. 1-5D). A diagonal at about 45 degrees provides the best bracing, but that is not always possible. A better bracing has two diagonal strips (FIG. 1-5E).

Some assemblies will appear to have four-sided frames, so there is no apparent triangulation, but that is not so if the joints are rigid. There is the effect of triangulation in the rails (FIG. 1-5F). The deeper a rail and its joints the more the triangulating effect. There is usually more than one rail, so triangulating occurs at both levels.

If the whole panel is solid wood, it obviously cannot be pushed out of shape (FIG. 1-5G). In effect, it is multiple triangulating. If a seat is made with many slats, each held by a single screw, the assembly could be pushed out of shape (FIG. 1-5H). If the joints are glued and two screws are spread at each joint (FIG. 1-5J), the assembly has a good resistance to distortion. A diagonal brace below would have

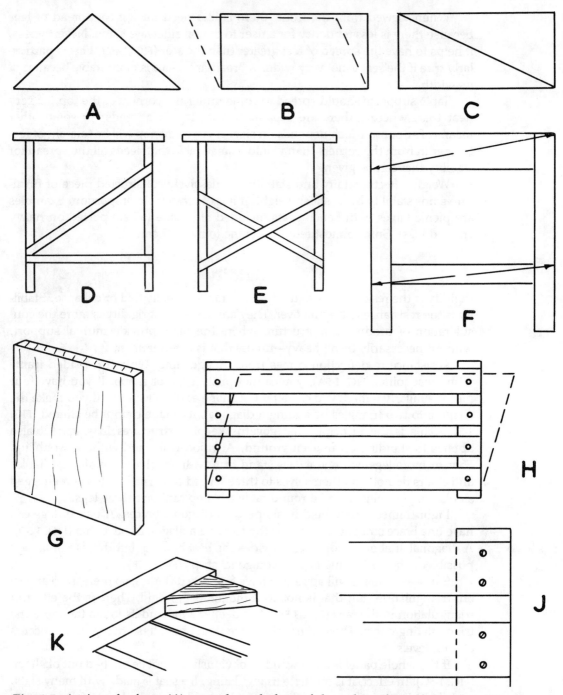

Fig. 1-5. *A triangular frame (A) cannot be pushed out of shape, but a four-sided one can (B) unless a diagonal divides it into triangles (C). This is seen in framing (D and E), but construction can provide an internal triangulation or the arrangement of nails or screws does the same (F through K).*

a similar effect, but that might not be practical. Corner blocks (FIG. 1-5K) would also resist distortion.

Crossed legs have a triangulating effect in themselves (FIG. 1-6A). Under a table they can be symmetrical, but they also can be altered to get better stability under a chair (FIG. 1-6B), with the rear foot coming further back.

If rails are added to an assembly, their stiffening effect can be judged. Suppose a lower rail or stretcher is to come low down between the ends of a table or bench. It might be put flat or on edge. In resistance to distorting the assembly lengthwise, it would be better on edge (FIG. 1-6C), where the triangulating effect would be wider. A flat rail would have negligible resistance (FIG. 1-6D).

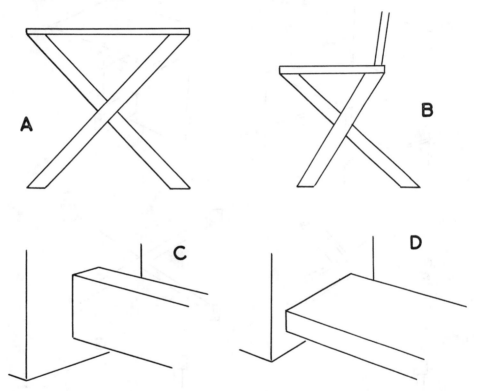

Fig. 1-6. *Rigidity is varied with leg arrangements (A and B). An upright stretcher (C) stiffens a table better than a flat one (D).*

Convenience

Some outdoor furniture might look good and be well made, yet not fulfill its purpose because it is impossible or inconvenient to use. Lower rails are necessary in many assemblies to give rigidity. Rails between front and back legs of a chair are not in the way of a sitter's legs, at whatever level they are put (FIG. 1-7A). Neither

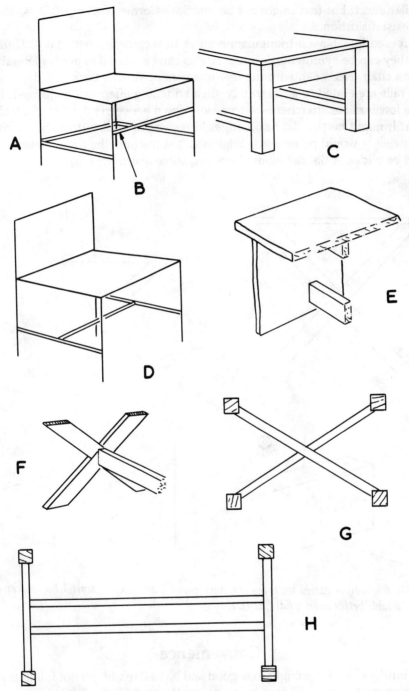

Fig. 1-7. *Rails and stretchers can be arranged in many ways to provide stiffness in the underframing of tables and chairs.*

would a back rail, but a low front rail—particularly in a chair used for sitting upright—would be a nuisance. A front rail could be high (FIG. 1-7B). The top rail could be deep, to give stiffness without the need for a lower one (FIG. 1-7C). Another arrangement has a crosswise rail between the side rails instead of the front legs (FIG. 1-7D) so that it is far enough back not to interfere with swinging legs.

A similar problem occurs with table rails. With slab ends, all the necessary bracing can come from a central stretcher (FIG. 1-7E). This leaves clearance for sitters' feet at each side. The crossed-leg sawbuck arrangement can also get all the stiffness needed from a central rail (FIG. 1-7F).

With corner table legs, stiffen with deep top rails only and dispense with lower rails. However, a sitter might not be able to get his knees under a deep rail. With the usual chairs and normal tables, you cannot have top rails deeper than about 5 inches, without meeting this problem.

Diagonal lower rails are kept away from feet (FIG. 1-7G), but then there are problems of strength on the crossing and the joints to the legs. Otherwise there can be similar arrangement to the chair, with the rail one way between the rails the other way, or even double rails (FIG. 1-7H). That still leaves rails far enough out to interfere with the feet of anyone sitting at the ends.

Appearance

Fitness for purpose is the main consideration in making outdoor furniture. Fortunately, if an item is functional and looks right, you can consider its appearance to be acceptable. In making furniture for use in the garden or yard, there is certainly no need to decorate for the sake of decoration.

There are some design considerations. A square is not considered as good looking as a rectangle. If you are making something that has a boxlike configuration, it looks better if all of its surfaces are longer one way than the other, and at no angle of viewing does the outline appear to be a square or cube. You may not consider that important in a functional piece of furniture, but if given the choice between a rectangle or a square, choose to make the item rectangular.

Curves are considered better looking than straight lines. Include many straight lines—wood construction is more easily done with straight pieces of wood—but consider adding curves. The arms of a chair can include curves. As the most prominent feature, curves will have a softening effect on the whole design. Cut the top of a chair back with a curve, and it will look better than with a straight edge. It is possible to cut curves into straight edges. This can also be functional, as at the bottom of a bench end, where the curve produces feet at the corners. A rectangular cutout would be less pleasing.

Color has a place in design. Do you want to draw attention to the piece of furniture, or would you rather it was inconspicuous? Most hardwoods left untreated will soon weather so they blend into their surroundings. At the other extreme, you might want to paint the wood in bright colors. Against the mainly green background of foliage, red and yellow are the colors that stand out. Paint your work bright red if you want it to shout, "Look, I made it!" Such a color might match the paintwork of an adjoining building and be justified.

Typical colors for furniture in a formal or cultivated garden or on a well-kept lawn are white and green. White looks attractive and inviting, but it needs to be kept clean, and you will have to touch up the paint frequently. Fortunately, there is no problem in matching the color. Green can be more of a problem for touching up. Supposedly there are more shades of green than any other color.

Treatments with linseed and other oils will preserve the wood as well as give it a mellow appearance. But oil takes some time to dry and you will not be thanked if someone gets it on their clothes. Varnish is another finish that lets you see the wood grain, but it must be the best quality outdoor varnish; that means asking for boat varnish. Then give the wood at least three coats. Be prepared to touch up as necessary or the wood rubbed bare will stain, and you cannot put that right.

Folding

All of the design considerations affecting rigid furniture have to be kept in mind when you are planning furniture to take apart or fold. Usually, folding furniture has to be light for portability. Select wood with reasonably straight grain and without flaws. There will be little margin to take care of weak parts.

The important thing concerning folding furniture is that there must be no fear of it folding or collapsing in use. When you are using it, you should be able to treat it in the same way as rigid furniture. Whatever locks the parts in place must always do so. Ideally there should be no loose parts. Loose pegs and other things can be lost and then the assembly cannot be put together. Worse are nuts and bolts that have to be taken out and wrenches are needed to tighten them.

Some folding furniture is never disassembled. Before making anything with the inherent complication of folding, consider if a rigid item might serve just as well.

Practicality

Designs in this book cover all manner of construction. If you do not think your skill level is appropriate, find a simpler construction technique for something serving the same purpose. When you design something yourself, think through all the steps in construction. Much of the skill in making anything is in anticipating the move after the next. Will you have all the tools needed for what you want to do? If not, it might be possible to buy wood already machined to suit, or you might have to pay someone to do work for you. Will that be worthwhile or is there some other way of achieving the same ends with your own tools and skills?

It is very easy to come up with a design that needs a different section of wood for almost every part. If you have your own circular saw and jointer, that might not matter, but if you have to pay for wood to be machined to many sizes it will be expensive. It is better to discover what stock sizes your supplier can provide and design at least most of the project around those sizes. Remember that bought planed wood is usually about $1/8$ inch under the specified size. It will not matter, for instance, if wood is $2^7/8$ inches wide or 3 inches wide, but if you insist on a finished size of 3 inches you will pay much more for it.

Do not underrate your own skill. If you have the tools necessary, tackle work you have not done before. It will take much longer for you to cut a particular joint than it would take an expert, but having plenty of time is an advantage for an amateur. You will experience a greater sense of achievement from being able to look at a piece of craftsmanship that incorporates a new skill than if you accepted some simpler alternative.

2

Tools and materials

The making of outdoor furniture is a branch of woodworking that embraces a large range of methods of construction. Considerable variations in the skills are needed, as well as in the equipment required. Opportunities for using woods exist that would not be suitable for use indoors. It is possible to use wood almost straight from the tree. At the other extreme are pieces of outdoor furniture made of woods that might also be used for indoor furniture. Some of the first woods can be made into crude, but satisfactory; furniture with very few tools and little precision. These tools and techniques would not be suitable for high-class work done with lumber that has been seasoned, planed, and made with cabinetwork joints.

There is no one tool kit to be recommended to anyone planning to make outdoor furniture. You have to consider what sort of work you intend to do.

In general, it is far better to work with a small collection of good tools than with a larger number of inferior ones. Also, consider a choice of tool for the same purpose. For instance, buy a pump-action screwdriver that certainly puts screws in quickly. However, for the same price, you could buy several plain screwdrivers of different sizes, that would be of more use to you.

Saws

Most of the cutting to size will be done by hand. A circular saw, either a portable one or one mounted in a saw bench, is useful, but it would not be a first priority in buying. Instead a good *handsaw* or *panel saw* about 20-inches long and with about 8 teeth per inch will do most cutting (FIG. 2-1A). Notice that the teeth are set in alternate directions, so the groove they cut is wider than the metal from which the saw is made. This *kerf* prevents the saw from binding in a deep cut—particularly important if there is still sap in the wood. Normal teeth are a diamond shape; these are designed for cutting across the grain. *Ripsaws* look the same, but their teeth are more upright on their leading edges, so they cut more efficiently along the grain; it should not be necessary to get one of these. The small amount of cutting along the grain can be done with cross-grain teeth.

For finer work consider a *backsaw*, 10 inches or 12-inches long, with a stiffening piece along the back. Teeth can be as fine as 16 per inch. A backsaw is the bench saw; it does not tear the grain much. In order to cut grooves across wood or make mortise and tenon joints, you must have a backsaw.

Use a panel saw with the wood supported at about knee height. Make a trestle, or use an old chair. Hold the wood with one knee while making cuts downward. Some sawing with the panel saw can be better done with the wood upright in a vise. Joint cutting with a backsaw can be done with the wood in a vise or held against a bench hook (FIG. 2-1B). Such a hook is easily made. A bench with a good vise helps in doing accurate work. Any table-size structure will do. Rigidity, and a front edge stiff enough and strong enough to stand up to hammering and planing is essential.

If you want to make furniture from natural wood—either slabs cut from logs or pieces of poles—the wood will probably still have sap in it. A saw suitable for dry, seasoned wood would not cut far without binding and coming to a halt. The saw teeth have to be fairly coarse and be given more set than the other saws, so that they make a wider kerf as they progress through the wood. Also, provide deep gullets at intervals to clear away sawdust (FIG. 2-1C). Saws are made with these teeth that look like panel saws, but it is more usual to have the blade narrow and tensioned in a tubular frame.

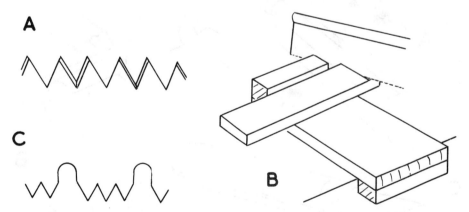

Fig. 2-1. Crosscut saw teeth are sharpened to points opposite ways to sever wood fibers (A). A bench hook is convenient for sawing parts (B). Saws for green wood can have gullets between groups of teeth to clear sawdust (C).

Chisels and Knives

For any sort of furniture you will need edge-cutting tools. In most situations, the tool of choice is a chisel; they are available in many widths. The general-purpose ones can be described as *firmer* chisels. Long thin ones are *paring* chisels; these are not meant to be hit and you are unlikely to need them. If you are buying new chisels, start with 1/2-inch wide and 1-inch wide chisels. The simplest chisels have square edges. Others have wide bevel edges. See FIG. 2-2A. With little difference in price, get bevel edges because they will do all the square edges well, and get closer into corners that are less than square.

For cutting mortise and tenon joints, it is helpful to have chisels the same width as the mortises. Usually, mortises are one-third the width of the wood. Much of your wood will be between 2 inches and 3 inches wide. There will be uses for 5/8-inch and 3/4-inch chisels. A very wide chisel is useful for paring broad surfaces, and you might want one that is 1 1/2 inches wide.

Modern chisels mostly have plastic handles that can be hit with a hammer without much risk of damage. Wood handles are better hit with a wooden mallet. In any case, a mallet has uses during assembly of many structures. The mallet can be quite crude, and it can be homemade.

A tool dealer has many different types of chisels. You will probably never need most of the special ones. A chisel curved in cross section is called a *gouge*. Delay buying one until you find a definite need for it. If it is sharpened on the inside of the curve, it is called *in-canelled* and is used for paring concave edges. If

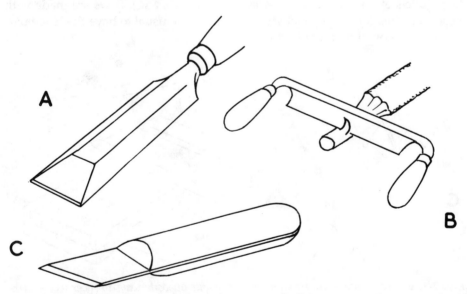

Fig. 2-2. A chisel can be bevel-edged (A). A draw knife cuts as it is pulled (B). A marking knife is sharpened on its end (C).

it is sharpened on the outside it is *out-canelled* and is used for removing waste from hollows.

There are uses for a good knife. It might be a hunting knife or a clasp knife. It is important to keep it sharp enough for whittling cuts. If you want to do upholstery with foam filling, a carving knife is the tool for cutting that material.

In some types of outdoor furniture, natural poles have to be tapered to go into holes to make something like a dowel joint. The traditional tool for tapering the ends is a *draw knife*. The wood has to be held in a vise or by other means. Then the tool is used in both hands to make cuts toward you (FIG. 2-2B). The edge is bevelled on one side—like a chisel. If it is used with the bevel downward, regulate the depth of cut by altering the angle of the handles.

If that is not the type of woodwork you want to do, but would prefer the cutting of joints in prepared wood, there is a use for a *marking knife*. It has its cutting edge at the end, and it could be made from a broken table knife (FIG. 2-2C). This is used, instead of a pencil, when marking a part of a joint that has to be sawn across the grain. As the knife severs the grain fibers, a much cleaner edge is left if the saw kerf is arranged against the waste side of the line.

Planes

Whether you need many planes or not depends on the types of furniture you want to make and in what state you obtain the wood. If you have a jointer or other power planer, deal with wood bought from the saw. Buy your wood already planed. If you only want to make rustic furniture from poles, you don't need a plane.

Machine-planed wood has a series of tiny ridges across the grain. The size depends on the coarseness of cut and how fast the wood was passed over the cutters. For much furniture, that sort of finish is all that is needed. For a better surface, hand plane the power plane marks away.

The most commonly used hand plane is the Stanley or Record *smoothing plane* (described as 4 or $4^{1}/2$ or a wider one). That should be the first plane you buy. It is intended for planing along the grain with fine cuts, but you can use it for trimming across the grain. With its mouth adjusted widely, it can be set coarse to take off thick shavings.

If you want to plane surfaces and edges straight, the plane should have a longer sole, to span inequalities. A very long plane is called a *fore* or *jointer*; your second plane could be the intermediate size called a jack plane. Occasionally, you need to straighten edges; it is easier to do with a long plane than with the shorter smoothing plane.

Another useful plane is the little *block plane*. Available in several versions, they are intended to be used in one hand. The block plane is used for dealing with a ragged end or to take the sharpness off the angle between two surfaces. Also, you can pick it up for small cuts.

A *spokeshave* is something like a plane. Its blade is in a narrow surface, controlled by a handle at each side. It is the tool for following curves, such as the shaped edge of a board. The modern metal version works like a plane. An older type has a blade something like a small draw knife, and it makes more of a slicing cut.

Sharpening

Everyone who has cutting tools should have the means and know-how to sharpen. A skilled man will pause for sharpening much more frequently.

Most edge tools, of the plane and chisel type, will have two bevels (FIG. 2-3A). The long bevel is put there by grinding. The short bevel is made on an *oilstone* or *whetstone*. The edge can be revived a great many times on the oilstone, but when its bevel gets very long, the tool is ground again. Therefore, you start with just a narrow bevel again on the oilstone.

Grinding can be done on a high-speed electric stone, but avoid overheating and keep the bevel true. Dip it frequently in water to cool the steel. If rainbow colors appear on the steel, that is a sign of overheating, which has drawn the temper (softened the steel). Professional grinding is done on a slower, larger stone that is kept wet. The need for grinding is so infrequent that you might prefer to pay for it and only sharpen on the oilstone yourself.

Plane blades and chisels are only sharpened on one side. The other side should be kept flat. The usual sharpening stone for these tools is a block about 8×2×1 inches, and it can be mounted in a wood case. Degrees of coarseness are obtainable. A coarse stone cuts quickly, but the edge given to the tool reflects the size of the grit and would appear to be like a saw edge under a lens. That sort of edge would be good enough for some rough work, but it is better to follow with a finer stone. It is possible to get combination stones, with fine and coarse grits on opposite sides, but most craftsmen prefer separate stones.

Most coarser stones are manufactured grits, but the finest stones are natural (such as Washita and Arkansas). For most outdoor furniture planing, there is no need to go down to the finest stones that are more appropriate to edges for finishing quality hardwoods in cabinetwork.

To sharpen a chisel or plane blade, apply a thin oil on the stone. Light lubricating oil or kerosene is better than motor oil (which would make a barrier between the steel and the stone). Some stones can be used with water. Have the bevel angled downward with one hand holding higher up, and the fingers of the other hand applying pressure (FIG. 2-3B). Rub the tool at a constant angle along and about the surface of the stone. The stone, as well as the steel, wears away. Keep it level and rub it all over the surface.

Wipe the oil off the blade, and feel the edge on the flat side. If there is a roughness there, that is a *wire edge*. This is a tiny sliver of steel rubbed off the sharp edge, but still clinging to it. It indicates that the edge is sharp. Put the flat of the steel on the stone (FIG. 2-3C) and give it a few circular rubs. That should remove the wire edge. If it does not, slice the edge across a piece of scrap wood.

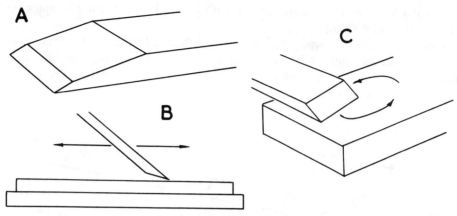

Fig. 2-3. *Edge tools, such as chisels and plane blades, can have a long grinding bevel and a shorter sharpening bevel (A). The latter is maintained on an oilstone (B) and any wire edge is removed by rubbing flat (C).*

If that sharpening was on a coarse stone and you want to follow with a finer stone, make sure the edge is clean. Then repeat all the sharpening on the fine stone. You only need to rub long enough to remove the scratches from the coarse stone.

To sharpen a knife, note the angle toward the edge at each side, and hold the blade at that angle on the stone. Again, control with one hand while the other puts on pressure. Move about if it is a curved edge, but maintain the angle. After rubbing well on one side, turn the knife over and do the same on the other side. Continue until you can feel a wire edge; then, slice across a piece of scrap wood to remove it.

Marking Out

A pencil is your best general marking tool, or you can use a knife for precision cuts across the grain. Measuring presents no problems, but remember that a rule is only a means of comparing things. Bringing two parts together for marking is better than using a rule.

Mark squarely at right angles. A try square that can be pushed against a straight edge, while you mark along its blade, is the standard tool, but there is a limit to its size. Several other things can be used. A sheet of plywood can be assumed to have square corners. Even the corner of a magazine page should be square. Other methods of squaring are described in Chapter 3.

An adjustable square can be used with a pencil for marking lines parallel with an edge. Its blade is adjusted to the distance, and a pencil held against the end is pulled along with it. The tool made specially for this purpose is a *marking gauge*, with a steel spur projecting to scratch from the stem. For mortise and tenon joints, there are mortise gauges with two adjustable spurs to mark both lines at the same time.

If you are planing wood true and to width and thickness, the first side is called the *face side* and the first edge, square to it, is the *face edge*. In subsequent marking out, work from these surfaces; there are conventional marks to pencil on them to indicate what they are (FIG. 2-4).

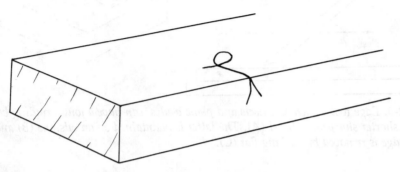

Fig. 2-4. *Marks are penciled to indicate face side and face edge as wood is prepared by planing.*

Holes

If you have only one power tool, it should be an electric drill. But it will not do all your drilling. Holes up to about 3/8 of an inch for screws and bolts can be made with drills originally intended for metal. Above that, use drills designed for wood. Some will fit the electric drill, but you will reach a stage where you must use a brace to drill by hand. If you buy one, pay a little more for a ratchet brace. It will allow you to work in a restricted space where you cannot sweep a complete circle with the handle. Besides making holes, the brace can be used with a screwdriver bit for the many large screws used in outdoor furniture. It will also countersink holes for screw heads or just to take off roughness around the hole.

A particularly useful tool for the holes needed in rural construction using natural poles is an *auger*. This is a bit extended to have its own lever handle. The working end is like a woodworking twist bit, but it is usually longer, so it can be used for deeper holes. It is not an essential tool, but a useful one.

Wood

Wood used for making furniture is broadly divided into *hardwoods* and *softwoods*. The names indicate the differences in most cases, but there are actually hardwoods softer than some softwoods. The names really indicate if the tree loses its leaves in the winter (as well as the general types of leaves). Coniferous trees with needle leaves produce softwoods. Hardwoods come from broad-leafed trees; most of these lose their leaves in the winter in temperate climates.

Most hardwoods are considerably stronger, harder, and heavier than most softwoods. Mostly they are more durable, but some hardwoods are prone to rot quite quickly. Some softwoods that contain plenty of resin are quite durable. Local suppliers will be able to suggest suitable woods. Local woods are probably less expensive than imported ones. One of the most durable woods for outside use is teak (which has to be imported). There are a few substitutes for it. The oaks are durable but beech is not.

As a tree grows, it increases in girth with the production of annual rings (FIG. 2-5A). As the tree gets older, the inner part becomes more compacted and that is the *heartwood*. The outer rings are the *sapwood*. The heartwood is stronger and more durable. Some woods can show little difference between sapwood and heartwood. Where there is any choice, use the heartwood for outdoor furniture.

Newly cut wood is quite wet with sap. Drying this out to an acceptable level is called *seasoning*.

As wood is dried it shrinks, mostly in the direction of the annual rings. Therefore, a board cut radially will get thinner, but remain flat (FIG. 2-5B). One cut further out will warp because shrinking is around the curve of the rings (FIG. 2-5C). Controlled seasoning minimizes the problem, but looking at the end of a board allows you to estimate what will happen to it with changes in moisture content.

As it is a natural product, wood is not a consistent material. Flaws must be accepted. The most common flaws are knots; these occur where branches leave the trunk. If the knot is small and solid with the surrounding wood, it does not matter. If there is a black edge to the knot, it will probably fall out and the wood will be weakened, probably only slightly. Avoid wood with knots half the width or more. A knot is a break in the lengthwise grain and does not provide much strength in itself.

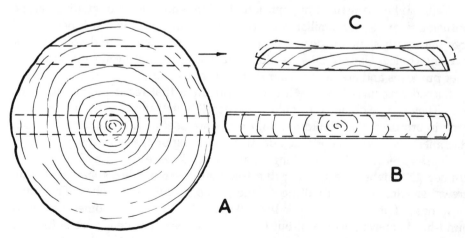

Fig. 2-5. When boards are cut across a log (A), shrinkage occurs in the direction of the annual rings (B) and can cause warping in boards cut further from the center (C).

Bark on the outside of the tree should be removed. There are a few trees where bark is so tight that leaving it on will not matter and it might be considered a design feature. Where bark tends to loosen as the wood dries, it will harbor insects and moisture; both of these can attack the wood. Remove the bark. The board will still have all the features of the waney edge and might need little treatment except the removal of sharp edges.

Nails and Screws

Many joints in outdoor furniture are made with nails, screws, or bolts. Consider the effects of corrosion. Pure iron has a good resistance to corrosion. Its initial light coating of rust resists further rusting. Very little pure iron is available now. What we loosely call "iron" is actually "mild steel." This is iron with a small amount of carbon in it. Rust on mild steel is an ongoing thing. Unprotected mild steel in damp conditions will eventually rust away.

Copper has a good resistance to corrosion, but it is soft and therefore not of much use. It can be alloyed with zinc to make brass or with tin to make bronze. Both of these alloys have a good resistance to the effects of moisture. Aluminum also resists moisture, but in its pure state it is soft. Other metals alloyed with it give hardness, but sometimes with reduced corrosion resistance. So-called stainless steel is not immune to all kinds of attack, but it can be alloyed to resist certain liquids. The usual variety should be satisfactory in normal weather.

Mild steel can be protected by plating. There is no need for some of the expensive plated finishes for outdoor furniture, but zinc gives fairly inexpensive protection. One such treatment is called *galvanizing*. Mild steel bolts buried in wood can have a long enough life. This is particularly true if their exposed ends are painted. There are rust-inhibiting fluids that can be used on steel fastenings before driving them and before painting.

Nails are best described by their length. The *penny system* of grading can be confusing if you are unfamiliar with it. For most furniture, you will need fairly large nails with standard heads. Diameters vary with length and you will not have any choice. Nails of other sections and with different heads are meant for other purposes and are not for your sort of woodworking.

Barbed ring nails have teeth cut around them that resist pulling out (FIG. 2-6A). They can be obtained in mild steel, possibly galvanized, but they are also made in bronze for boatbuilding. Both types are useful where you need a firm attachment, yet there is not much depth for holding or space for many nails.

Screws are made in many lengths and in thicknesses described by a gauge number (the higher the number, the thicker the screw). Sizes start with tiny screws, smaller than you will need, and go up to quite large ones. The usual screw has a flat or countersunk head (FIG. 2-6B). You might sometimes need round-head screws (FIG. 2-6C), but for most purposes flat heads are sufficient. Screw length varies with the parts being joined. Within each length there will be at least three gauge thicknesses available. In general, you want the thicker ones.

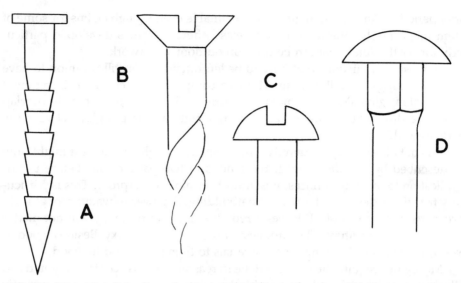

Fig. 2-6. The grip of a nail can be improved with annular rings (A). Screws can have flat (B) or round heads (C). A square neck under a bolt head prevents it from turning in wood (D).

In any case, avoid slender screws that will shear off when being driven. Typical useful sizes are: 8 gauge × 1^1/$_2$ inches, 10 or 12 gauge × 2 inches, 12 or 14 gauge × 3 inches. In longer screws, you will not usually need too much larger than 14 gauge. Brass screws are not as strong as steel ones. Therefore, they will have to be thicker, or you could drive a steel screw first, withdraw it, and then replace it with the brass screw.

In heavy construction, the best fastening method is to bolt right through. The term *bolt* means a fastening with a screw thread only a short distance from the end. If the thread goes for nearly all the length, it is an *engineering screw*. To avoid confusion, the screws for driving into wood can be called *wood screws*.

Quoted lengths are from the surface, which would be under a hexagonal or square head, but from the top of a countersunk one. A carriage bolt is particularly intended for woodwork. It has a shallow "snap" head and a square neck under it (FIG. 2-6D). The square pulls into the top of the drilled hole and resists turning when the nut is tightened on the other end. Normal bolts require a wrench at both ends. When choosing bolts, it is usually better to have one large bolt through a joint than several smaller ones. Quoted diameters are fractional. You will not usually need ^{1}/$_4$-inch bolts. The general sizes are ^{3}/$_8$ inch or ^{1}/$_2$ inch, but for large work you will have to choose larger bolts.

Glue

Not so long ago, the use of glue on outdoor woodwork would not have been considered because there were no glues able to withstand moisture for more than brief periods. Many modern glues are unsuitable even though claims for some of them might imply otherwise. Nevertheless, there are glues developed particularly for boatbuilding that can be used on outdoor woodwork.

In most constructions that have to be left outside, it is still common to have metal fastenings as well as glue. The two complement each other. In tenoned construction, glue alone will provide security. It is where parts merely overlap that there should be screws or bolts through. But you can put glue between the parts as well.

It is not always easy to identify a fully waterproof glue because it might only be described by a trade name. If the glue is in two parts to mix before use or application to meeting surfaces, it is almost certainly waterproof. This is particularly true if it is described for use in boatbuilding. A powerful waterproof glue (in two parts) is "resorcinol." It leaves a red glue line that normally will not matter for this type of furniture. The strongest of these glues is epoxy. Besides wood to wood, it will also join many other materials to themselves and to wood.

Most glues require the surfaces to be in reasonably close contact. If you try to fill a gap with glue, it will not provide any strength. In that case, you can mix sawdust with the glue. This bonds the glue and particles to the surfaces to make a stronger joint. At the other extreme, do not tighten a close-fitting joint so hard that most of the glue is squeezed out. There must be enough glue left to make a bond.

There is not much need for stoppings in outdoor woodwork. The older putty and similar things that set hard have been superseded, but make sure you buy an exterior stopping. Some are only intended for indoor use. For filling holes over punched nails, there are stoppings to press in and sand level. They appear to set hard, but actually they remain slightly flexible to allow for movement of the wood. They can be used in cracks, but larger gaps are better filled with a more flexible stopping sold for the purpose. These synthetic stoppings are superior to any you might mix yourself.

Finishes

Some woods can be left untreated and they have sufficient resistance to rot to last a long time. They will take on a weathered appearance that you might want. Otherwise, you have to apply a finish.

For wood preservatives to be effective, the wood has to be soaked. Obtain some protection by brushing on the preservative. Some preservatives are clear. Others are colored, often green, but that is translucent and it fades fairly rapidly. It is unwise to rely on the preservative to provide much contribution to appearance. Most preservatives can be followed by paint, but check the directions on the can. Some take a long time to dry before the furniture can be used or before paint should be applied.

Most paints now available are synthetic. They are superior in durability and quality of finish to the older paints made from natural materials. Read the instructions on the can. There might be a limit to the amount of brushing advised. Too much will alter appearance by causing air bubbles. Most paints must dry between coats, but there are some where a further coat must be put on before the earlier one is fully dry. There might be a maximum or a minimum time between coats.

The best protection comes with a gloss finish. This is usually what you want in any case, because it looks good and is easily kept clean. The effectiveness of the finish depends on what is applied underneath, as much as on the quality of the final coat.

The first coat on bare or preserved wood has to make a bond with the wood grain. This is a *primer* that is thin, so it penetrates. Its color is not important, but is usually white or pink. There might have to be a second coat of primer. Follow with an undercoat that is a matt finish of a color compatible with the *top coat*. It is better if it is not exactly the same shade as the top coat; then you can see how you are progressing on the final coat.

It is the undercoat that provides the body in the paint system. You might need to apply two coats because this is where thickness is made (not at the final stage). In some paint systems, the primer is the same as the undercoat—probably thinned. Get thinners recommended by the paint manufacturers; use them sparingly.

If the undercoat is not as smooth as you prefer, use wet-and-dry, medium abrasive paper, with water. The top gloss coat is a once-only coat. Buy more undercoat than top coat. If you apply a second top coat, it tends to run on the earlier gloss and finish unevenly. Do not mix different makes of paints. Most paint manufacturers recommend complete systems of finishes.

Check that the paint offered is intended for exterior use. The most durable paint is produced for boats, and it can be used on furniture. Check that it is intended for use on wood and not fiberglass. There are some boat paints, supplied in two parts, that have to be mixed before use. There is no need to use them on furniture. They make a very hard skin on a boat and they are intended for immersion in water.

Paint obscures the grain of the wood. If you want to protect the wood, but still see the grain details, use varnish. Be careful what you use. Some varnish is intended for indoor use only. Avoid anything with shellac in it because it will not stand up to even slight dampness. Like paints, most varnishes are now synthetic. Not only has this given them better protection, but it makes application easier.

A varnish described as "exterior" might be satisfactory, but a boat varnish should be even better. Some of it is described as "spar varnish." That has good weather resistance. There are no primers or undercoats for varnish. The first coat should be thinned, using the thinners recommended by the makers; further coats are made with the varnish as supplied.

3
Basic techniques

The most basic furniture is formed from natural poles or slabs of wood. Often the bark is left on and the parts are either nailed or assembled with a simple peg arrangement. Little regard is provided for the niceties of squaring and exact size. Other furniture is comparatively massive and made of wood that has been sawn to squared sections, but not finished in a way that would make it suitable for indoor furniture. Sometimes the wood is used almost directly from the tree, and it does not season until after it has been made into furniture. In other situations, the furniture is made of planed, seasoned wood; it would be acceptable to use the items inside the home as well as outside.

There is room in the making of outdoor furniture for a wide range of skills. It is possible to make satisfactory furniture if all you can do is saw wood to length and nail parts together. For that work the range of tools needed is also slight. With more skill and more tools, it is possible to produce more advanced furniture. Anyone experienced in making indoor furniture of good quality will probably feel happier producing outdoor furniture of almost cabinetmaking quality.

Nailing

Most nails used in outdoor furniture are fairly large. You must take into consideration other things besides being able to hit the nail every time.

If the wood is not very hard and the nail not too large, you could just position the nail and drive it. If it is near an edge you might split the wood. Usually, if you are dealing with nails 3 inches or more long, drill a starter hole for each nail. When nailing two pieces of wood together, it is the grip of the nail in the lower piece clamping the upper piece to it under the nail head (FIG. 3-1A) that counts.

You do not gain anything by having the nail tight in the top piece (as it would be if you nailed without drilling). In smaller sizes that does not matter.

For much nailing, you can drill an undersize hole through the top piece and partly into the bottom piece. How much undersize and how far depends on the size of the nail and the wood. If it is very hard wood, the hole in the top piece can be the same size as the nail and a smaller drill can be used to continue into the bottom piece. Usually one drill size will do (FIG. 3-1B). Even in very hard wood, stop the drill short, so the nail makes its own way into the last short distance. Even if you are dealing with an assembly where you can drive nails, drill nail holes near the edge of the board so that there is less risk of splitting.

It is not easy to decide on the length of nails and spacing. It is largely a matter of experience. Remember it is the length of nail in the lower piece of wood that provides the grip. About three-fourths of the way through the average board will be about right. About twice the depth of the upper piece of wood is another guide for thinner parts. A minimum of three nails in any joint should be used, but in many furniture constructions a 2-inch spacing is appropriate. Try to avoid driving nails close by in the same line of grain; this encourages splitting. If there is space, a zig-zag line (FIG. 3-1C) makes a stronger joint and spreads the nails in the grain. If the lower part of a nail is going into an end grain, it should go about twice as far into it as it would in a side grain, if possible, or there will have to be more nails going to a lesser depth.

If nails have to be driven in a row, there is a gain in strength when you drive at alternate angles to provide *dovetail nailing* (FIG. 3-1D).

Nail heads normally finish level with the surface. For neatness, the heads can be punched below the surface and then the hole can be filled with a stopping material (FIG. 3-1E). In furniture with wood that has not been fully seasoned, assume that a board will probably get thinner as it dries out. In that case, punch nail heads below the surface, so that they are not left standing and liable to snag clothing as the wood surface shrinks.

In some places, the greatest strength will come from taking the nail right through and turning over the point. This is particularly so where the wood is thin and where there would not be much grip with normal nailing. This clench nailing is not just a matter of hitting over the projecting nail end. The neatest way to bury the point is along the grain, but it is stronger to go squarely or diagonally across the lines of grain (FIG. 3-1F).

Bury the point rather than merely turning it over. Drive the nail through. Then, support the head with an iron block or a heavy hammer. Put a spike beside the projecting nail point and hammer the end to a curve over it (FIG. 3-1G). Pull out the spike, and hammer the nail point into the wood (FIG. 3-1H).

Screws

Compared with nailing, screwing parts together has the advantage of exerting a clamping action. The force of hammering at one place can cause nails to loosen at

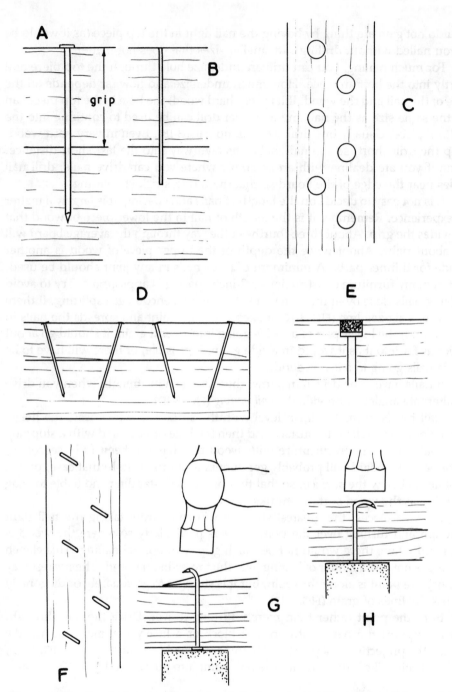

Fig. 3-1. A nail grips between its head and the lower part (A). A hole will be needed (B). Staggering nails reduces splitting and adds strength (C); so does dovetail nailing (D). A nail set below the surface can be covered with stopping (E). Nails can be taken through and clenched (F, G, and H).

another place. That does not happen with screws. It is possible to pull parts together progressively by going back over screws for further tightening. If it is expected that parts will have to be disassembled later, screws can be withdrawn without damaging the wood. With nails there would be damage even if nails could be pulled out.

For each length of screw, there are several gauge thicknesses available. For most outdoor work, choose the thicker screws. Thicker screws are stronger and they grip better; they need not be spaced as closely. As with nails, avoid getting close screws in the same line of grain (because of the risk of splitting). A zig-zag arrangement can be used.

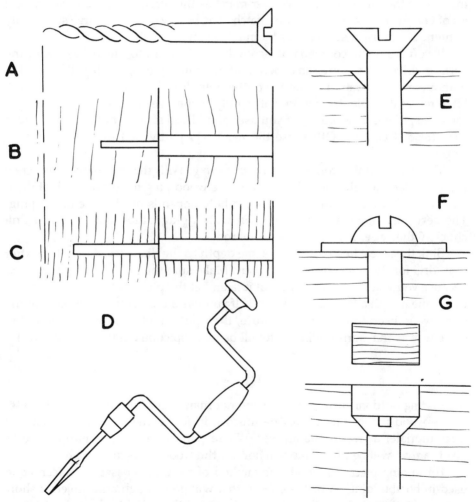

Fig. 3-2. Screws need holes (A, B, and C). A screwdriver bit in a brace is useful for large screws (D). A hole can be countersunk (E). A washer spreads pressure (F). A plug in a counterbored hole hides a screw head (G).

Screws in the sizes used in building furniture must have starter holes drilled. The clearance hole in the top piece of wood allows the screw to pass easily and be drilled right through, even if part of the screw thread comes within it (FIG. 3-2A). What size and length of hole to drill in the lower piece depends on the screw and the wood. In soft wood, the hole can be quite small in relation to the screw and only be taken about half as far as the screw will go (FIG. 3-2B). In hard wood, it should be bigger and be taken deeper (FIG. 3-2C). But even then, leave a short distance for the screw to make its own way.

Large screws are difficult to drive tightly. It helps to rub wax or a candle on a screw before driving. That is cleaner than using lubricating oil or grease. Even with a large screwdriver, it might be difficult to exert enough torque. In any case, make sure the end of the screwdriver matches the screw head. You will waste a lot of energy if the driver does not match. The best way to get a large screw fully tightened is to use a screwdriver bit in a brace (FIG. 3-2D).

If you are using countersunk screw heads that are to finish flush with the surface, drive one screw as an experiment. In many woods, it will pull its head in without any preparation of the top of the hole. If it does not, use a countersink bit to recess the hole. Do not do that as fully as the size of the screw head. Allow for some pulling in (FIG. 3-2E). If you use round head screws, put a washer under each head (FIG. 3-2F). Otherwise the head will partly pull in and it will look sloppy.

The neatest finish comes from *counterboring*. With this technique, the screw heads are far enough below the surface for a wood plug to go over each of them (FIG. 3-2G). The size of the counterbored hole depends on the size of the plug. The best plugs are cut across the grain with a plug cutter that fits into a drill chuck. Otherwise, use a piece of dowel rod.

Sink the screw head about the same depth as the diameter of the plug. After that, drill for the screw in the usual way. Make sure the screw is fully tightened because you will not be able to get at it later. Let the plug stand high so that you can plane it level after the glue has set. If you use a plug cutter on a piece of the same wood used to make the furniture, then put the plug in with its grain the same way as that surrounding it; it will be inconspicuous in the finished work.

Rivets

In building outdoor furniture, there are not many uses for rivets. Nevertheless, where wood is too thin to provide much grip for screws, and bolts would be inappropriate, a rivet is the answer. Where parts of folding furniture have to pivot, a rivet will be preferable to a bolt for the wood parts to turn on.

For joining pieces of wood, the method of riveting is based on a technique used in boatbuilding. A nail is chosen that will go through and project a short distance (FIG. 3-3A). A small washer is driven over the nail. Ideally, it should have a hole that needs forcing on the nail. Therefore, a hollow punch is needed (FIG. 3-3B). The nail head is held by an iron block. Then the end of the nail is cut off a

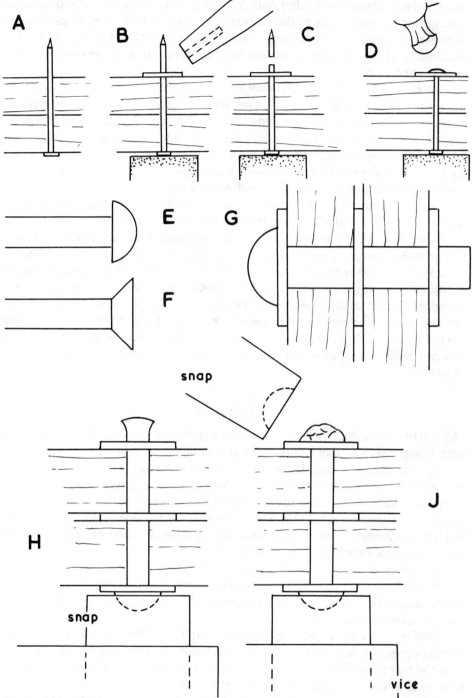

Fig. 3-3. *A nail can be riveted through a washer (A through D). Rivets can go through washers to make pivots for moving parts (E through J).*

short distance above the washer (FIG. 3-3C). You must judge the amount left as enough for hammering onto the washer. Use a small ball peen or cross peen hammer to spread the end tightly onto the washer (FIG. 3-3D). Aim to form a rounded head, by hammering around the end, rather than on top only to get a broad flatter head.

For furniture pivots, the diameter needs to be $1/4$ inch or more. Therefore, nails cannot be used. Some rivets come with round, (FIG. 3-3E) or countersunk heads (FIG. 3-3F) already made on one end. You can usually arrange for the manufactured head to come on the more prominent side; the head you make need not have such a good finish. Never have a rivet head directly on the wood. If you try to spread a rivet head over a loose-fitting washer, much of your effort will go into spreading the neck of the rivet to the washer hole size.

Normally there will be washers each side and between the moving parts (FIG. 3-3G). Cut the end of the rivet to allow enough for forming the second head. There are tools called rivet *sets* or *snaps* that are like punches with hollowed ends to match rivet heads. If one of these is available, the manufactured head can be supported in it, while the other end is formed (FIG. 3-3H). Otherwise a lead block is an alternative support that will hold the rivet against hammering without damaging the head. Hammer all around the projecting end to make the new head. For any riveting through wood, do not hammer too hard, or you will bend the rivet in the wood. Try to make a head that matches the one on the other side. If you can hammer it approximately to shape, you can round it by hitting a rivet snap on it (FIG. 3-3J).

Bolts

Many parts of outdoor furniture are held together with bolts. If you use bolts with hexagonal or square heads and nuts to match, include washers under the heads and nuts (FIG. 3-4A). If the threaded part extends some way through the nut, saw off fairly close in. If the bolt is through moving parts, there is a risk of the nut working loose. The traditional way of locking it is with a locknut. This is a second, thinner nut (FIG. 3-4B). Do not merely tighten one on top of the other, but hold the lower nut with a wrench while the other is tightened. Then turn the wrenches toward each other, so that the nuts jam.

It is possible to get nuts with a friction arrangement built in; these are sometimes called *stiff nuts*. They lock well enough without further action (FIG. 3-4C). A simple method of securing is to hammer over the end of the bolt so that the nut cannot come off (FIG. 3-4D).

Carriage bolts are popular for outdoor furniture. The shallow, round head does not project much, and the square neck under it pulls into the wood to prevent the bolt from turning as the nut is tightened (FIG. 3-4E). For this and other bolts, drill a hole the same size as the bolt diameter.

For some assemblies, you will want a bolt action, but the length will be more than a normal bolt will reach. In that case, there can be a rod screwed at both

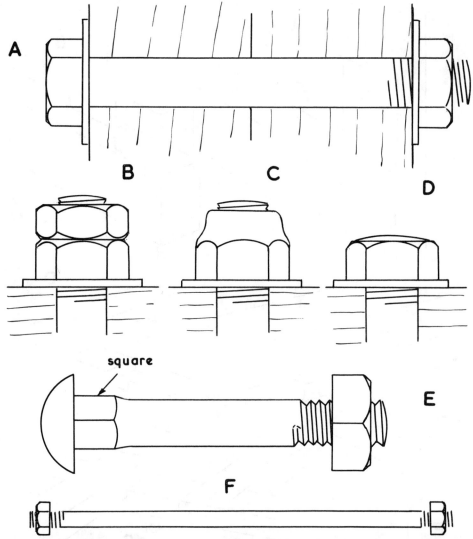

Fig. 3-4. Bolts through wood need washers (A). Nuts can be locked in several ways (B, C, and D). A square neck prevents a bolt turning (E). Threaded rod can be used instead of long bolts.

ends so that nuts and washers can be used (FIG. 3-4F). If screwing tackle is available, such a rod can be made when required. Otherwise, a craftsman could easily make up what you need.

Notched Joints

Some joints are made by putting one piece of wood on another and nailing or screwing, but if a sliding movement has to be resisted, one or both pieces could

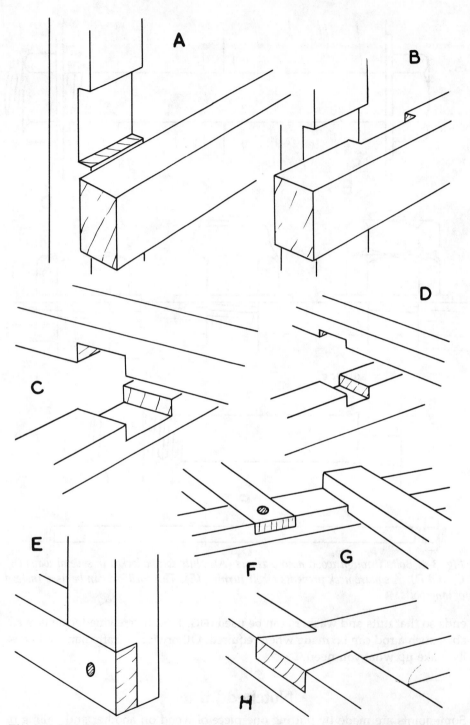

Fig. 3-5. Notching parts together prevents them from sliding over each other and can bring them to the same level. They can be secured by dowels or dovetailing.

be notched. If a rail under load might try to slide down an upright there can be a shallow notch to supplement screws or a bolt (FIG. 3-5A). If there is a risk of movement in both directions notch both pieces (FIG. 3-5B).

Those notches can be shallow, but if two crossing pieces of the same thickness must come level, cut half out of each piece (FIG. 3-5C). With parts of different thicknesses, do not cut too much out of the thinner piece (FIG. 3-5D). Use similar joints when parts do not cross squarely.

Notched joints can be used at corners (FIG. 3-5E), or cut them where one piece meets another (FIGS. 3-5F and G). If one piece has to resist a pull, dovetail its end (FIG. 3-5H). A slope of 1/4 inch in a 2-inch board is satisfactory.

Mark and cut notched joints carefully for close fits. Mark one piece from the other, squaring on all faces (FIG. 3-6A). If cutting by hand, tilt the saw and cut from opposite sides (FIG. 3-6B). Slice as you chisel away the waste (FIG. 3-6C), working upwards from each side in turn before leveling the bottom of the joint (FIG. 3-6D).

A less-common notched joint is like an indoor furniture dado joint. You can let an end into a notch (FIG. 3-7A). It may be easier to cut a V-shaped notch (FIG. 3-7B). A nail or screw driven diagonally (FIG. 3-7C) will be hidden, and produce a stronger joint than a nail endwise (FIG. 3-7D). If you use notches in natural round poles, they will prevent movement (FIGS. 3-7E and F).

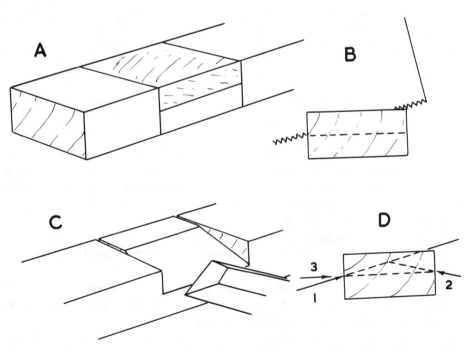

Fig. 3-6. Notches are marked out, and then cut by sawing and chiseling from opposite sides.

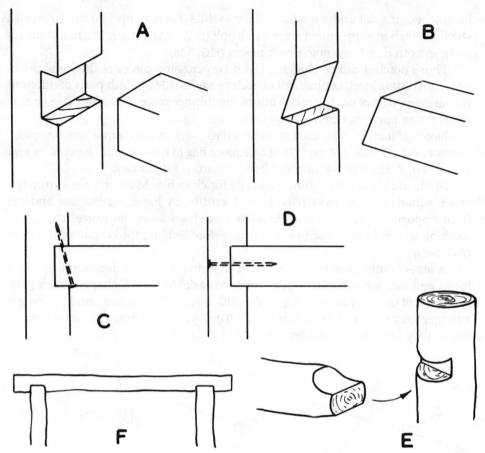

Fig. 3-7. Parts can be notched together in several ways.

Mortise and Tenon Joints

The most-used woodworking joints are mortise and tenon, with the projecting tenon fitting into the hollow mortise (FIG. 3-8A). If the tenon does not go right through, it is a stub or stopped mortise and tenon joint (FIG. 3-8B). It is usual to make the tenon one-third the thickness of the wood.

Mark both parts all around (FIG. 3-8C). Some of the waste in a mortise can be removed by drilling, but finish it with a chisel. Be careful to match mortise and tenon thicknesses.

Use waterproof glue in these and other joints, and also wedge them. Drive wedges outside the tenon (FIG. 3-8D), but it will be stronger to drive wedges into saw cuts (FIG. 3-8E). Plane level after the glue has set.

Strengthen a joint with a dowel across it (FIG. 3-8F). Make a dowel do the work of a clamp in pulling a joint together. Drill across the mortised part for a dowel. Mark this position on the tenon, but drill the dowel hole slightly nearer

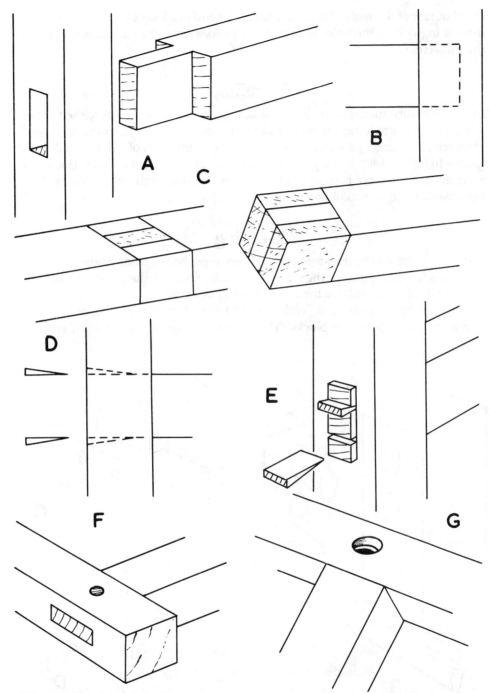

Fig. 3-8. Mortise and tenon joints are commonly used in furniture. They can go through or be stopped. The tenon is often one-third the thickness of the wood (A, B, and C). Wedges or dowels hold and pull the joints together (D through G).

the shoulder of the wood (FIG. 3-8G). Taper the end of a long piece of dowel; then drive it in, to force the holes in line and therefore close the joint tighter. Cut off the projecting ends.

Doweling

In outdoor furniture, glued dowels might be used more to strengthen other joints than to form joints themselves, but in some situations use dowels instead of mortise and tenon joints (FIG. 3-9A). If you taper the ends of a dowel and put a groove in it (FIG. 3-9B), it will go in with less risk of splitting the wood. Use dowels instead of screws or bolts in a joint (FIG. 3-9C), and strengthen a dowel by driving a wedge into a saw cut in its end (FIG. 3-9D).

Clamping

Although there will be uses for ordinary C-clamps, bar clamps or other versions of clamps to fit on pipes or the edges of boards, much of the assembly work in outdoor furniture is outside the reach of these devices.

Wedges have some uses. With a rigid board longer than the parts to be clamped, nail or screw on blocks. Then, drive wedges at one or both ends to

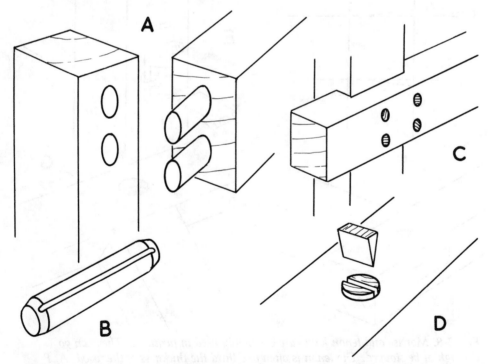

Fig. 3-9. Glued dowels are an alternative to tenons or can strengthen other joints.

tighten the joints (FIG. 3-10A). A similar idea employs two long boards and bolts. Then, the wedges are driven against the bolts (FIG. 3-10B).

Single wedges do not put on direct pressure, and driving them will tend to move the parts. It is better to use pairs of similar wedges called *folding wedges* (FIG. 3-10C). By driving them alternately against each other, a parallel thrust is applied (FIG. 3-10D).

Instead of wood you can use rope, by tightly lashing around the work over scrap wood. Then, you drive wedges under the wood (FIG. 3-10E).

Another way of using rope is as a *Spanish windlass*. Use one turn of thick rope, or many turns of thinner rope with the ends tied together. Put a rod through the rope loops and twist (FIG. 3-10F). This puts a considerable load both on the parts being clamped and on the rope. Make sure the rope is strong enough. Stop the rod against an adjacent part (FIG. 3-10G), or by tying it to the turns (FIG. 3-10H) to keep on the pressure.

The Spanish windlass could go around the four sides of an assembly, such as a seat, as well as be used across a flat frame. Several clamping arrangements might have to be used together to get all parts tight. At the same time, remember to watch squareness (as described in the following section).

Squaring

Absolute squareness of all parts of a piece of outdoor furniture might not seem so important as when indoor furniture is being assembled, but it is surprising how lack of truth in some part will become rather obvious. Check the squareness of most things as they are assembled. If possible, work on a flat floor even if the furniture will eventually be used on uneven ground. Then check that such things as seats and tabletops are parallel with the floor when the legs are standing level. In the final situation, leveling will bring these important parts true. However, without the initial test, you do not have a basis for comparison.

A spirit level is a useful tool. Try it in all directions on a tabletop or anything else that should be level. If it seems to show a persistent error, turn it end-for-end in case the fault is in the level. The longer the level, the more accurate your result. This is particularly true if you are dealing with a surface that is something less than flat. If you use a small level, put it on a straightedge that will bridge over unevenness.

Where possible, check squareness with a try square; there is a limit because of its size. If you try to extend the blade of a 12-inch try square with a straightedge, the trouble is that a negligible error at its tip becomes a large one at 48 inches, for instance. Corners of sheets of plywood and other manufactured boards can be assumed to be square; use one of these sheets to check squareness within its limits of size.

Most assemblies are rectangular. If they are not rectangular they are usually symmetrical. In this case, it is easier to check squareness by comparing diagonals. If you have a four-sided frame that should be square, measure corner to

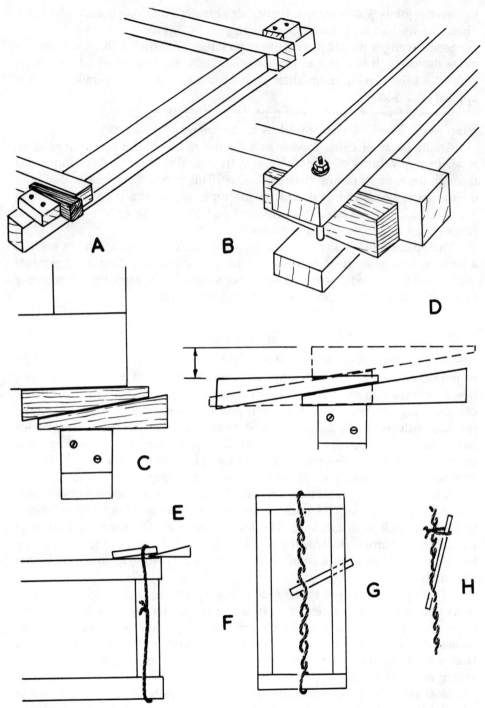

Fig. 3-10. Wedges can provide considerable clamping pressure (A through E). A Spanish windlass made from rope will also serve as a clamp (F, G, and H).

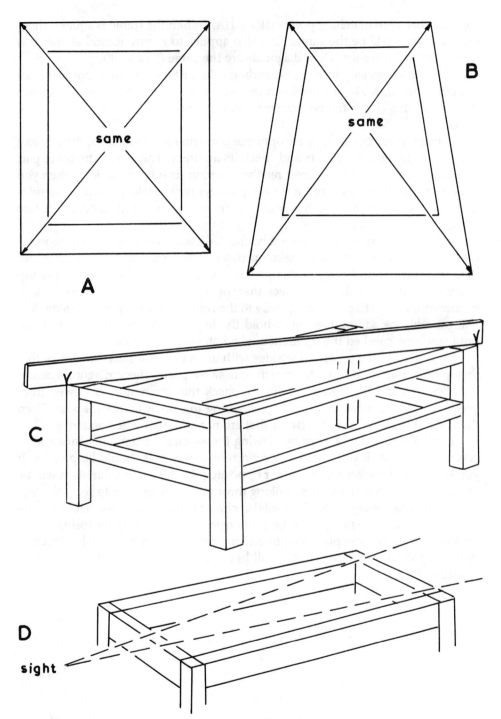

Fig. 3-11. Squareness or symmetry can be checked by comparing diagonals (A, B, and C). Twisting or winding can be checked by sighting across.

corner or between matching points (FIG. 3-11A). When the frame is square, these measurements will be the same. This also applies to a symmetrical shape. It is true about its centerline when diagonals are the same (FIG. 3-11B).

Measure diagonally with an expanding rule, or tape measure, but it is safer to mark a board. Make *peck marks* on the edge (FIG. 3-11C) and compare the two directions. This avoids the possible error of misreading rule divisions or confusing them.

In many assemblies, there are opposite parts that have to match, usually as a pair. Normally, make one part and check its accuracy. Then, true the other part by putting it over it in the correct relative position (inside to inside). When you have an assembly to make up, it is nearly always best to take two opposite sides with more parts than the other way. Get them together and matching before bringing in the parts the other way.

As you progress with the assembly, check diagonals as often as the opportunity occurs. For instance, you make up two end leg assemblies for a table and then you have to add a top built up of strips. Check the diagonals of the top assembly as it is added. Then, check that the legs are perpendicular to the top, by measuring from their feet diagonally to the corners of the top at each side. You will probably be adding bracing to hold the legs, but do not secure any brace until you have checked the squareness of whatever it is to hold.

For a chair, make up opposite sides with arms and seat rails. You know that they match, but as you join them with crosswise parts, check diagonals across the back legs and the front legs. Finally, check the squareness as viewed from above. Usually this can be done by measuring diagonals across the seat. Even then, stand back and look for twists that are not apparent when squaring.

Twists can usually be seen by viewing the assembly from a distance and in several directions. It does help to view across things that should be parallel. If you sight one thing across its partner opposite (FIG. 3-11D), any variation will be obvious. This also applies when looking through a table or chair to see if the legs match. If the assembly is glued, do all this checking before the glue has started to set. Then, you can usually pull the parts true. If they still try to spring to the incorrect positions, you put a weight on top or clamp diagonally in the direction that will pull the shape right. You will have to overcorrect slightly to allow for springing back.

4

Simple seats

Something to sit on is the most needed type of outdoor furniture. It does not necessarily have to be anything elaborate. Often, places and circumstances where a top firmly supported at the right height is all that is needed. This is particularly so in the natural surroundings of trees, bushes, and paths where there is a need for an occasional place to rest. The sort of chair or lounger that would be right on a patio or in a formal garden would not look right, particularly if it had brightly colored cushions.

At other areas simple seating is all that is required. Examples are in a play area, or where the seats are likely to get rough use or suffer from neglect. You can leave a simple bench or stool out in all types of weather. Something more elaborate and valuable would have to be put under cover or taken indoors when out of use.

From the practical point of view, simple seating is easier to make. The structures are rather basic. The joints are simple. Usually there does not have to be much regard for precision. Some simple seats can be made with only a few tools.

Many simple seats can be made with wood that might not be suitable for anything more advanced nor for making indoor furniture. There is much wood that is sound and durable, but it is normally discarded when converting lumber to standard-size boards. This can be obtained inexpensively or for free. Some of it has the waney edges of the outside of the tree where it has been cut right through the log. This can be regarded as a design feature for a seat to be positioned among natural surroundings.

Rustic Bench

A free-standing bench seat can be made in a size to suit its surroundings and the available materials. It uses wood in as near its natural state as needs permit. The bench can be positioned in a field or woodland where it will match surroundings. Almost any wood can be used, but for the strongest and longest-lasting seat it should be a hardwood free from large knots. If softwood is used, sections should be thicker and a very long life should not be expected. Treat the wood with a preservative to lengthen life. If the wood has been recently felled, allow sap to dry before preservative is applied.

When a log is prepared for cutting into boards, it is first cut to an approximately square section (FIG. 4-1A). The curved pieces removed are usually discarded, but many of them are suitable for seat tops. This will apply to the first board cut as well if it has a wandering, waney edge. This would make it uneconomical to convert to a parallel board (FIG. 4-1B). Both of these scrap pieces can be suitable as bench tops.

Remove any bark that remains. The traditional tool for doing this, a *spud*, was a long-handled tool—something like a broad chisel—with a thin, but not sharp, cutting edge. Instead, manage with an ax or a large chisel. If bark is left, it harbors insects and it will trap water that might introduce rot. It could also mark clothing. Except for removing bark, the waney edge should be left. Level sharp edges or projecting parts.

The top surface should be made reasonably flat, but the perfection of surface required for indoor furniture is unnecessary. A coarsely set plane, used diagonally to the grain, will usually level unseasoned wood. Remove any sharpness around the edges, but otherwise leave the natural appearance.

The legs are also natural pieces of wood that are cut from poles. Their size depends on the overall sizes of the bench, but a diameter of about 2 inches should suit most constructions. Remove any bark. The knots left by small branches can be leveled, but do not use pieces with large knots. Make the legs too long at this stage, and bring them to matching lengths after assembly.

The legs fit into holes in the top. The size of holes will depend on available equipment, but they should be at least 1 inch and preferably up to 1½ inches. Arrange the holes depending on the shape of the board section. If it is a parallel thickness, you can mark out a regular arrangement. With an irregular shape, such as the outside curved section, the holes do not have to be arranged squarely or in line. Aim to spread the feet at least as wide as the board. If it is narrower, let them be about 15-inches apart on the ground (FIG. 4-1C) when you have cut them to the correct height. At the ends of the bench, the feet should not be very far in from the end of the seat. Otherwise, someone sitting on the end could tip the bench (FIG. 4-1D).

Drill from the top, diagonally outward. You might be able to estimate the angle—particularly as each leg can slope differently on an odd-shaped piece—or

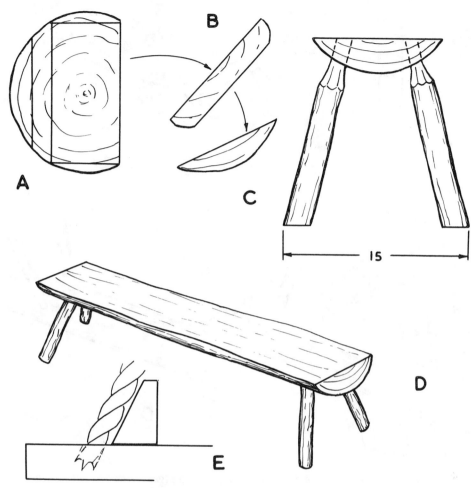

Fig. 4-1. Parts of logs and branches can be made into stools and benches.

you could cut a scrap-wood template as a guide (FIG. 4-1E). If the grain breaks out as the drill goes through the underside, that should not matter.

Taper the end of each leg to drive into its hole (FIG. 4-2A). It will be stronger if you do this gradually on a long slope than if you have a more abrupt change of section. The traditional way of doing this is to use a draw knife (FIG. 4-2B), while the wood is held diagonally in a vise, but get a similar effect with a broad chisel used with its bevel downward. It will help to draw a circle of the right size on the end. Have a piece of scrap wood with a hole of the right size drilled in it to slide over the end, so that you can see that it is down to size for a sufficient length to go through the seat. There is no need for absolute precision, but aim to get a reasonable drive fit.

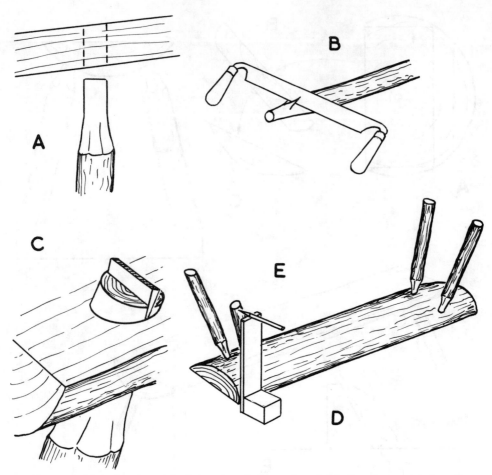

Fig. 4-2. Tapered ends can be driven into holes and wedged, then legs cut to length.

Make a saw cut in the end to take a wedge. Assemble the joint with the cut across the seat grain. Let the leg end project slightly. Then, drive in the wedge (FIG. 4-2C). Decide if you want to use glue. If you do use glue, it must be a waterproof type, preferably a boatbuilding grade. If the wood is still green or only partly seasoned, assemble each joint dry. Wedging will tighten it and the shrinkage that occurs as the wood dries should further tighten it. Wood that is still wet with sap does not bond well with any glue.

With all four legs in place and their tops planed level, invert the bench, so you can mark the leg lengths. Make a simple gauge with a strip of the right height attached to a base block (FIG. 4-2D). Use this with a pencil on the end to mark as far around each leg as you can (FIG. 4-2E) as a guide to sawing off. Take off any raggedness from the end, and bevel all around so the risk of splitting (if the bench is dragged over concrete or stones) is reduced. The bench is now complete.

Rustic Stool

A long bench will find its own level when standing on four feet, but if you bring the legs closer together it gets increasingly difficult to make them stand level if the ground is uneven. Because of this, stools and small seats were once made with three legs. A tripod arrangement will stand without wobbling on any surface. In the old days of earth floors in the home, and particularly in the milking shed, three-legged stools were standard. Stools made in this way will produce individual seats to match the rustic bench.

The top can be a piece of waney edged wood that is cut to about the same length as its width and with the corners trimmed off (FIG. 4-3A). Cut the ends at

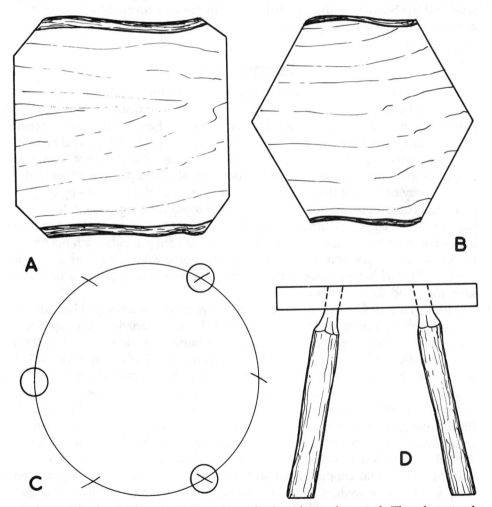

Fig. 4-3. *Waney-edged wood can have its ends shaped to make a stool. Three legs stand better than four on uneven ground. Legs should be splayed at least to the limits of the top.*

two angles so that the final shape is approximately hexagonal (FIG. 4-3B); this would match the three-legged arrangement.

The arrangement of holes for the legs does not have to be equally spaced, but they should not be too far out. What is more important is equal spacing on the ground. With an awkwardly shaped top, alter the angle of a leg to fit it into the top shape, yet bring it to part of a regular pattern at the floor. A top in its natural form will be more interesting than a piece of wood that fits into a symmetrical shape.

The way to get even spacing is to draw a circle and step off the radius around the circumference. It will go six times, so legs come at alternate marks (FIG. 4-3C). Fit and level the legs in the same way as for the bench. Try to finish with the top level and the bottoms of the legs fairly close to the area covered by the top (FIG. 4-3D) for reasonable stability, if the user leans or tries to tilt his seat.

Fixed Bench

Alongside woodland paths there might be a need for simple seats that are secured to the ground. A simple bench top can have vertical end legs that are held down in some way (FIG. 4-4A). The top should be hardwood about 2-inches thick. It can have waney edges or can be trimmed parallel. Its top should be level and reasonably smooth, but if the underside is rough that does not matter. It needs no special preparation except for the removal of sharp edges all around.

One way of making the bench is to let the legs into the ground—by digging holes and compacting the soil firmly—then the tops of the legs are cut level and the seat is nailed on. A firmer support can be obtained from using concrete instead of compacted soil around the legs. There is a snag to either arrangement. Buried wood will rot, sometimes quite rapidly. Some woods, such as oak, will withstand burial longer. Soak the wood in preservative first, but it is better to keep the wood above ground.

To do that, the bench is made as an above-ground assembly and held down in some way. The simplest assembly is nailed. If the underside of the top is uneven, make a groove across parallel with the top surface for the leg to fit into (FIG. 4-4B). Usually the leg is the same thickness as the top, but if you have thicker wood it can be used as it is. Drill the top for the nails to reduce the risk of splitting. The hole should be the same size as its nail or only very slightly smaller. Because you will be driving into end grain in the legs, they need not be drilled. Ideally, use galvanized nails. Plain iron nails should provide a reasonable life.

A better way is to tenon the legs into the top (FIG. 4-4C). Two square tenons should be enough unless it is a very wide seat. Remove the waste from the mortises by drilling and chopping out with a chisel. Make the tenons slightly too long. Cut them for wedges that can come across the grain or might be arranged diagonally (FIG. 4-4D). As with the rustic bench, assemble the joints dry, particularly if you are working with green wood. Or use a waterproof glue.

You can attach the legs to the ground in many ways. If the ground is level and

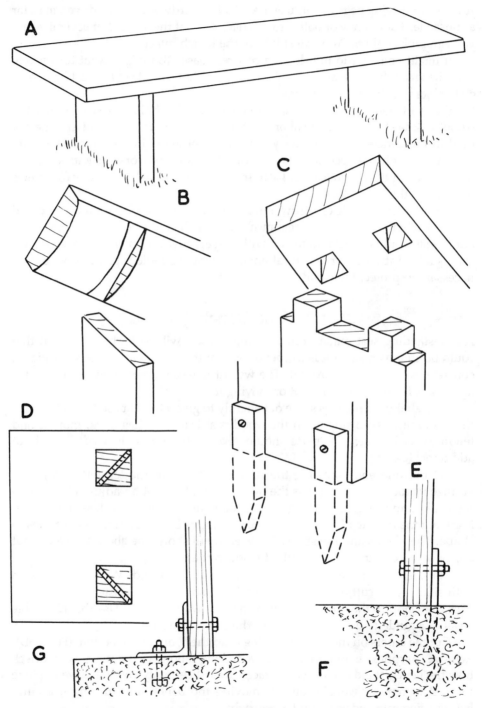

Fig. 4-4. *Bench ends can enter the ground (A). Their tops can be notched (B) or tenoned (C and D). Feet can be pegged or bolted down (E, F, and G).*

suitable for driving pegs into it, use oak or other hardwood pieces driven in as far as possible. Then screw or bolt through (FIG. 4-4E). If these rot after several years, you can replace them. You will still have the bench intact.

It might be better to put down a concrete base. You might want to concrete over the area where users' feet will come. It might be sufficient to just have concrete blocks under the bench legs.

Strips of metal can be let into the concrete with holes for screws into the wood (FIG. 4-4F). Bend the metal or chop teeth into it with a cold chisel to help it hold in the concrete. Alternatively, put pieces of angle iron on top. These are held down with the special bolts intended for concrete work, or with ordinary bolts buried in the concrete (FIG. 4-4G). In both cases, have holes ready for screws driven into the bench legs.

If the bench is made of hardwood, it will probably look best if untreated and left to weather to a natural appearance. The bench could be made of softwood, but then it would be better to treat it with preservative and paint it. Dark green is the usual paint color for a natural environment. Periodic repainting would be necessary to protect the wood.

Slab Bench

A free-standing seat made from very thick wood will be fairly heavy, but that could be an advantage if it is to spend most of the summer outside standing on concrete, wood, or level ground. The weight makes for steadiness and discourages users from tipping the seat or moving it.

For stability, let the legs slope out slightly to give a broad base (FIG. 4-5A) with the minimum risk of tipping. If the wood is at least 2 inches thick, mortise and tenon joints between the parts should give all the strength needed—without additional bracing.

Set out one end, showing the proposed angle of the leg (FIG. 4-5B), and arrange its foot almost as far as the overhanging top. Set an adjustable bevel to the angle, and use it for marking out the joint and the foot of each leg (FIG. 4-5C). Mark out the outline of each leg, but cut the joints before cutting the outsides to shape. The tenons and the spaces between them should be about the same, but adjust this according to the width of wood you are using.

Mark tenons and mortises on both sides of the wood. Watch the lines on both sides when cutting the tenons. Drill out some of the waste from the mortises, but chop to the outlines from both sides with a chisel. Use the adjustable bevel as a guide to the angle you hold the chisel and saw.

Cut the tapers on the sides of the legs and the V out of the bottom (FIG. 4-5D). Remove sharpness before assembly. Wedge the tenons in the usual way. Check how the bench stands on a level surface. Almost certainly you will have to plane the feet to remove wobble, but try moving the bench and turning it around before being satisfied that you have it right.

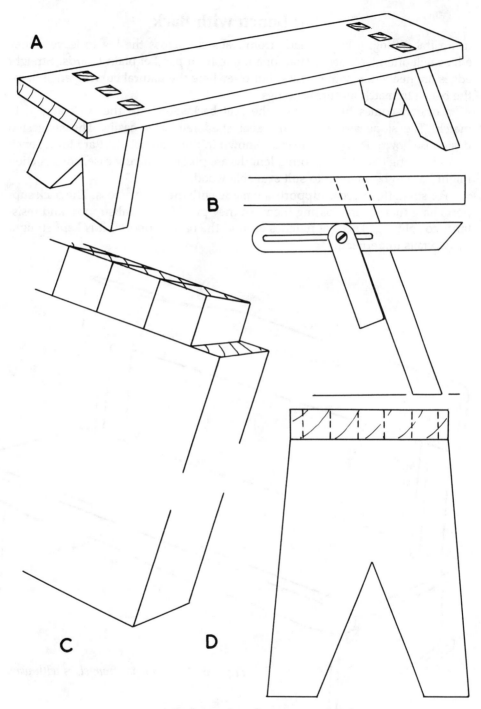

Fig. 4-5. Sloping and cut legs provide stability.

Slab Bench with Back

In a rural setting, a bench made from slabs cut across the log to leave waney edges will often look better than one made from parallel plain boards. Straight edges are needed in some places, but elsewhere the natural curving edge helps the bench to match its surroundings.

Comfort comes from sloping the seat backward with the back angled to match. The slope also makes the seat shed rainwater easily. The suggested design is shown (FIG. 4-6). The sizes shown in the Materials List are for a bench 48-inches long (FIG. 4-7), but other lengths are possible. In any case, construction might have to be adapted to suit available wood.

For strength, the seat supports are made with the grain across. The back supports have their grain crossing them, so they provide mutual support and resistance to splitting. The seat notches around the back supports; it is kept straight by two rails underneath.

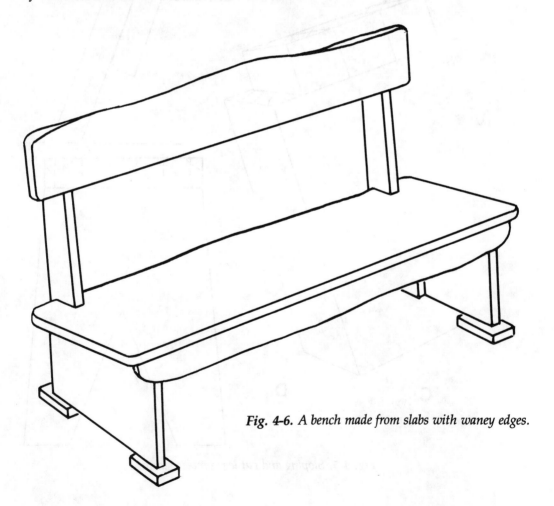

Fig. 4-6. A bench made from slabs with waney edges.

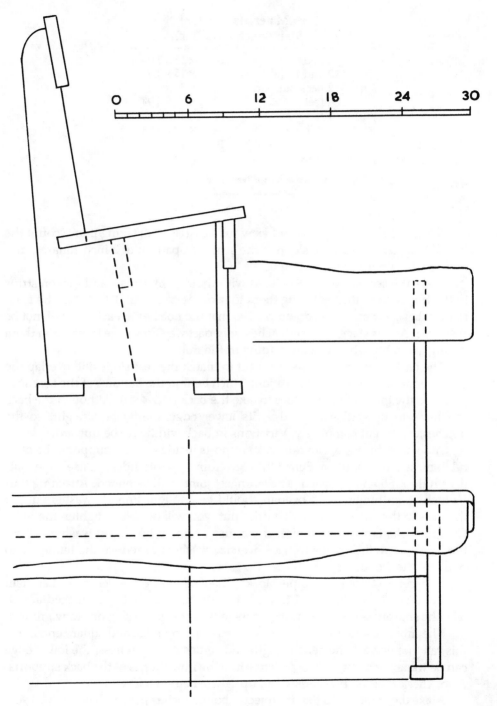

Fig. 4-7. Suggested sizes for a slab bench.

2 ends	14	$\times 15 \times 1^{1}/_4$
2 end fronts	1	$\times 15 \times 1^{1}/_4$
2 back supports	7	$\times 30 \times 1^{1}/_4$
4 feet	$2^{1}/_2 \times$	$5 \times 1^{1}/_4$
1 rail	4	$\times 42 \times 1^{1}/_4$
1 rail	4	$\times 49 \times 1^{1}/_4$
1 seat	16	$\times 49 \times 1^{1}/_4$
1 back	6	$\times 49 \times 1^{1}/_4$

(no allowance for waney edges)

It will help if you draw an end view full size (FIG. 4-8) taking into account the available materials. Get the slope of the seat on a pattern of 2-inch squares, and draw in the other parts to match it.

Make the seat supports (FIG. 4-9A) with their grain across, and nail on strips to the front edges after notching them to take the front rail (FIG. 4-9B). The front rail will have a waney edge downward so that the notches at each end will not be the same. At this stage, cut the notches only part way down the front. Trim them during assembly when you are putting in the rail.

The back supports (FIG. 4-9C) are cut to match the seat slope and overlap the seat supports. Rear edges finish about 1 inch behind the bottoms of the seat supports. At the top, notch the edges to take the back (FIG. 4-9D). Although the back can have an upward waney edge, its lower edge should be straight, so the notches can be cut completely. Variations in back width will be upward.

Assemble the ends with the back supports inside the seat supports. Be careful to make a pair of them. Screw through from opposite sides, or use large nails driven through and clenched. The strongest joints will be bolted. Attaching four $1/4$-inch bolts through each overlap should be enough. Provide washers under the nuts. If the wood shrinks as it dries out, you will be able to tighten the nuts. Carriage bolts are a good choice. If you use ordinary bolts, put washers under the heads as well. It helps to have oversize washers to reduce the tendency to pull into the wood.

The feet (FIG. 4-9E) are simple blocks nailed or screwed underneath. Let them extend about 1 inch back and front. If the bench is likely to be dragged about, take the sharpness off edges and corners to prevent splintering on stony ground.

The inner seat rail (FIG. 4-9F) needs a straight top edge and square ends. It is this rail that decides the bench length and settles its squareness; the lower edge can be waney or straight. Nail or screw it to the inner edges of the back supports. Also, check that the two ends stand upright when on a level floor.

Make the front rail so that it projects about 3 inches past each end (FIG. 4-9G). Its top edge needs to be straight, but bevel it to suit the seat angle. Round the extending ends and take off any sharpness of the waney edge, so that a hand put

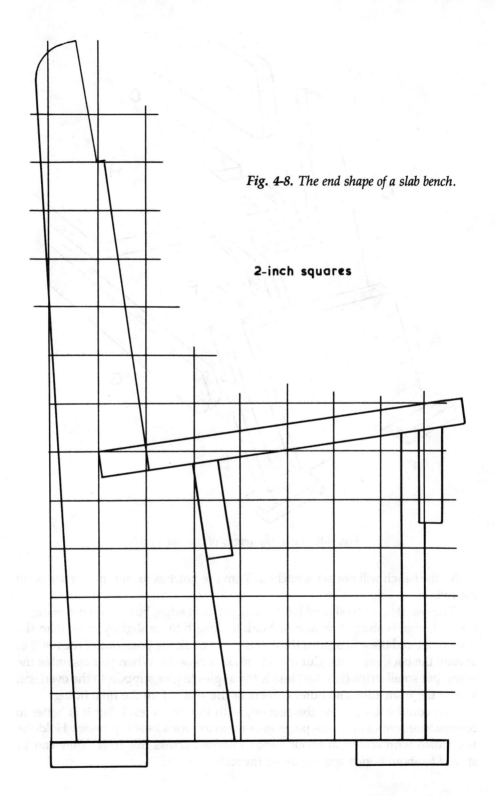

Fig. 4-8. The end shape of a slab bench.

2-inch squares

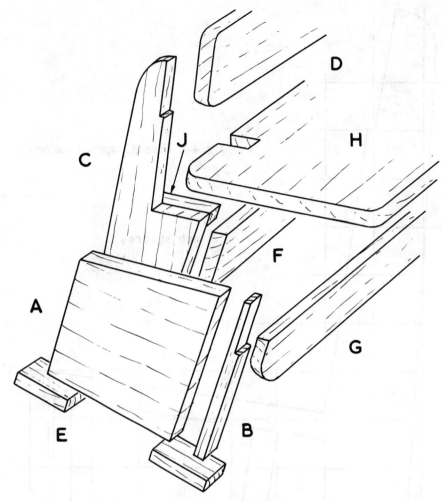

Fig. 4-9. Assembly details of the slab bench.

under the bench will not get scratched. Trim the notches to suit; nail or screw on the rail.

The seat (FIG. 4-9H) should have a straight front edge, but it does not matter if the rear edge is straight or waney. Mark its length to be slightly more than the front rail. Hold the seat against the assembly to mark the positions of the notches around the back supports. Cut them to make a close fit. When you assemble the piece, put small strips (FIG. 4-9J) inside the angles to give support to the overlaps. Round the front edge and outer corners of the seat before the final fitting.

You could nail or screw the seat on, with the heads level, but it is better to counterbore screws and glue plugs over them to give a neat top finish. Hold the seat down with screws at about 2-inch intervals across the ends. They can be spread to about 6-inch spacing along the rails.

The back can be the width you like, but it looks best if the waney top edge is higher near the center. Make it the same length as the seat. Round ends and exposed edges. Attach it to its supports the same way as the seat.

This type of bench can be made more attractive by having something carved at the center of the back. It might just be the date cut in with a knife. A motif could be formed from the initials of the maker or owner; it might be the badge of an organization. Keep it simple and bold. Natural wood, probably not fully seasoned at the time of carving, does not accept fine detail carving without the risk of breaking out.

Dual-purpose Stool

A stool at normal seat height has many uses and is particularly welcomed by anyone unable to stand for long. This stool (FIG. 4-10) has a seat 12 inches × 20 inches, 15 inches from the ground (FIG. 4-11). The handles at each end can be used for carrying and will also be valuable for pushing yourself up if your legs are weak (FIG. 4-10A). Additionally, the stool can be turned on its side and used as a kneeler for gardening, giving ample knee area about 6 inches from the ground (FIG. 4-10B). Hand holes near the edges serve the same purpose in this position, as the handles do with the seat at the top. A cushion can be transferred between the positions.

The stool is made from 1-inch boards. Ideally, these should be a durable hardwood that can be left outside. Use softwood for a lighter stool, protected by paint and stored inside. The suggested construction is with wedged tenons; this makes an extremely strong assembly with a traditional appearance. It would be possible to use 5/8-inch dowels, with two in each end of the rails and at least four in the ends of the top. The instructions assume you will use tenons. Exact sizes of the stool are not important, but if you alter them, be careful not to make the seat too narrow and unsteady.

The key parts are the pair of ends (FIGS. 4-12 and 13A). Mark them out, using the pattern of squares to get the outline of the shaped top (FIG. 4-12A). Check the actual thicknesses of the lengthwise pieces when marking the mortises and the dado grooves for the top. Make the grooves 1/4-inch deep (FIG. 4-13B). All mortises are 2 inches wide (FIG. 4-12B). Mark the mortises, but do not cut them until you have prepared the tenons and can compare sizes for good fits.

The hand holes are made by drilling holes and cutting between them. Make the holes 1 1/4 inches in diameter, if possible. If you do not have a drill bit larger than 1 inch, you can use that, but do not cut the hand holes any narrower. Smooth inside the slots and round the edges for a comfortable grip.

Cut the seat (FIG. 4-13C) with tenons to match the mortises. Make the tenons in the seat and rails about 1/8 inch too long, for leveling after assembly. The three rails are identical (FIG. 4-13D). Arrange the top rail to come close to the seat. Remember that the rails are shorter than the seat by the amount it goes into the grooves in the ends.

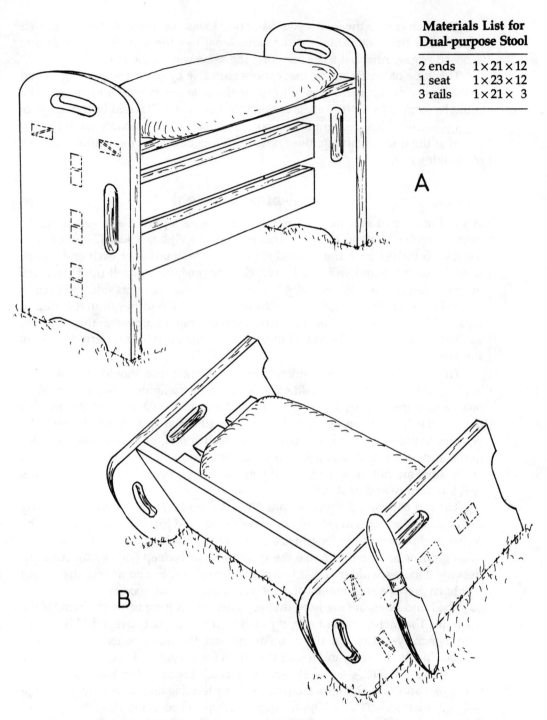

**Materials List for
Dual-purpose Stool**

2 ends	$1 \times 21 \times 12$
1 seat	$1 \times 23 \times 12$
3 rails	$1 \times 21 \times 3$

A

B

Fig. 4-10. The multi-purpose stool can be used upright as a seat or on its side as a kneeler.

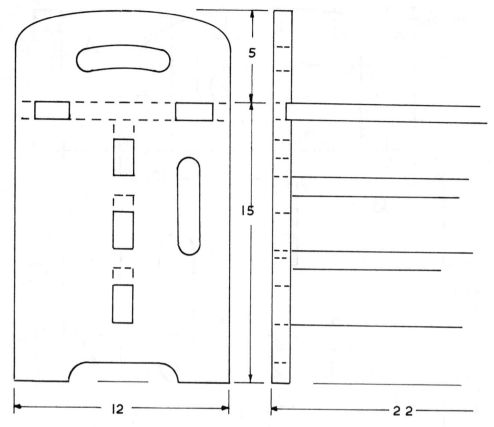

Fig. 4-11. Suggested sizes for the multi-purpose stool.

Cut the mortises to match the tenons. Round edges of the seat and take sharpness off other parts that will be exposed. Make saw cuts in the tenons for wedging (FIG. 4-13E). Those in the seat tenons can be diagonal for a decorative effect (FIGS. 4-12C and 13F). Make wedges from the same wood as the other parts, if they are hardwood, but if the stool is softwood, hardwood wedges will be more effective than softwood ones.

Use waterproof glue in all joints and on the wedges. Glue the top rail to the seat. The parts should pull the assembly square, but work on a level surface to guard against twist. Drive in wedges tightly. Make sure each tenon is fully home in its mortise as you wedge it. Leave the wedges projecting until the glue has set; then, cut them and the tenon ends level. Check that the stool does not wobble. If necessary, correct a wobble by planing one or more feet.

Leave a durable hardwood untreated and allow it to weather. It might benefit from rubbing with oil. Paint softwood and touch it up when it becomes worn in use; otherwise, there is a risk of rot due to water penetration.

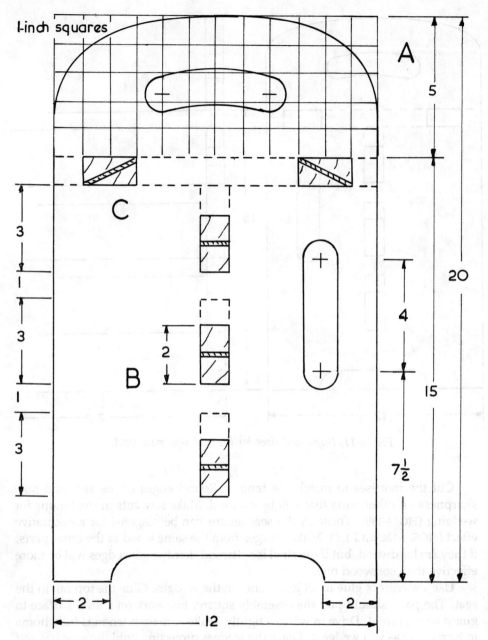

1-inch squares

A

5

C

3

1

3

1

3

B

2

20

4

15

7½

2

12

2

Fig. 4-12. The shape of an end of the multi-purpose stool.

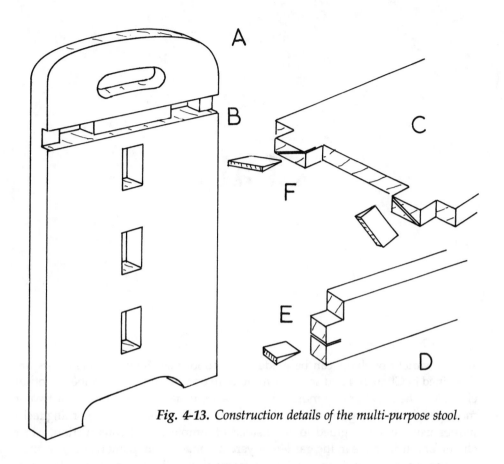

Fig. 4-13. *Construction details of the multi-purpose stool.*

5

Chairs

A great variety of chairs can be made for outdoor use. Some simple chairs are described in Chapter 4 and seats for more than one person are described in other chapters. The rougher and more rustic seats are usually large enough for two or more people. Building chairs includes rather more advanced woodworking techniques using cut and glued joints instead of simple nailed construction. Most chairs for outdoor use in the garden or yard are made from planed and seasoned wood with mortise and tenon joints in many, if not all, meeting places between parts.

Chairs are often made to match tables, using generally similar layouts and construction, so there is a balanced appearance when several chairs are grouped around a table. Some seats for more than one person can be made to match as well. Assess your probable needs, and keep in mind a general pattern, even if you are only making one chair at first.

If chairs are made from prepared wood, stock sizes of sections can be less than specified because the quoted size is before it is machine planed. For example, you will find that 2×2 inches quoted is actually not much more than 1³/₄ inches finished. Allow for it when marking out. Where joints have to be cut, mark from the actual pieces of wood, rather than rely on measurements for widths of cuts.

In better quality chairs, use galvanized nails or otherwise protect nails from corrosion. Iron screws should also be protected; they can be counterbored, where the wood is thick enough, so that plugs can be glued over their heads. Modern waterproof glue, particularly the type intended for boatbuilding, will help to make strong weatherproof chairs.

Side Chair

The outdoor side chair has a normal sitting height (FIGS. 5-1 and 5-2) for use with a table outside. With cushions it provides a certain amount of relaxation, but not

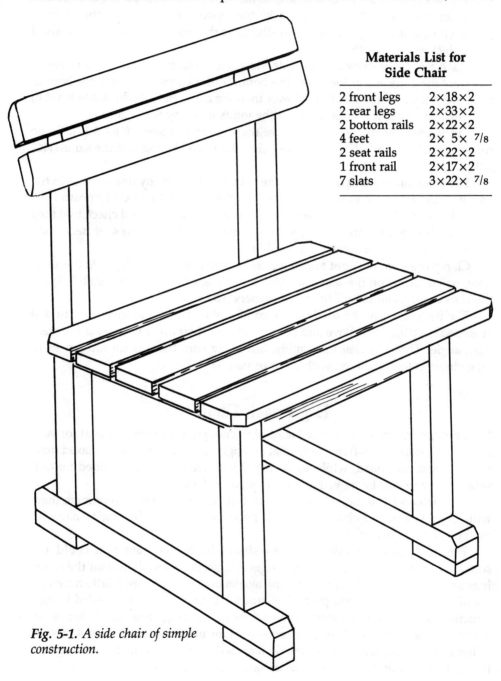

Materials List for Side Chair

2 front legs	$2 \times 18 \times 2$
2 rear legs	$2 \times 33 \times 2$
2 bottom rails	$2 \times 22 \times 2$
4 feet	$2 \times 5 \times \frac{7}{8}$
2 seat rails	$2 \times 22 \times 2$
1 front rail	$2 \times 17 \times 2$
7 slats	$3 \times 22 \times \frac{7}{8}$

Fig. 5-1. A side chair of simple construction.

as much as those chairs shaped for lounging. It is more appropriate for working at a table or for having outdoor meals.

The seat is made of slats (FIG. 5-2A) and the back is similar (FIG. 5-2B). Firm attachments of the slats gives stiffness to the chair. The other parts have mortise and tenon joints (FIG. 5-3A). Do not take the tenons right through; they will be strong enough if they go in about two-thirds of the thickness, and are one-third of the thickness in width.

Make a full-size drawing of a side view (FIG. 5-3B) to get the sizes of parts. Mark out the pairs of legs together. The bottoms of the legs tenon into the bottom rails. The back of the seat is 1 inch lower than the front. Set an adjustable bevel to this angle, and use it for marking out the joints made by the seat rails.

Cut the tops of the rear legs to give the back slats a slope (FIG. 5-3C). Some corners are shown cut off. For neatness they should all be marked the same (FIG. 5-3D).

The chair might stand directly on the bottom rails, but any unevenness in the ground would cause it to wobble. To reduce this risk, put feet underneath (FIG. 5-2C). Assemble the two chair sides over the fullsize drawing, and check that they match each other. Clean off surplus glue and level the surfaces, if necessary, before going on to complete the assembly.

Clamp the front rail tight and check its squareness with the legs. At the same time, nail or screw on the seat slats; check that the sides are kept parallel. Space the slats evenly, and cut off the front corners (FIG. 5-2D).

The back slats can be made more comfortable if they are given a rounded cross section (FIG. 5-3E) above and below. Take off their outer corners at the standard angle. That completes assembly, but make sure there is no roughness or raggedness before finishing with paint or varnish.

High-back Chair

Most outdoor chairs do not have backs high enough to provide support for your head. This chair (FIG. 5-4) is arranged at an angle, so you can sit in a relaxed position and rest your head, while still being able to read or knit. Intended for outside use, it can also be moved about the yard or deck.

Sizes (FIG. 5-5) should suit most users, but you might wish to compare them with other chairs and change them, if necessary, without having to alter the method of construction.

The best chair is made of a rot-resistant hardwood, but you could use softwood treated with preservative. Suggested sections are shown on the drawings and in the Materials List, but if the available stock sizes are a little different, it will not matter. Use wood planed all around. Some screws are needed in construction. They should be steel protected by galvanizing or other treatment, or you could use brass or other corrosion-resistant metal screws. Many joints are either mortise and tenon or doweled, with waterproof glue in all meeting surfaces. A chair built in this way should have a very long life.

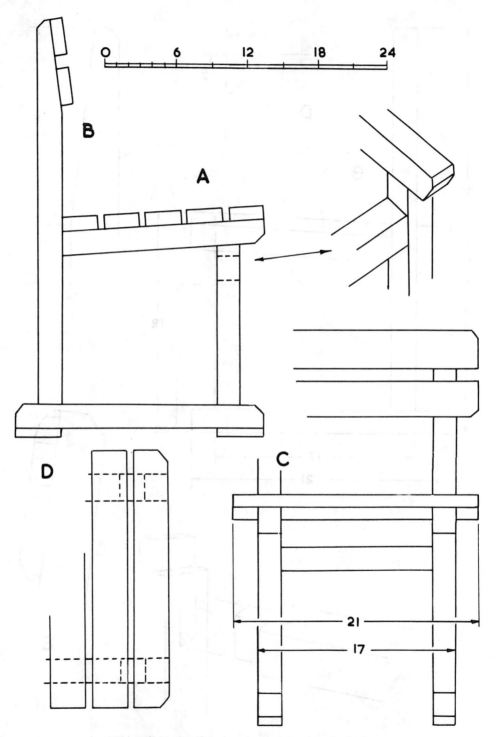

Fig. 5-2. Suggested sizes for the simple side chair.

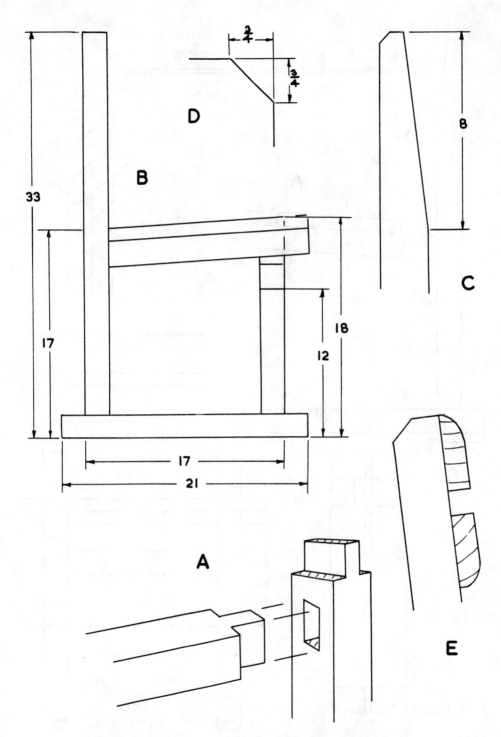

Fig. 5-3. Main sizes and construction details of the side chair.

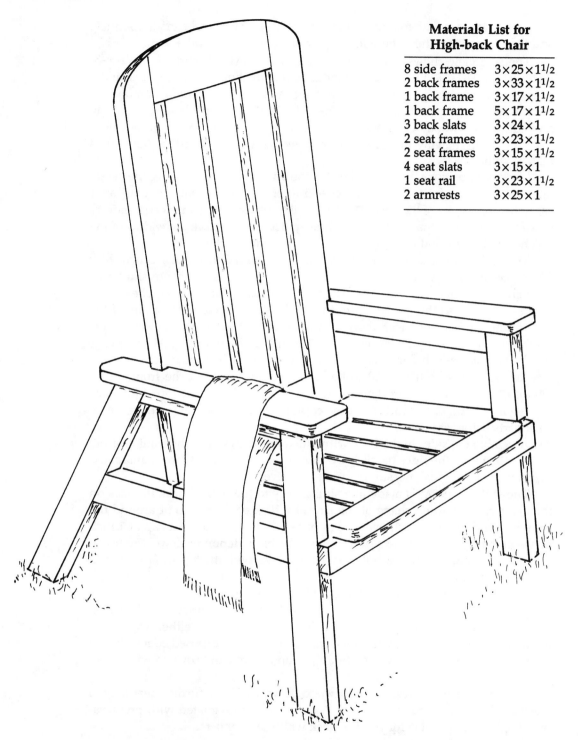

Materials List for High-back Chair

8 side frames	$3 \times 25 \times 1\frac{1}{2}$
2 back frames	$3 \times 33 \times 1\frac{1}{2}$
1 back frame	$3 \times 17 \times 1\frac{1}{2}$
1 back frame	$5 \times 17 \times 1\frac{1}{2}$
3 back slats	$3 \times 24 \times 1$
2 seat frames	$3 \times 23 \times 1\frac{1}{2}$
2 seat frames	$3 \times 15 \times 1\frac{1}{2}$
4 seat slats	$3 \times 15 \times 1$
1 seat rail	$3 \times 23 \times 1\frac{1}{2}$
2 armrests	$3 \times 25 \times 1$

Fig. 5-4. The high-back chair is stable and provides good support.

Construction is with four main sub-assemblies, which can be made complete and then joined together. These are: a pair of sides, a back and a seat.

The side view shows the leg assemblies (FIG. 5-5A). All parts are $1^1/_2$-×-3-inch section (FIG. 5-6A) with halving joints at the junctions (FIG. 5-6B). Leave the wood for the joints slightly too long, so you can plane it level after assembly. Set out the shape of the parts on scrap plywood; use this as a guide when marking and cutting the wood. Cut notches for the seat crossbar in the front legs (FIG. 5-6C). Glue the halving joints; screw or dowel as well. Check that both sides match, without a twist.

Mark the positions of the notches for the back before assembling the sides, but you might prefer to leave final checking of the in line notches until after assembly. The angle of the back (FIG. 5-6D) will probably suit your needs; modify this if you wish. Cut the notches $1/_2$ inch deep (FIG. 5-6E). Check the widths of the notches with the wood that will be used for the sides of the back.

The back is a frame of wood $1^1/_2$ inches thick with 3-inch slats, 1 inch thick (FIGS. 5-5B and 7A). Vary the height, if you wish, but what is shown should be enough for most users. The 19-inch width of the back fits into the notches in the side assemblies, so the usable width in the chair is 18 inches. The parts of the back frame can be joined with mortise and tenon joints, in the same way as seat parts (FIG. 5-8B), taking the tenons about 1 inch into the mortises. Alternatively, use $1/_2$-inch or $5/_8$-inch dowels, with at least three in each joint.

Arrange the slats (FIG. 5-7B) to be level with the frame at the front, using tenons (FIGS. 5-7C and 8C) or dowels (FIGS. 5-7D and 8D). Cut the top of the back to a regular curve, or just round out the corners. Also, round out the edges of all back parts before assembly.

Assemble the sides to the back with glue and screws; add the front seat rail (FIG. 5-5C) to hold the sides parallel. Do this on a level surface. Check squareness by comparing diagonal measurements at seat level.

The seat (FIG. 5-8A) is made in a similar way to the back. Check its sizes on the chair. Make it to overhang at the sides by $1/_2$ inch. Notch to fit around the front legs and project 1 inch over the front rail. There should be a gap of 1 inch between the rear edge of the seat and the chair back. Tenon or dowel the frame parts, and arrange the slats evenly spaced and level with the top surface. Round all edges before assembly.

Fit the seat in place with waterproof glue and screws.

Make the armrests (FIG. 5-5D) to fit level with the inner surfaces of the sides. Make them parallel or reduce them in width towards the back, either with a simple taper or with a curve. Round the front corners and all exposed edges. Join to the sides with glue and screws, preferably counterbored and covered with wood plugs.

If you have used rot-resistant hardwood, leave it without further treatment to weather. Otherwise you can paint it. A softwood, impregnated with preservative, might be unsuitable for paint. Check with the suppliers.

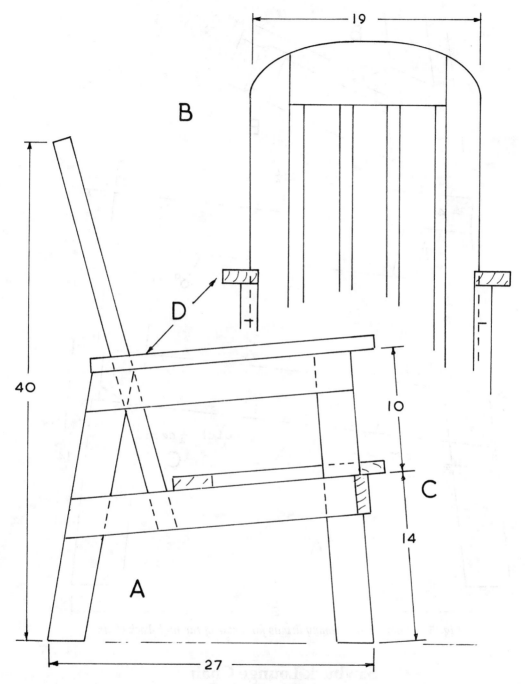

Fig. 5-5. Main sizes for a high-back chair.

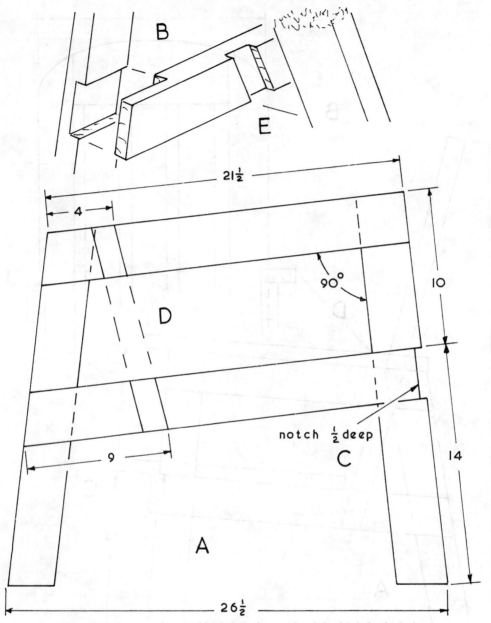

Fig. 5-6. Shape and assembly details for a side of the high-back chair.

Sawbuck Lounge Chair

The chair shown in FIG. 5-9 is intended to fill the need for a light comfortable small chair with a lounging angle. Its shaping allows it to be used without padding (although cushions could be added). It can be carried easily, so several of

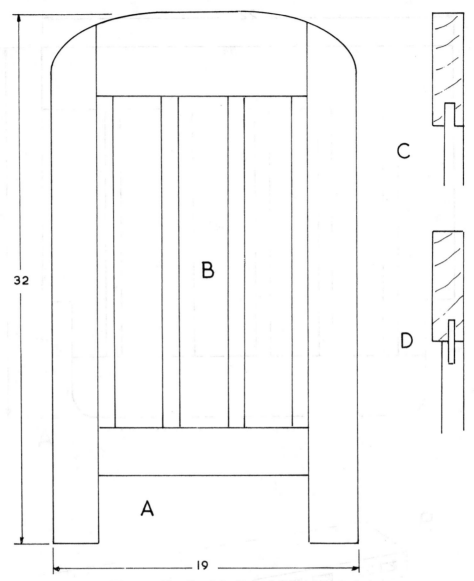

Fig. 5-7. Details of the back of the high-back chair.

these chairs could be provided for guests to move around as they gather into groups. If made of good quality wood and given a suitable finish, the chair could also be used indoors.

The main structure consists of two crossing frames, joined with a few cross-bars; then the seat and back are curved plywood. The wood should be hardwood and the crossing pieces should have a reasonably straight grain without knots. Select pieces with the grain following the curve of each piece. The plywood

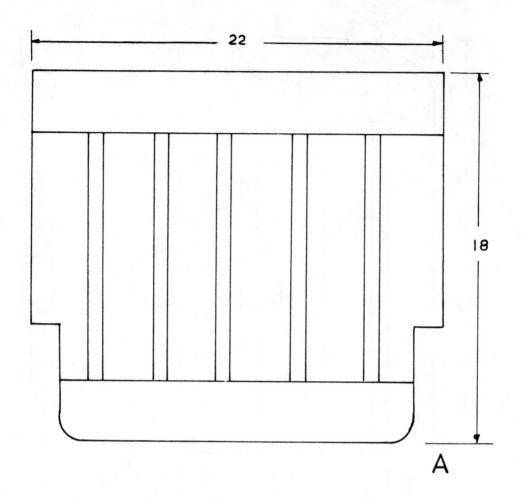

A

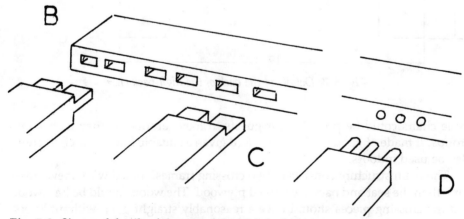

Fig. 5-8. Sizes and details of the seat of the high-back chair.

Fig. 5-9. Sawbuck lounge chair.

should be exterior or marine grade. If you use veneers, bond with waterproof glue.

The sizes shown in the Materials List and FIG. 5-10 give a chair of relaxing proportions to suit an adult. A slightly smaller version could be made for a child. In particular, the front edge could be lowered to suit shorter legs. In that case, the seat would also have to be reduced back to front.

Materials List for Sawbuck Lounge Chair

2 inner legs	$5 \times 34 \times 1$
2 outer legs	$4 \times 34 \times 1$
4 rails	$2 \times 20 \times 1$
1 seat	$18 \times 21 \times 1/4$
1 back	$8 \times 21 \times 1/4$

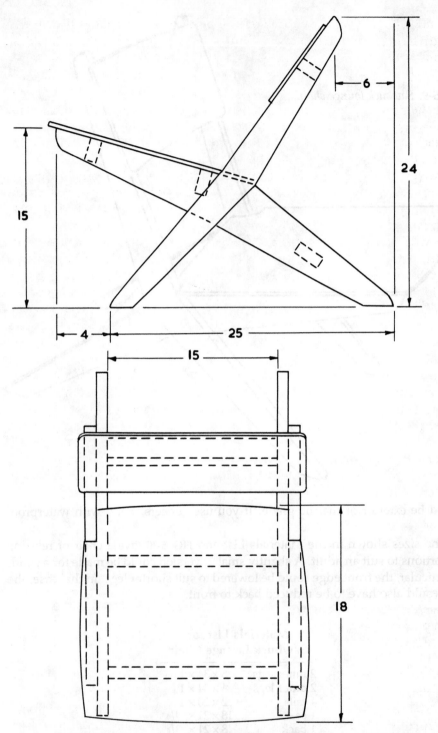

Fig. 5-10. Two dimensioned views of the sawbuck lounge chair.

A full-size drawing is essential; draw it on a pattern of squares (FIG. 5-11A). Strength has to come where the parts cross; do not reduce sizes there. Mark the locations of the two supporting pieces under the seat and the single one at the back. There is also a rail between the rear legs. The surfaces toward the sitter are straight, but the other surfaces can be curved (except where the parts cross).

Where the pieces cross, notch them into each other, but do not use full halving joints to bring the parts to the same level. That would remove too much wood from each piece. Instead, cut not more than 1/4 inch from each piece (FIG. 5-11B) so that the back legs come outside the seat legs.

The seat and back have similar curves. A simple way of forming them is to use two thicknesses of 1/8-inch or 3mm plywood. Cut this with the grain of the outside veneers the straight way of the parts—the short direction—two for each part slightly too large at this stage.

Provide two stiff boards that will not deflect when clamping over them and four strips longer than the width of the pieces being shaped. Take off any sharpness of the edges that will come against the plywood. Put the plywood between the strips and boards; then squeeze with clamps (FIG. 5-11C). The exact amount of deflection is not important, but aim to push in about a 1-inch curve. If that dry trial is satisfactory, open up and coat the meeting surfaces with waterproof glue. Then clamp again. If the plywood is rather unyielding, dry clamp and leave the assembly overnight. Preferably you should curve it a little more than you will eventually want, so that the plywood becomes accustomed to curving. Then when you make the glued assembly, the seat or back will hold its shape.

An alternative is to make your own curved plywood from veneers. If possible, get veneers at least as thick as those used in plywood (which are between 1mm and 2mm, or 1/16 inch upward. The thinner veneers used in cabinetwork would require too many thicknesses to be glued. To get a smooth, curved shape, you have to make a jig or former. It can be a frame with thin plywood sprung to shape on it (FIG. 5-11D). There will probably have to be at least one intermediate crossbar to keep the plywood to a regular curve. Provide another piece of flexible plywood ready for applying pressure.

Prepare enough pieces of veneer to make up nearly a 1/4-inch total thickness, but make it an odd number so that both outside veneers have their grain the short way. Put newspaper over the former, so the veneers will not become attached with any surplus glue. Apply glue to the veneers and bring them together. Put the loose plywood over the top, with newspaper underneath; then, put on pressure with strips of wood and C-clamps. Leave it until you are certain the glue is hard. Some glues appear to be hard in a few hours, but they need a day or more to build up their full strength.

Whichever method of shaping is used, trim the back piece parallel and to a length that will overhang the supports slightly. Round the outer corners (FIG. 5-12A). The seat also overhangs, but it looks better if the edges are cut to curves. At the rear, you have to shape the seat to fit between the outer legs (FIG. 5-12B). Round all edges.

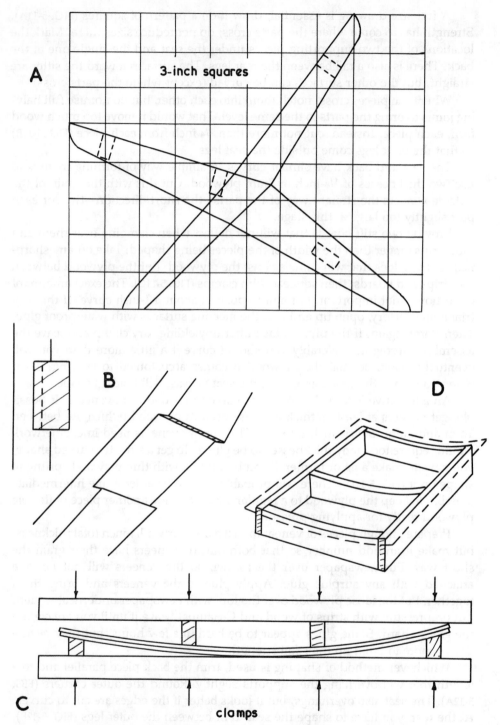

A

3-inch squares

B

D

C

clamps

Fig. 5-11. Shaping the parts of a sawbuck lounge chair.

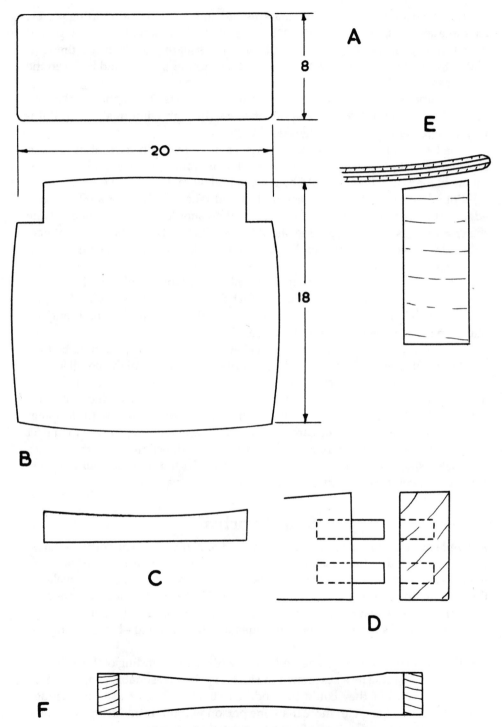

Fig. 5-12. Seat back, and rails of the sawbuck lounge chair.

Use the back as a template for marking the hollows in the supporting pieces. All three are the same curve (FIG. 5-12C). They could be tenoned into the legs, but dowels are suggested (FIG. 5-12D). Cut the ends squarely to fit inside the legs. Make the one behind the back longer than those under the seat and between the inner legs.

The curved parts have to bear against their supports. The slope of the meeting surfaces is not much, and you might screw through without shaping. But it would be better to bevel the edges (FIG. 5-12E).

The lower rail between the rear legs is a simple piece doweled at its ends or tenoned into the legs. Round its edges. If you want to follow on the curved theme of the seat edges, it could be given a hollow in its width (FIG. 5-12F).

Round all ends of the side assemblies and take the sharpness off exposed edges. The tops project above the back, so they should be well rounded. Glue the crossed legs. Waterproof glue should be sufficient. For additional reinforcement, drive two screws into each joint from inside—where the heads will not show. Check to make sure that opposite sides match.

Join these parts with the crosswise members (pulling together with clamps). Check squareness at seat level and see that the chair stands upright. The plywood parts will hold the chair in shape; for additional strength, glue triangular blocks in the corners of the framing under the seat.

Leave this assembly for the glue to set before adding the plywood parts; they can be glued down. If you can get close fits, glue alone might be all that is needed; then there will be nothing to mar the surfaces. Glue does not hold well if the joints are less than perfect. You will probably need to use fine nails with small heads. They can be punched below the surface and covered with stopping. If you prefer to use screws, be careful to get them level with the surface for a neat effect. You might even get their slots all in the same direction across the chair.

For outside use, finish with varnish or paint. For both indoor/outdoor use, stain it to match existing furniture, and finish it with varnish.

Strip Armchair

A simple robust armchair can be made of hard or soft wood. The softwood must be well protected with preservative and paint or varnish. All of the parts are made of wood of the same section. In the simplest form, it is possible to make all the joints with screws using just two, 10-gauge-by-2^1/$_2$-inch, flat-head screws at most crossings. If several chairs are to be made, prefabricate the parts for all of them to standard sizes—with edges rounded and holes drilled—before doing any assembly work.

The chair (FIG. 5-13) has a squared shape with some rounding of the arms and a slope to the back. The sizes shown in FIG. 5-14 give a reasonable proportion for most purposes, but they could be modified slightly. Do not use an extended design to make a bench for more than one person without introducing additional lengthwise members to give rigidity to the extended shape.

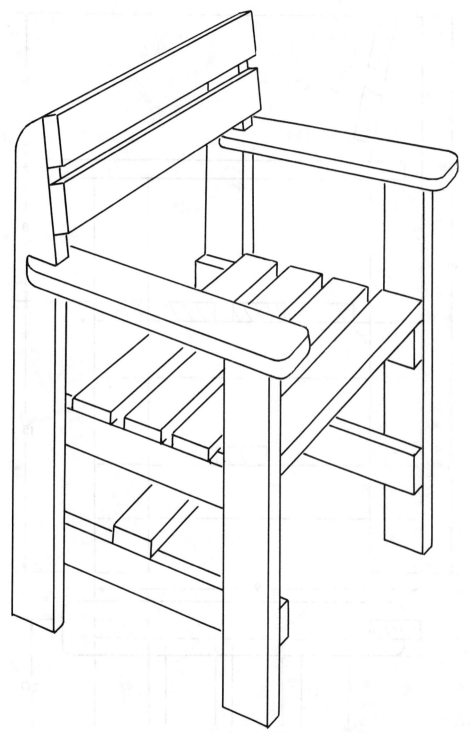

Fig. 5-13. An armchair mostly made of similar strips.

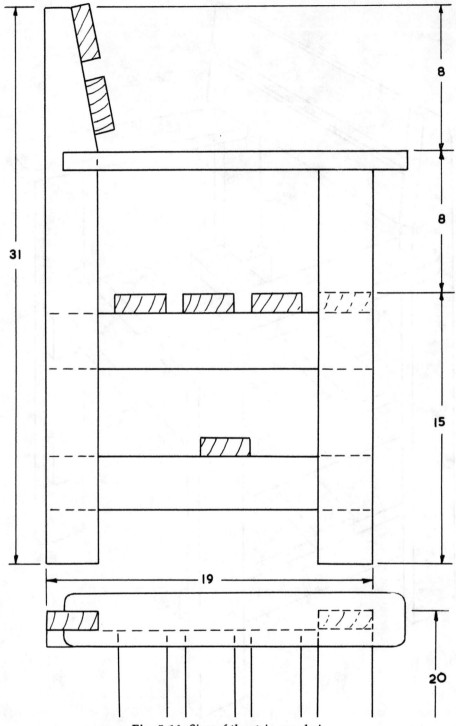

Fig. 5-14. Sizes of the strip armchair.

2 rear legs	$3 \times 32 \times 1$
2 front legs	$3 \times 23 \times 1$
4 side rails	$3 \times 20 \times 1$
2 arms	$3 \times 21 \times 1$
5 cross pieces	$3 \times 20 \times 1$
2 cross pieces	$3 \times 21 \times 1$

Make all four legs (FIGS. 5-15A and 15B). Make the side rails (FIG. 5-15C) with screw holes arranged diagonally. Make the arms to match (FIG. 5-15D). At the rear, the slot should make a close fit on the leg and be drilled for two screws (entered at opposite sides to miss each other). Round the edges and corners of the arms. Assemble the sides with the crossbars inward. Check that they are square and match each other. If you prefer, use glue as well as screws.

Prepare the five pieces that make the seat and lower rail (FIG. 5-15E). Round the top edges of the seat. Have the front rails level with the legs, and space the others evenly. The back rails (FIG. 5-15F) are longer, but check the final length on the chair before cutting and fitting in place. The lower rail is screwed to the side rails.

A simple arrangement of lap and screws at each crossing might be adequate, but anyone wanting a more craftsmanlike construction will prefer to include some fitted joints.

The lower rail would be better arranged upright and tenoned (FIG. 5-16A). Tenons taken through and wedged would be strongest.

If the joint between each arm and its rear leg is altered to include a shallow notch in the leg (FIG. 5-16B), the arm is positively located, and the screws are relieved of downward strain.

The screws through the arm into the front leg should be counterbored (FIG. 5-16C), but they go into the end grain, which might not provide a good grip on the screw threads. For a tighter screwed joint, put dowels across so that the screw threads pull into them across their grain (FIG. 5-16D). Preferably, use mortise and tenon joints instead of screws between the arms and the front legs. Take the tenons through and wedge them (FIG. 5-16D). Make stub tenons if you do not want their ends to show.

Slab Armchair

Wide boards, cut straight across a log, are often available from a saw mill. The chair shown in FIG. 5-17 is intended to make use of these slabs (which can be $1^{1}/_{2}$ inches thick or more). The finished chair is intended to be kept outdoors almost indefinitely. Its sawn surface will weather to blend in with its surroundings. Some woods will benefit from treating with preservative, but oak and other durable hardwoods can be left untreated. The chair is shown free-standing. It

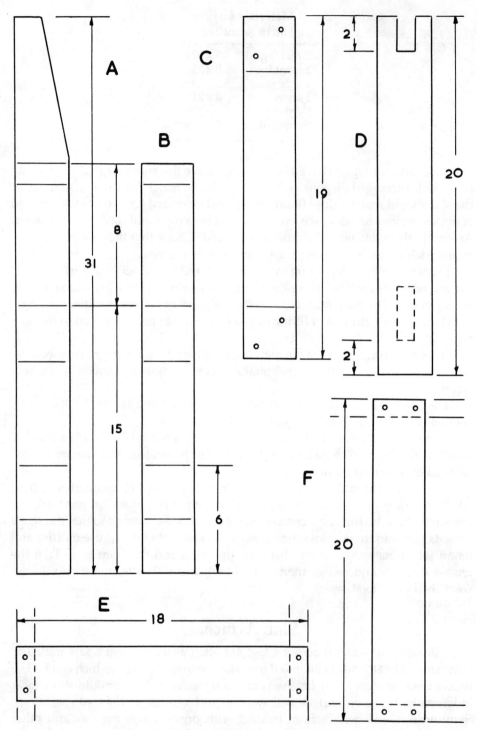

Fig. 5-15. Main parts for a strip armchair.

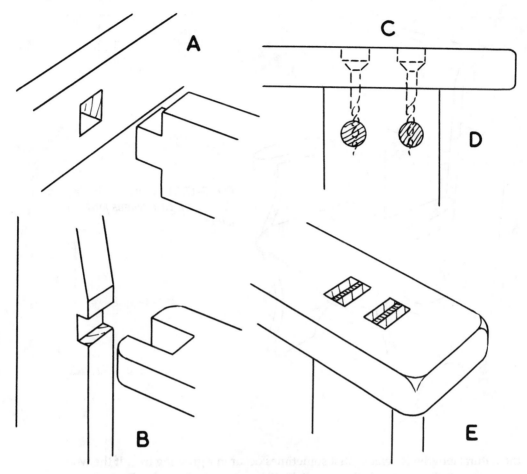

Fig. 5-16. Construction methods for the strip armchair.

can be moved about, but if its position is settled, it could have the legs extended to go into the ground. Alternately, it might be held down by pegs into the ground or brackets to a concrete base.

Sizes are not crucial; they can be adapted to suit available wood. Refer to the Materials List. It is possible to make use of waney edges as decorative features. You do not need to plane straight edges where they would match surroundings better if left to the natural curves. Only the joints and the bottom edges need accurate cutting. The sizes shown in FIG. 5-18 give a seat of comfortable proportions. If you vary them to suit your wood, keep the seat about the same area and height. Fix the back at a moderate slope and a position to come below the shoulder blades.

Examine the wood for flaws. Knots that are obviously well bonded to the surrounding wood will not matter if they come in the body of a part, but they would be weak if they have to be cut to make joints. Look for shakes; these are

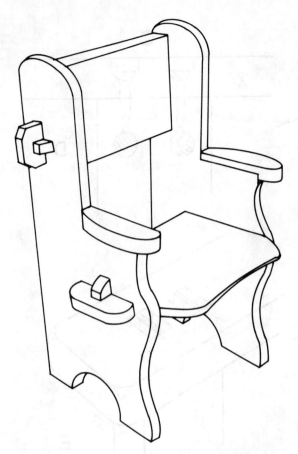

Fig. 5-17. An armchair, made from slabs, with tusk tenons for the main joints.

the natural lengthwise cracks that sometimes occur in a growing tree. If the wood has not yet fully seasoned, they are liable to open as the wood dries further. A shake that goes through to the end of the wood will not matter, but it would be an unacceptable weakness in a short part such as the front of the seat or toward the edge of the back piece.

With wood of uneven width, accurate assembly includes the positions and angles of the seat, back, and arms in relation to the floor (FIG. 5-19A). This can be

Materials List for
Slab Armchair

2 sides	$20 \times 38 \times 1^{1}/_{2}$
1 seat	$15 \times 31 \times 1^{1}/_{2}$
1 back	$12 \times 31 \times 1^{1}/_{2}$
2 arms	$3 \times 13 \times 1^{1}/_{2}$
4 wedges	$2 \times 5 \times 2$

(approximate only)

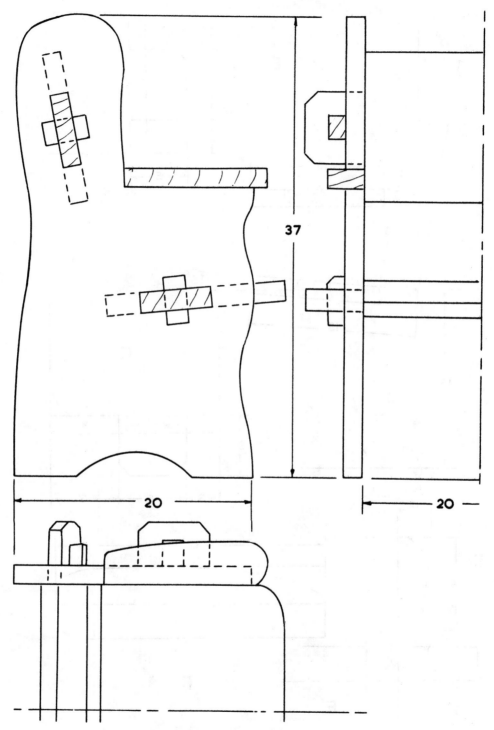

Fig. 5-18. Sizes for a slab armchair.

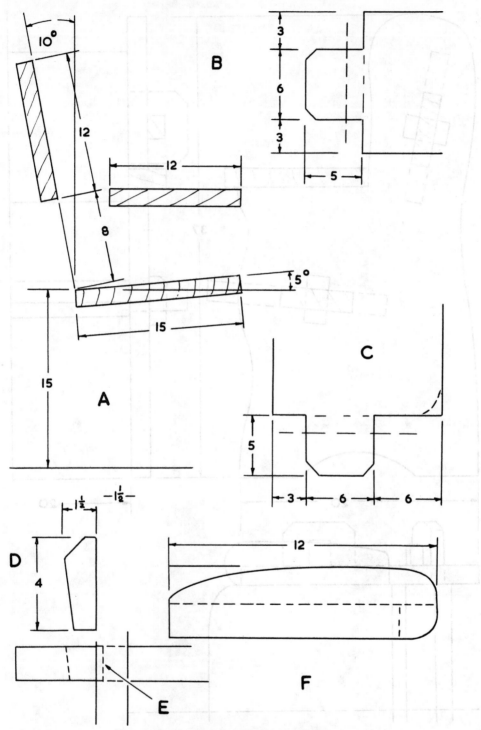

Fig. 5-19. Detail sizes of a slab armchair.

set out on a side that has its bottom edge cut straight. Make sure there is enough wood around the marked positions to provide strength. If you have to alter sizes to suit the wood, give the seat a slight tilt (5 degrees to horizontal is shown) and slope the back rather more (10 degrees to vertical is shown). Keep the arms horizontal.

Mark the full widths and then the mortises. Both are 6 inches wide, but the ones for the seat are offset in its width. Prepare the seat and back; mark the chair width across both pieces the same, so that they fit evenly between the sides. Then, mark the tenons, centrally on the back pieces (FIG. 5-19B) and toward the back on the seat (FIG. 5-19C).

Remove the waste from the wide mortise carefully. Drill out as much as possible. Then, trim with chisels from both sides toward the center of the thickness, so as not to break out the grain fibers. The holes should be a reasonably tight fit on the tenons. Deal with each joint independently, and mark them so the same parts go together during assembly. This is particularly important if the wood varies in thickness—as newly sawn wood often does.

Prepare the four wedges (FIG. 5-19D). Give them a slight taper (1/4 inch in 4 inches is about right) and bevel the top, which will be hit during assembly. Cut the tapered holes to match the wedges, but have the inner edges slightly inside the thickness of the mortised part (FIG. 5-19E), so the tightening wedge pulls the tenon into the mortise without itself coming against the inner edge of the hole in the tenon.

Some parts of the wood can be left with waney edges, but those edges that will come into contact with a user should have any sharpness removed. Use a waney edge at the fronts of the chair sides, but otherwise you can bandsaw to a curve (FIG. 5-18). Round out the front corners of the seat and remove any sharpness along its front edge.

The arms (FIG. 5-19F) are nailed or screwed on to the sides with their inner edges level. Make their widths about twice the thickness of the wood. Round out the fronts and outer edges; take off any sharpness around the sides. Although a natural and rather rustic appearance is a feature of the other parts of the chair, the chair arms should be shaped and cleaned up so they are comfortable to the touch.

6

Other seating

There is no clear line between what are simple seats and what are more complicated seats. Also, it is difficult to draw a line between chairs and other seats. If a chair is made longer, it is no longer a chair, but the constructional work will be the same. Most of the seats described in this chapter require more advanced techniques than those in Chapter 4, but the work is still not very difficult.

Most seats in this group are larger than chairs (they can seat two or more people), but they have backs and they can have arms like chairs. The general form can be like some of the simple seats with these additions.

The provision of seating is one of the main requirements of outdoor furniture. If a seat can be made to serve more than one person, it will be more economical of space and will usually mean less work for the craftsman than if he made individual seats.

Tusk-tenoned Bench

Much medieval furniture was held together with what are now called *tusk tenons*. Such a tenon goes right through a mortise and is held tight with a wedge. This was a satisfactory way of putting together furniture when proper seasoning was not understood. Joints could be tightened easily if the wood shrank. It also allowed furniture to be taken apart. When a feudal lord traveled, he took much of his furniture with him and his staff put it together at any of his stopping places.

It is possible to make a bench where the lengthwise parts are all tusk tenoned into the ends. It can be made of parallel planed pieces of wood, but the example shown in FIG. 6-1 is made of slabs of waney-edged wood.

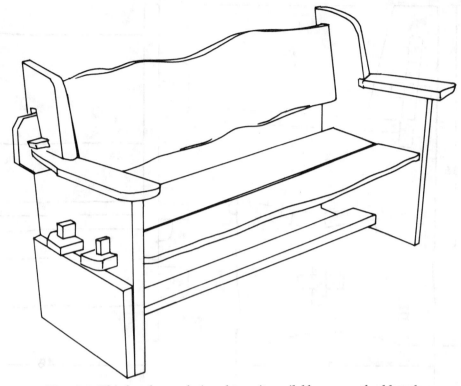

Fig. 6-1. *This bench was designed to suit available waney-edged boards.*

Sizes depend on available wood, but you can obtain a reasonable proportion by using wood about 1¹/₂ inches thick (see the Materials List and FIG. 6-2A). Although edges may come indiscriminately you have to establish straight lines where the joints come, to get proper fits. Wide boards with the grain vertical make up the ends (FIG. 6-2B). If there is no straightedge to work to, draw a line through the slope of the back to act as a datum from which other parts can be measured. The back should be between 10 inches and 15 inches wide (FIG. 6-2C), with its tenon about half that width. The seat is shown as two boards dipping in

Materials List for
Tusk-tenoned Bench

2 ends	22 × 36 × 1¹/₂
1 back	12 × 57 × 1¹/₂
2 seats	9 × 57 × 1¹/₂
1 stretcher (optional)	6 × 57 × 1¹/₂
2 arms	4 × 22 × 1¹/₂

(Approximate sizes for guidance)

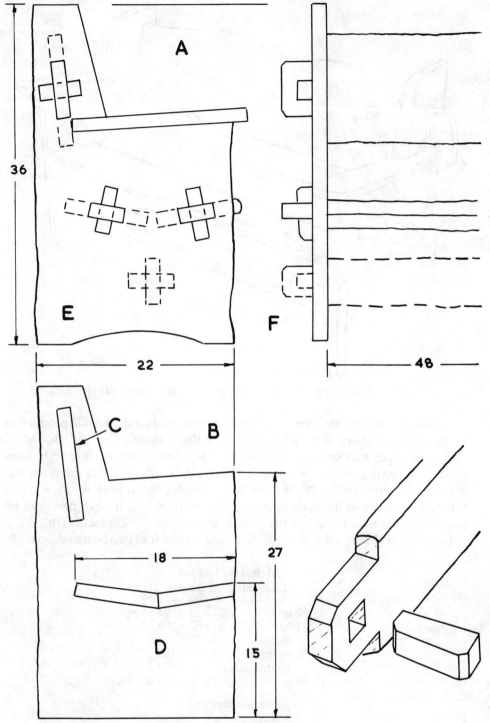

Fig. 6-2. A tusk-tenoned bench.

a shallow V to give an approximation of a curved seat (FIG. 6-2D). Make the tenons about half the width of each board.

With the general arrangement marked on one end, its mortises can be cut. If you are using parallel planed wood, the shapes can be continued over each of the edges to the other side. Then cutting can be done a little from each side. For rougher wood, it should be satisfactory to do most of the cutting from the one marked side. A small amount of breaking out on the far side will not matter. Drill through near the corners of each mortise. Then, more holes can be drilled inside the lines (FIG. 6-3A). In that way, only a small amount of chopping with a chisel will be needed to remove the waste center. Square the edges by further chopping with chisels. The mortises do not have to be close fits on the tenons; leave finishing the mortises until you have the tenons ready to try in them. Bring the second end to the same stage as the first.

Lay out the back and seat boards, so you can draw parallel lines across, to mark what will be the insides of the ends (FIG. 6-3B). The meeting edges of the seat boards should be fairly straight. A slight waneyness of the seat front edge will not matter, but if it is very uneven it would be better to straighten and round its section.

The tenons must go through far enough to take the wedges and have enough wood beyond to avoid the grain breaking out when a wedge is driven. Allow for the wedges being fairly thick and about the same distance of solid wood on the tenon beyond them (FIG. 6-3C). Cut the wedge slots to match their slope. Since the wedge must tighten against the bench end, cut the slot back, so some of it remains within the end mortise. If the wedge ever hits that surface, it will cease to tighten.

Leave some excess wood on the tenons; they can all be trimmed to matching lengths later. Similarly, make the wedges overlong at first. Then they can be trimmed to about the same length and penetration after assembly. Otherwise, you can get one wedge much further in than another. This might not matter except for a uniform appearance.

Make a trial assembly. Mark the cuts on the tenons and wedges. Then dismantle and cut off these parts. Take off the sharpness of the corners and edges (FIG. 6-3D).

Arms on the ends can prevent warping and provide comfort (FIG. 6-3E). Nail or screw the arms in place. Carrying them back to the rear mortise, providing it does not interfere with wedging, will increase stiffness.

If the bench is to be held down with stakes or other attachments to the ground, the bottoms can be left flat. If moved about, it will be more likely to stand level on uneven ground if the bottoms are cut away to make feet (FIG. 6-2E). The three boards making the back and seat should provide enough stiffness, but if you feel that more is required you could add a stretcher underneath (FIG. 6-2F). This is held at the ends with tusk tenons and wedges, the same as the other parts.

Even if the bench is to remain in one place, the wedged tenons can be

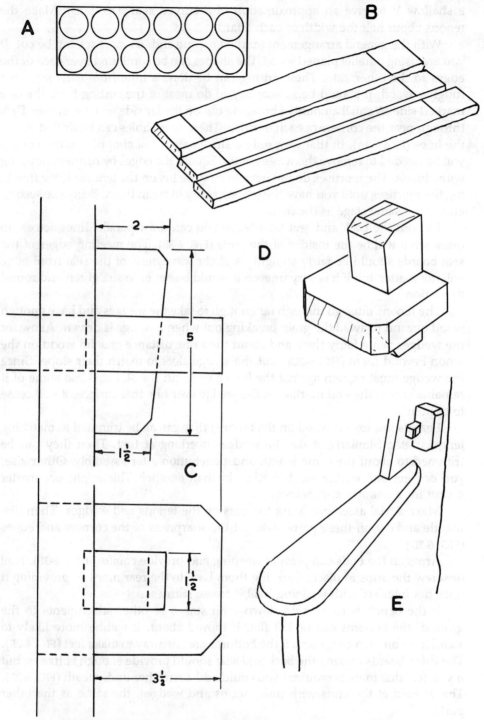

Fig. 6-3. Construction details of the tusk-tenoned bench.

regarded as a design feature. They also allow you to tighten the structure by driving the wedges further, if the seat becomes shaky.

For storage purposes, knocking out the wedges allows you to separate it into its component parts. If that is your intention, take care to get the slots and wedges sufficiently alike for them to reassemble in any place satisfactorily. Otherwise, mark the wedges and tenons so they are brought back to the same places.

Bench without Arms

This is a simple seat that could be made to any length. It is shown 48 inches long, but it could be short enough to be a single chair. It could also be lengthened to seat more people. If it is very much longer the wood should be thickened to prevent the seat and back springing too much. If the seat wood seems too flexible, the boards could be linked with one or more battens underneath. For a very long seat, there could be another upright arrangement at the middle.

The ends are shown sloping inward (FIG. 6-4A). This gives a greater spread of the feet with good resistance to tipping endwise. Nevertheless, with the small amount of overhang there is little risk of tipping and the ends can be made upright if you prefer. Fitting the ends at a slope means cutting bevels instead of square edges at some places; otherwise there is no difference. The slope is not enough to alter sizes for practical purposes.

Because the ends are 24 inches wide, it is unlikely that single boards can be obtained, so two or more pieces will have to be joined. This also avoids cutting out a large waste piece. Arrange the joints so that they avoid the mortise for the stretcher and preferably do not come directly under, where the back extends upward. This shape (FIG. 6-5A) will allow you to plan the joints economically.

You can join the boards with simple glued joints, using a fully waterproof glue. If you are doubtful about the dryness of the wood, it would be advisable to reinforce the joints. Putting battens across would be unsatisfactory, as swelling and shrinking of the wide boards later might cause cracking. You could put dowels between the board edges (FIG. 6-6A); 3/8-inch dowels taken about 1 inch into each board should be sufficient. Use a jig when drilling, or mark out the edges carefully (FIG. 6-6B).

Materials List for
Bench without Arms

2 ends	$24 \times 34 \times 1$
1 back	$9 \times 49 \times 1$
2 seats	$8 \times 49 \times 1$
1 stretcher	$3 \times 40 \times 1$

(from narrower boards)

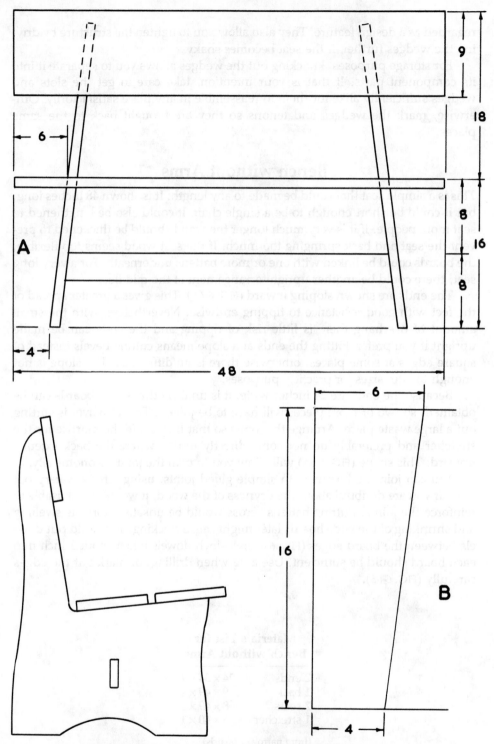

Fig. 6-4. A bench with splayed legs, but without arms.

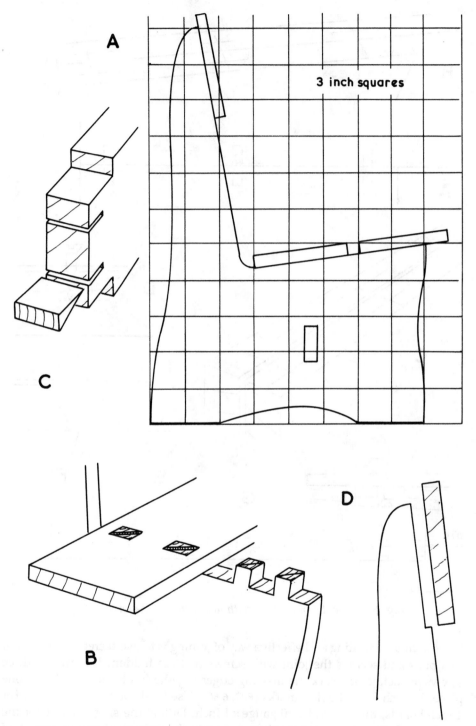

A

3 inch squares

C

D

B

Fig. 6-5. The end shape and method of assembly of the bench without arms.

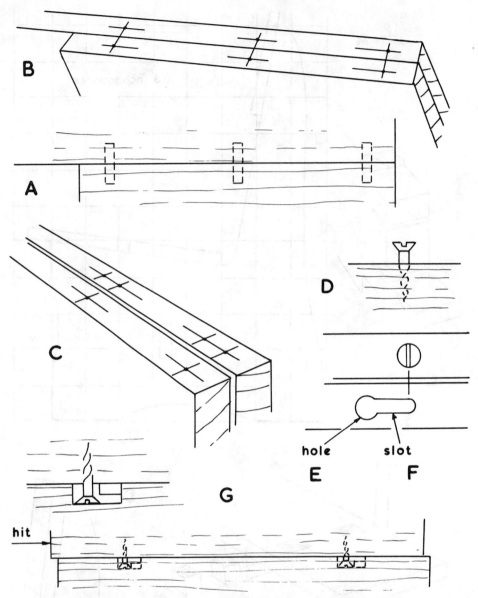

Fig. 6-6. How to join boards with dowels or secret-slot screwing.

Another interesting and effective way of joining is to use secret slot screwing; this pulls and secures the joint with screws that are hidden. Use two or three screws in each joint. Mark the meeting edges together with extra marks on one piece, 1/2 inch from the first marks (FIG. 6-6C). Use flat-headed steel screws. For 1-inch boards, they could be 10 gauge×1 inch. Drill at the single marks for the screws, and drive them until the threaded part is buried and not more than 1/4 of an inch projects (FIG. 6-6D). On the other board, drill holes at the second marks large enough to clear the screw heads (FIG. 6-6E). Go deep enough to let the head enter.

At the other marks, drill holes that will clear the necks of the screws. Remove the waste between the holes by drilling and chiseling out to make a slot (FIG. 6-6F). Bring the boards together so that the screws go into the opposite holes. Then, drive one board along the other until the screw heads have cut their way along the bottoms of the grooves to the other ends (FIG. 6-6G). If that assembly of the joint is satisfactory, drive the boards back again until the screws will lift out. Give each screw a quarter tightening turn. Apply glue to the surfaces, and drive the joint together again. The screws act as clamps as well as reinforcements.

The shape shown (FIG. 6-5A) allows for a tilted seat and a back that slopes at about 100 degrees to it. The outer edges could be straight, but they look better with curves. Do not cut in too much at the back because that could weaken it. The curve at the bottom helps in providing feet that stand a better chance of coming level on uneven ground than a broad straight base. Note the small curve between the edge under the seat and the upright part. A curved inside corner is always stronger than an angular cut because there is less risk of a split developing.

If the ends are to slope, set out the angle (FIG. 6-4B), and use an adjustable bevel when cutting joints. The seat boards could be nailed or screwed down, but for the best quality work they are tenoned. Two tenons at each place should be sufficient. Allow the tenons through with diagonal saw cuts for wedges. Then, trim level (FIG. 6-5B).

Cut the stretcher at an angle on each end with tenons through. Keep the full thickness of the wood, and tighten with double wedges (FIG. 6-5C). Take the sharpness off the edges before assembly.

The back is a single board. It could be screwed directly to its supports, but it is a better fit if they are notched (FIG. 6-5D). Counterbore and plug the holes for the best appearance.

In its basic form, the bench has parallel lengthwise parts (with the sharpness taken off their edges and corners). The seat boards could have their edges fully rounded and the corners given a good curve (FIG. 6-7A). The back would be treated to match in the same way.

The back provides an opportunity for decoration. Edges could be curved (FIG. 6-7B) or the top edge shaped (FIG. 6-7C). Do not use elaborate decorations that have angular corners. They may be uncomfortable against shoulders. You could cut out the center of the back (FIG. 6-7D), or it could be carved (FIG. 6-7E). Use a fairly bold treatment of a leaf or something similar. This is not the place for very detailed or deep carving. Use incised lettering with a name or initials or just the assembly date (FIG. 6-7F).

The stretcher tenon could be carried through and rounded (FIG. 6-7G). It could have a tusk extending far enough for a wedge to be driven across, but that would just be for decoration because the furniture could not be disassembled.

A problem with end grain resting on the ground is the absorption of mois-

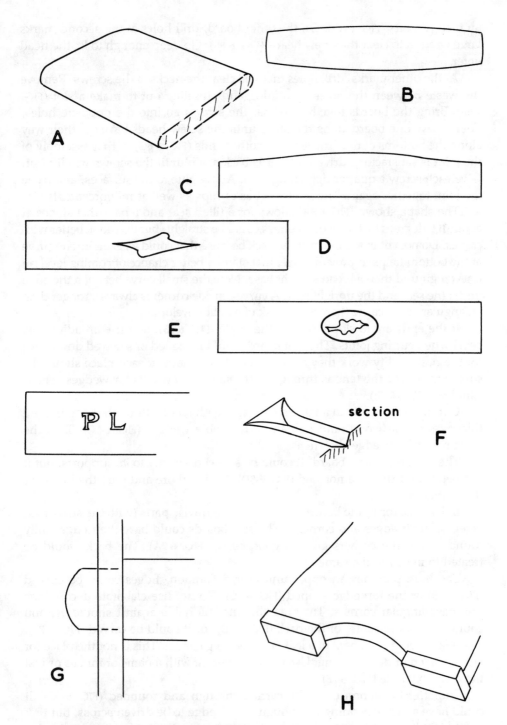

Fig. 6-7. Bench parts can be shaped, or the back can be decorated with a cutout or carving. Tenons can project and feet can be added.

ture; it will eventually lead to rot. Absorption into side grain is much less. One method of protection is to paint the end grain with waterproof glue, but that does not penetrate very far and could get rubbed through if the bench is dragged on stony ground. It is better to screw on feet with their grain across and the screws far enough below the surface to be clear of the ground (FIG. 6-7H). When these get worn, they can be replaced.

Park Bench

A strong bench similar to the types often used in public parks, is equally suitable for a garden or yard. If made of teak or another wood that withstands any weather, it can be untreated and left in place year-round. If made of other wood, it should be treated with preservative and paint. It is not too heavy for two people to carry, so it can be moved under cover in bad weather. The shape is intended to provide reasonable comfort without cushions or other padding (FIG. 6-8). Padding can be added for longer use.

Sizes are for a 60-inch bench designed to seat three people (see the Materials List and FIG. 6-9). The seat is made of slats arranged on a curve and the back is inclined to give a restful position.

The front legs are 1³/4 inches square (FIG. 6-10A), and the back legs are cut to that bent section from a wider piece (FIG. 6-10B), to provide the slope of the upper part. Note that the bend comes just above the seat level and the change of direction should be curved—not an abrupt angle. Mark the legs together to get the

Fig. 6-8. A park bench of a popular type.

Materials List for
Park Bench

2 front legs	$1^3/4 \times 23 \times 1^3/4$	
2 rear legs	$3^1/2 \times 34 \times 1^3/4$	
2 bottom rails	$1^3/4 \times 20 \times$ $5/8$	
4 seat rails	$3 \times 20 \times$ $7/8$	
2 arms	$3^1/2 \times 23 \times$ $7/8$	
2 seat rails	$3 \times 60 \times 1^1/8$	
2 bottom rails	$1^3/4 \times 60 \times$ $7/8$	
2 back rails	$3 \times 60 \times$ $7/8$	
11 back slats	$2 \times 13 \times$ $1/2$	
5 seat slats	$2 \times 61 \times$ $5/8$	

seat and bottom rail joints level. Mark the two rear legs together to get the back rail positions the same. Note that they must be in the same plane to match the back slats.

Nearly all joints are with stub tenons; they should go about $1^1/4$ inches into the $1^3/4$-inch legs (FIG. 6-10C). For most parts, the tenons can be $1/2$ inch thick.

Mark the seat and lower rails together (FIG. 6-10D). The top of the seat rails dip to 2 inches thick with a fair curve. The two intermediate seat supports must have the same curves. Mark them at this stage, but do not cut them to length yet. Cut the mortises and tenons for the bottom and seat rails at each end.

Make the armrests (FIG. 6-10E). They are parallel, except for tapering to the rear legs, where they tenon in. At the front, there is not much depth for tenons. You might prefer to screw downward into the tops of the legs. If tenons are to be used, it is best to use twin ones to get enough glue area (FIG. 6-10F).

Prepare the lengths. Get all the distances between shoulders the same (FIG. 6-11A). The seat front rail comes almost level with the front of the legs, and it can be given a barefaced tenon. This allows for curving the front edges adequately (FIG. 6-11B). The seat back rail also comes near the front of the rear legs, but it does not need rounding. Its purpose is to take the ends of the intermediate seat supports.

Top and bottom back rails are the same with tenons into the legs and a number of light slats arranged ladderlike along them (FIG. 6-11C). Because they are thin, mortises could be cut to take the full thickness, or they could be shouldered on one side only (FIG. 6-11D). The back assembly can be made up, but be careful that it is square. Get diagonal measurements the same. Note that it is the squareness of this assembly that controls the squareness lengthwise of the rest of the seat.

Make up the pair of ends. Check squareness and check that opposite ends match. The arms and seat are parallel with the floor; they should be square to the legs. Let the glue set on the end and back assemblies before going further. As far as possible, pull the joints together with clamps. If you prefer, dowels could be put through the main joints; two $1/4$-inch dowels set diagonally would be right (FIG. 6-11E).

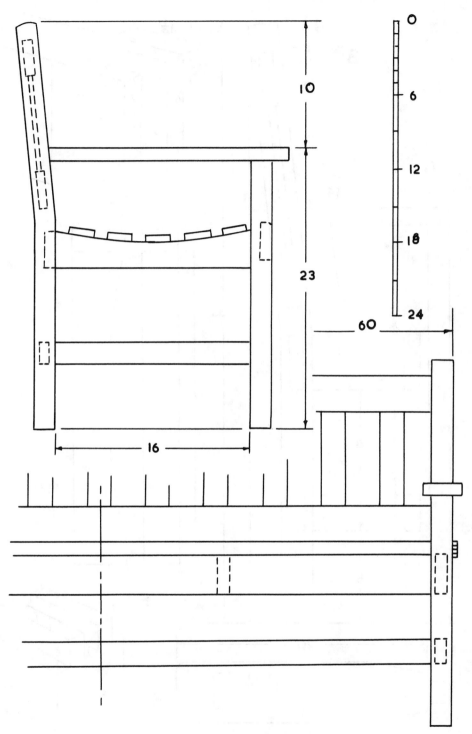

Fig. 6-9. Suggested sizes for a park bench.

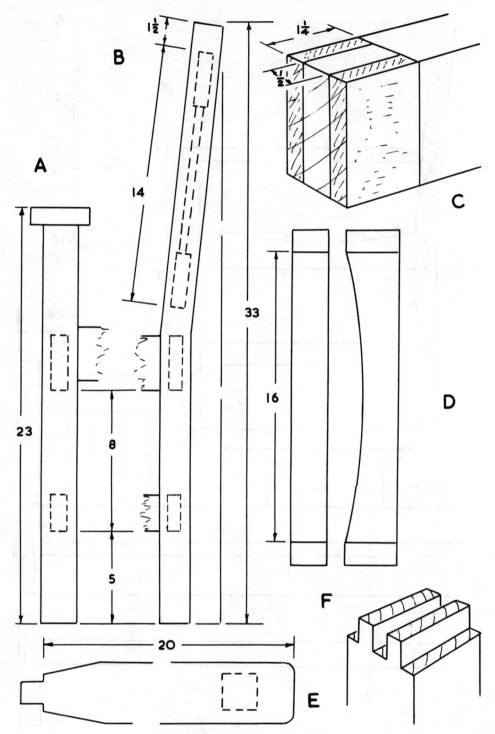

Fig. 6-10. *Sizes of parts for a park bench.*

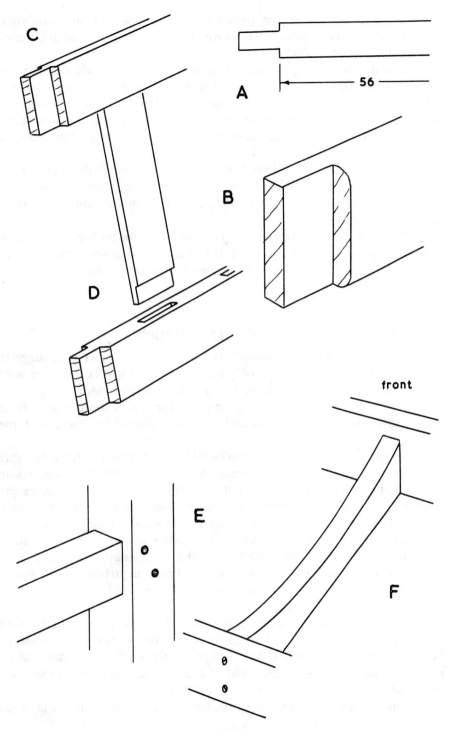

Fig. 6-11. Assembly details of a park bench.

Join the ends with the lengthwise parts while the ends are standing on a level surface. Check squareness as viewed from above, as well as in other directions, before the glue sets.

The seat slats will go past the ends a short distance and will need intermediate supports. Make the supports to fit between the seat rails where they can be screwed (FIG. 6-11F). They could be tenoned or doweled, but screws should be sufficient. Use a long, straight piece of wood between the end seat rails as a guide when fitting the intermediate supports, so that you can get the curved tops in line.

Make the seat slats with rounded tops and ends. Attach them with a central screw at each crossing. Space them evenly. As far as possible, have the gap behind the front seat rail the same as the gaps between the slats (for the sake of a uniform appearance).

Take the sharpness off exposed edges, but except for the tops of the rear legs, there is no need for much rounding. If it is a wood that will suffer from water absorption, treat the bottoms of the legs with waterproof glue.

Back-to-Back Bench

This bench can be nailed or screwed (FIG. 6-12). The sizes given are suggestions (see the Materials List and FIG. 6-13) and the method can be used for seats of many other sizes. For very long seats, there must be intermediate supports that can be repeats of the end frames. Even when the seat is short enough for only two or three each side, the seat and back slats should be linked with pieces across.

The shapes of the end frames can be laid out from the general drawing (FIG. 6-13). The sloping center pieces taper to a total 3-inch width at the top. Assemble the parts by nailing or screwing (FIG. 6-14A). Nail the beveled center pieces together. Make sure the opposite ends match with their cross members inward.

Make the front rails (FIG. 6-14B). They finish the same length as the seats, but the end frames join them 3 inches back from their ends. Bevel the under surfaces at the ends. The capping over the backs is the same length (FIG. 6-14C). Join the end frame with these parts, and make a central piece to go between the seat rails. It could be doweled or tenoned into them, but it should be satisfactorily nailed (FIG. 6-14D).

Four struts provide resistance to sideways loads; it is easiest to fit them at this stage. They each go from the lower rails of the end frames to the central piece between the seat rails (FIG. 6-15A). Arrange their positions so they will come under seat slats. Although they could be kept in line, it is easier to make strong nailed joints if they are staggered slightly (FIG. 6-15B).

Before making and fitting the struts, have the assembly standing level. Once

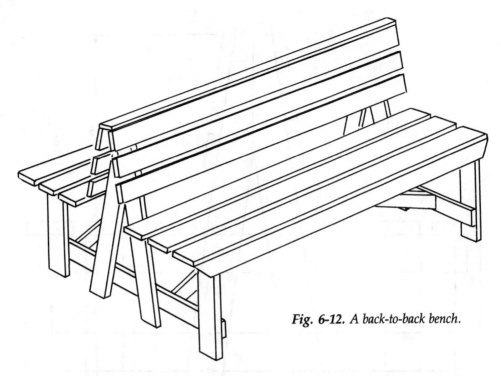

Fig. 6-12. A back-to-back bench.

the struts are added the shape will be held. Sight along to see that one end is not twisted in relation to the other. Measure diagonals at seat level.

Cut the struts to size to fit closely in place. They should all be the same; make a template from scrap wood (so as to get the lengths and angles correct). Attach with nails through the meeting surfaces.

Round the exposed ends and edges of the back slats; they will be spaced with 1-inch gaps between them. The braces that held them in place at the centers cannot be fitted after nailing to the end frames. Therefore, position them with nails from the back before attaching them to the end frames (FIG. 6-15C). Finally, round the seat slats and nail them to the end frames and the central rail. Nail the front slat along the seat rail each side as well.

Materials List for
Back-to-Back Bench

4 backs	3×32×1
5 cross rails	3×36×1
2 front rails	3×76×1
7 back slats	3×76×1
2 back braces	3×12×1
6 seat slats	4×76×1
4 struts	3×36×1

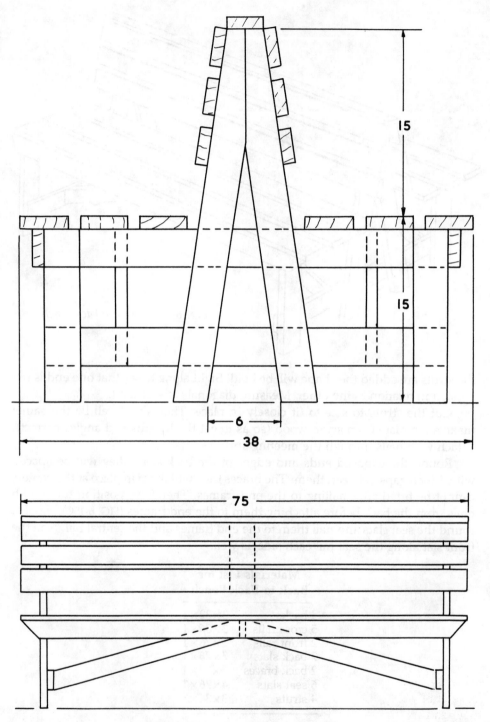

Fig. 6-13. Sizes for a back-to-back bench.

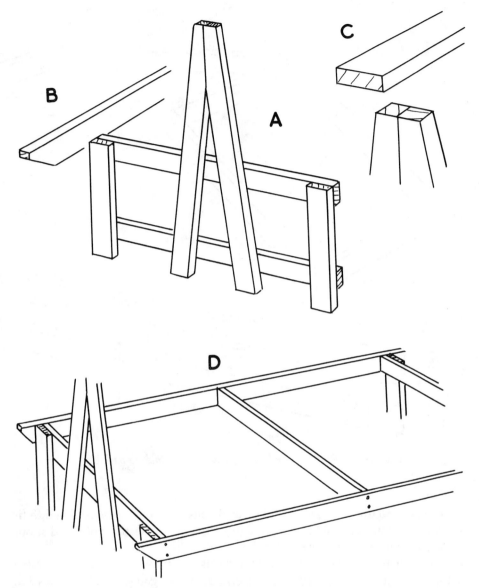

Fig. 6-14. Construction details for a back-to-back bench.

Batten Bench

This is a light bench seat that is made entirely from wood of 1-×-3-inch section. A total of 48 feet will make 48 inches long. Although construction is light (FIG. 6-16) and the bench is easily moved, it is rigidly braced and able to stand up to plenty of use.

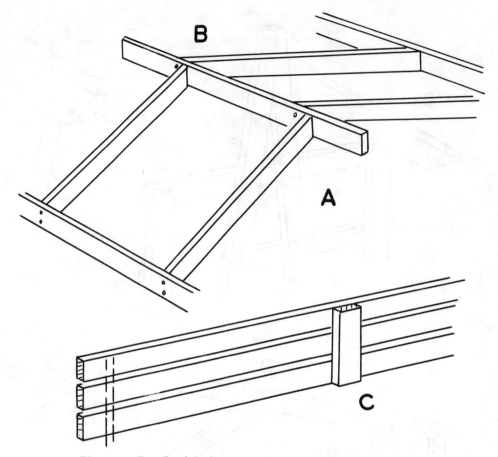

Fig. 6-15. Details of the bracing and set of a back-to-back bench.

The general drawing (FIG. 6-17A) gives details of a bench proportioned to finish 48 inches long. It could be made slightly longer, but sections of wood should be increased for anything over 60 inches.

The end frames (FIG. 6-18A) are made as a pair with the cross members inside. If the laps are glued, three screws about 10 gauge × 1³/₄ inches long should be strong enough at each joint. That size screw could be used throughout. Cut the tapered pieces that provide a slope at the back diagonally through a 3-inch width (FIG. 6-18B). Nail them to the back legs. Assemble the ends squarely and check that the pair match.

Prepare the wood for the seat and back battens. Round all exposed edges and corners. Drill for two screws at each end. Cut the pieces for the seat first and make the back pieces longer—to reach the back legs. With the ends upright, screw on the seat battens; keep their spacing even and the assembly parallel. Fit the back top two battens, but leave the bottom one until the arms are being fitted.

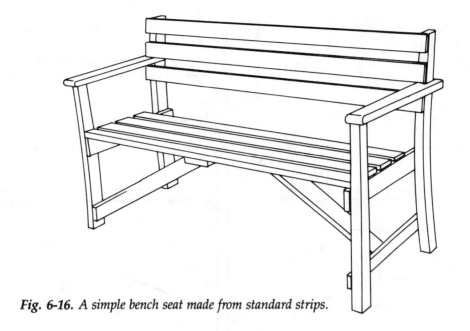

Fig. 6-16. *A simple bench seat made from standard strips.*

The arms go on top of the front legs (arranged centrally). Let them extend forward of the legs and cut away round the rear legs (FIG. 6-18C). Mark the back legs where the arms are to come, and fit the remaining back batten immediately below this.

Screw the arms downward into the front legs. These are the points of greatest twisting loads, and some strengthening might be advisable. Glue blocks of wood in the angles (FIG. 6-18D). Dowels in place of screws would be stronger (FIG. 6-18E). Tenons though make an alternative (FIG. 6-18F). Glue and screw the other end of each arm to its rear leg.

Underneath, the struts go from the lower rails at the ends to a strip brace beneath the seat battens (FIG. 6-17B). Notch the lower ends over the rails, and notch the tops at the brace. Stagger them, so they overlap (FIG. 6-18G). Then, screw them to each other as well as to the brace; the two struts should be the same. Try standing the bench level and upright. You might have to manipulate it

Materials List
for Batten Bench

2 back legs	$3 \times 34 \times 1$
2 front legs	$3 \times 24 \times 1$
2 seat rails	$3 \times 22 \times 1$
1 seat brace	$3 \times 18 \times 1$
2 arms	$3 \times 23 \times 1$
2 backs from one	$3 \times 13 \times 1$
2 braces	$3 \times 28 \times 1$

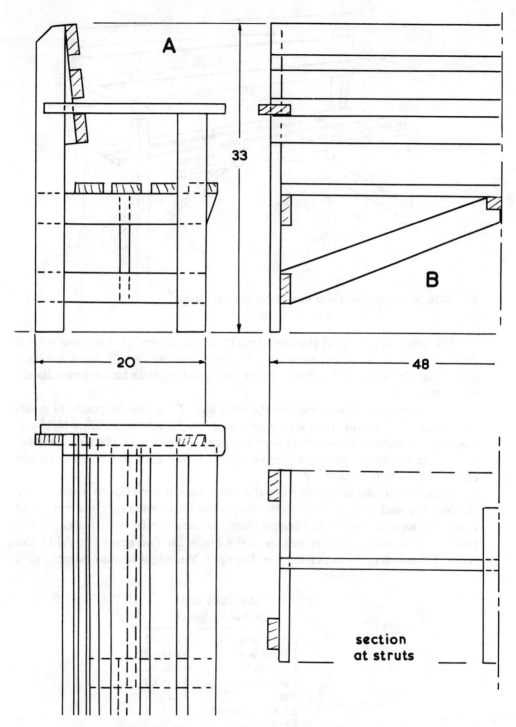

A

33

20

B

48

section
at struts

Fig. 6-17. Sizes for a light strip bench with arms.

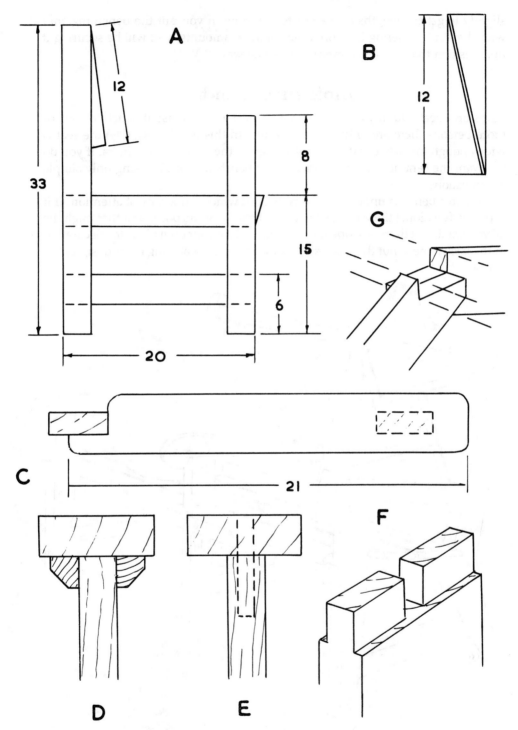

Fig. 6-18. *Construction details of the light strip bench.*

slightly to get the lengths of the struts the same. If you put the bench together with the struts differing by more than minimal amounts, you will be securing it in a position that is not symmetrical in some way.

Triple-armed Bench

Arms on a seat add to your comfort when sitting. In the usual bench for two or more persons there are only the outer arms. In this bench (FIG. 6-19) the seat is wide enough for two, but the central arm gives the effect of two chairs. If you do not want the central arm you can make the bench without it, using only simple modifications.

When a bench is unoccupied, it is its back which attracts most attention. If it is purely functional there can be beauty in fitness for purpose, and that might be all you want, but there is scope for decoration. Use your own ideas for decoration in the back panels, but there is a suggestion for an eye-catching open design (FIG. 6-20A).

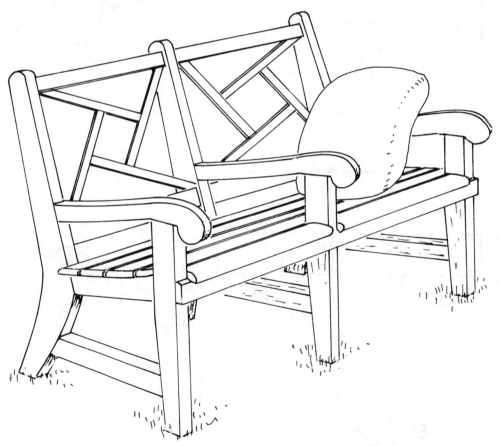

Fig. 6-19. A triple-armed bench has the comfort of two armchairs.

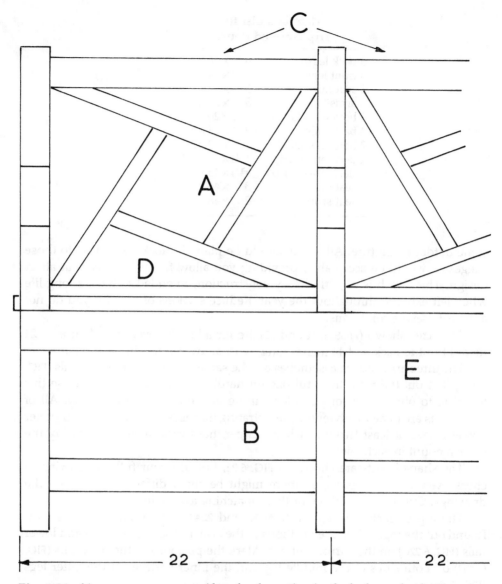

Fig. 6-20. *You can use your own ideas for decoration in the back panels, but here is a suggestion for an eye-catching open design.*

This bench is intended to be made of hardwood, using traditional methods, with mortise and tenon joints where appropriate, although you could substitute dowels. Any screws should be counterbored and plugged. A good hardwood will look best if your workmanship allows the finished bench to be left untreated or given a transparent finish. This means working to a high standard as you would with indoor furniture, rather than in the cruder way that is acceptable for

Materials List for Triple-armed Bench

3 back legs	6	$\times 34 \times 2$
3 front legs	3	$\times 24 \times 2$
3 seat rails	3	$\times 17 \times 2$
3 arms	3	$\times 24 \times 2$
3 bottom rails	2	$\times 20 \times 2$
4 back rails	2	$\times 23 \times 2$
2 bottom rails	2	$\times 23 \times 2$
4 decorative strips		$1^{1}/_{4} \times 18 \times 1^{1}/_{4}$
4 decorative strips		$1^{1}/_{4} \times 15 \times 1^{1}/_{4}$
1 seat rail	3	$\times 46 \times 1^{1}/_{2}$
7 seat strips	2	$\times 48 \times 1$

some outdoor furniture. All wood should be planed. Stock sizes close to those suggested would be acceptable, providing you allow for differences that affect design. This bench is of fairly heavy construction, intended to have a long life when left exposed throughout the year. Reduce sections of wood if you do not anticipate severe conditions.

The sizes shown (FIGS. 6-21 and 22) are for a bench covering a floor area 21 inches front to back and 44 inches long, with an overall height of 33 inches.

The three arm and leg assemblies are the same, except for minor details (FIG. 6-21A). Set out the main lines fullsize on hardboard or plywood; then use this template to obtain sizes of parts for cutting and for accurate assembly. All of these parts are joined with tenons, penetrating mortises $1^{1}/_{4}$ inches. If you prefer dowels, have at least two $^{3}/_{4}$ inch, or larger, hardwood dowels extending the same amount in each joint.

The shaped parts are shown in FIG. 6-22, but use your fullsize drawing to check overall sizes of parts, as there might be slight differences between the drawings. Cut parts to outline for three matching assemblies.

The top of each rear leg (FIGS. 6-21B and 22A) is vertically above its foot. Round out the tops. Mark the positions of the arm and seat (FIG. 6-22B) and lower rails (FIG. 6-22C) on the narrow surface. Mark the positions of the back rails (FIG. 6-22D) on both sides of the middle leg and the inner surfaces of the outer legs (FIG. 6-23A).

The front legs (FIGS. 6-21C and 23B) are straight, but tapered to the foot. Allow for tenons into the arms at the top. Mark mortise positions on the inner narrow surfaces.

The seat rails (FIGS. 6-21D and 23C) fit between the legs, but the curved shape of the seat (FIG. 6-22E) has to be continued over the front leg to support seat rails. This is done with shaped blocks (FIG. 6-23D) screwed to the legs after the frames are assembled. Allow for tenons on the ends of the seat rails.

The arms (FIGS. 6-21E, 22F and 23E) will be prominent in the finished bench, so be careful in shaping and round the exposed edges uniformly. Keep the parts

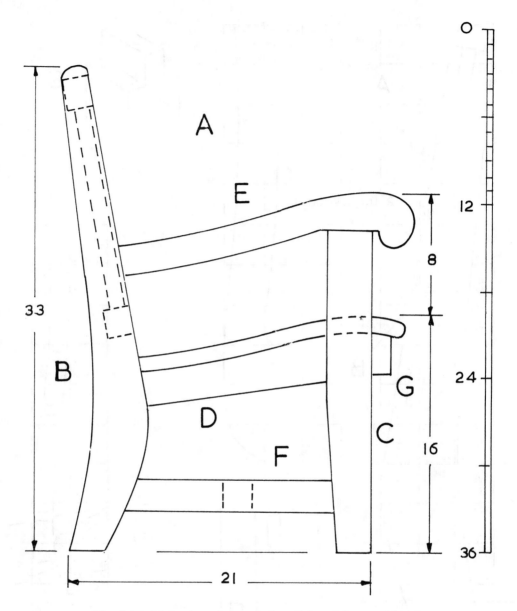

Fig. 6-21. Main sizes of an end view of the triple-armed bench.

that will join the front legs flat and allow for tenons at the inner ends. Do most smoothing and rounding before assembly.

The bottom rails (FIGS. 6-21F and 23F) have ends sloping to match the legs. Allow for tenons. Mark centrally for the lengthwise rails (FIGS. 6-20B and 23G). There will be mortises on the inner surfaces at the outer frames and right through the rail on the central frame.

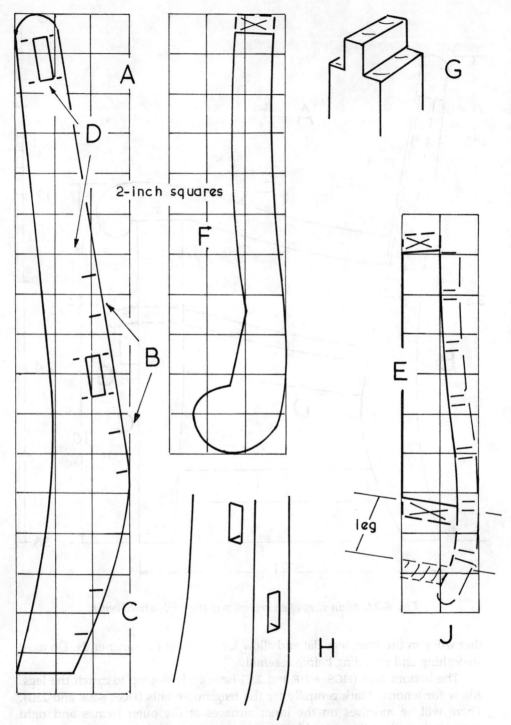

2-inch squares

Fig. 6-22. *Shapes and joints of bench parts.*

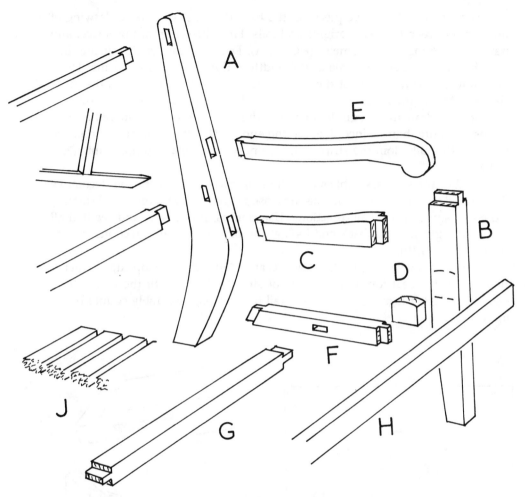

Fig. 6-23. Assembly details of one end of the triple-armed bench.

Mark tenons and mortises all together to ensure uniform joints. Tenons and mortises should be about one-third the thickness of the wood (FIGS. 6-22G and H), but modify this slightly to suit your tools.

Assemble a frame over your fullsize drawing, using waterproof glue. Put a 1/2-inch dowel across each joint. This is not essential with a good glue, but it helps in showing that the bench was built in the traditional way.

If you want to make a bench without the central arm, stop the front leg at seat level and do not cut the mortise for the arm at the back of the middle frame.

The main lengthwise parts are the back rails (FIGS. 6-20C and D) and the bottom rails (FIGS. 6-20B and 23G). They are all 2 inches square and have tenons 1 inch long at each end. Make sure there are identical lengths between shoulders to keep the bench symmetrical.

To set out the decorative pieces in the back (FIG. 6-20A), make a drawing of the space between the rear uprights and rails. Find the center of this space, and draw a circle 6 inches in diameter (FIG. 6-24A). Draw another circle outside this, with the gap between the same as the width of the wood you are using. Draw lines from the corners against the circles (FIG. 6-24B). Two lines go to the outer circle and two to the inner one. Complete marking the widths of the wood.

With this drawing as a guide, mark out the strips. Allow for tapered narrow tenons, no more than 1/2 inch deep on the ends (FIG. 6-24C), and cut mortises to match on the rails. Join the strips with ordinary mortise and tenon joints (FIG. 6-24D).

Join the three leg assemblies and the lengthwise rails, with the decorative pieces fitted into the back as the rails are closed together. Work on a level surface, and check squareness in all directions. Use clamps, if possible, and see that all joints pull tightly. Stand back and look at the bench from all directions, before the glue starts setting.

Make the front seat rail (FIGS. 6-20E, 21G and 23H). Bevel the top edge to match the curve of the seat top. If you have not already done so, fit the blocks (FIG. 6-23D) to the front legs. Screw the seat rail to the legs, preferably counterbored and plugged.

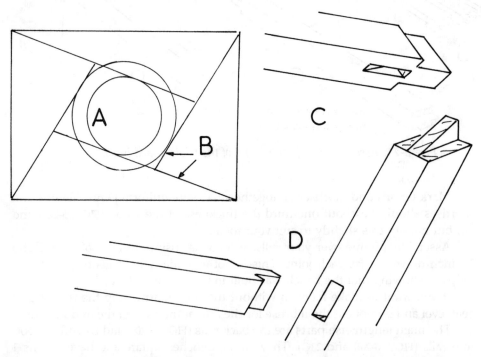

Fig. 6-24. How to lay out the decorative parts of the back of the triple-armed bench and details of their joints.

The seat is made of 1-inch- × -2-inch strips (FIG. 6-23J), spaced so the front one can overlap the front rail and have a rounded edge (FIG. 6-22J). Arrange gaps about 1/2 inch. It does not matter if the rear strip does not come close to the rear legs. Make the main seat strips long enough to go through the outer assemblies and project 1/2 inch. Cut those near the front to fit between the legs. Glue and screw the strips in position, preferably counterbored and plugged.

Remove any excess glue. Round all edges and corners. Check that the bench stands on all six legs on a level surface. If the bench might be pulled about on concrete or stone, bevel all around the bottom of each leg to reduce the risk of splintering. Any finish depends on the wood. A suitable wood could be left untreated to weather. Others might be better with preservative, varnish or paint.

Sociable Seat

In the stately homes of Europe a piece of furniture often found in drawing rooms was a double seat in which the occupants sat alongside each other, but facing opposite ways. A similar type of seat was made for outdoor use. Users could look at each other, lean across the central arm or use it as a common table; such was a sociable seat.

Fig. 6-25. A sociable seat is a combination of two chairs facing opposite ways, with a common arm between.

4 legs	$2 \times 27 \times 2$
2 end rails	$2 \times 20 \times 2$
4 end rails	$1 \times 20 \times 2$
4 lengthwise rails	$2 \times 54 \times 2$
2 central posts	$2 \times 16 \times 2$
2 central rails	$1 \times 22 \times 2$
2 back supports	$2 \times 29 \times 2$
8 seat strips	$1 \times 25 \times 5$
8 seat backs	$1 \times 27 \times 5$
4 seat rails	$1 \times 22 \times 2$
2 armrests	$1 \times 24 \times 4$
1 armrest	$1 \times 24 \times 6$

This double seat (FIG. 6-25) serves as an armchair for each occupant. Seats are flat and the backs are sloping. There is reasonable comfort without padding, but loose cushions might be used. Each position is at a satisfactory height for most people with ample width and depth. The arms are flat and level, so they can be used for food and drink. The wider central arm would allow papers to be spread for discussion or a modest meal laid out.

The end view (FIG. 6-26) shows a squared assembly, whichever way the backs slope. In the length (FIG. 6-27) the assembly is squared except for the S-shaped arrangement of the alternating back supports and the central arm when viewed from above. The suggested sizes will produce a seat for most situations, but this is the stage where you can make modifications to suit your needs or to match other furniture.

Most of the structure is 2-inch square wood, which could be a durable hardwood or softwood treated with preservative. Rigidity and long life depend on tightly-fitting glued joints, which can be reinforced with screws or dowels. Many joints are notched like halving joints, but do not completely halve the parts, as that might weaken them. Cut notches only one-fourth the thickness of the wood (FIG. 6-28A), so each jointed part extends halfway over the other. This applies at crossings within the length of the wood or at corners. If you use screws, arrange two diagonally on a joint (FIG. 6-28B). Screws #12 gauge $\times 2^{1}/_{2}$ inches would be suitable. Alternatively, put a $^{3}/_{4}$-inch dowel through each joint (FIG. 6-28C).

Mark out and cut the four legs together, so they match. They are the same, except that each rear leg (FIGS. 6-26A and 29A) has to take a back support rail; this is omitted at the front (FIGS. 6-26B and 29B). Because of the opposing seating arrangements, both ends are the same. Arrange the seats so the sitter's right sides are towards each other, or the opposite way around.

Make the lower end rails (FIGS. 6-26C and 29C), notched to fit the legs and with notches to take lengthwise rails. Cut 1-inch-$\times$-2-inch strips to the same length to go across at seat and arm level (FIGS. 6-27A, B and 6-29D, E). Screw or

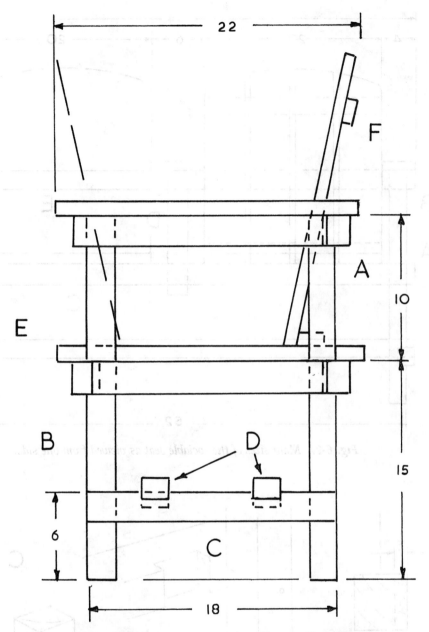

Fig. 6-26. Main sizes of an end of the sociable seat.

dowel the crosswise pieces to the legs, checking squareness and seeing that the opposite end assemblies match.

Cut two full-length seat rails (FIGS. 6-27C and 29F) to fit the notches in the legs and with central notches for the divider posts. Cut two bottom rails (FIGS. 6-26D and 29G) the same length, but without the central notches.

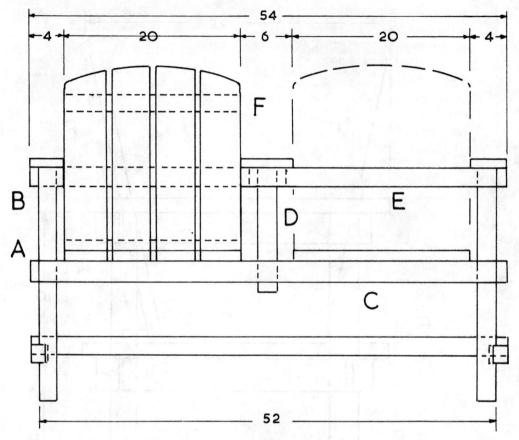

Fig. 6-27. Main sizes of the sociable seat as viewed from one side.

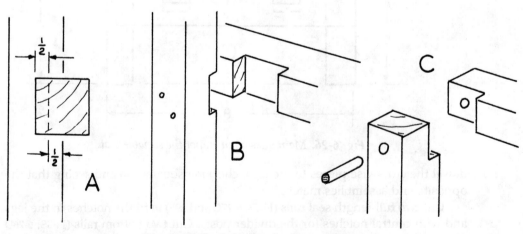

Fig. 6-28. Typical joints in the sociable seat.

The two dividing posts (FIGS. 6-27D and 29H) match the top parts of the legs and extend 1 inch below the seat rail notches. The back support rails (FIGS. 6-27E and 29J) are on opposite sides of the seat, with notches to suit.

Join the end assemblies with the lengthwise parts. Add the dividing posts and the back support rails. Check that the framework stands level and all parts are square. Put 1-inch-×-2-inch pieces across each side of the tops of the central posts (FIG. 6-29K). See that all top surfaces to take armrests are level and in line with each other when sighted from one end.

Make the armrests (FIG. 6-29L) to extend 1 inch over the framework at the back and front. The two outside pieces are 4 inches wide and will fit level with the inner surfaces of the legs and top rails, so they extend 1 inch outside. The wider central armrest extends 1 inch each side of the supporting parts. Round the corners and edges of the armrests. Fit them with glue and by screwing downwards at about 6-inch intervals. Leave screw heads level with the surface, but it would be better to counterbore the holes, so you can sink the screw heads and cover them with plugs.

Each seat and back assembly is made up of four, 1-inch boards. Widths are controlled by the spaces between the armrests, which should be 20 inches. Do not arrange the boards closely. It is better to leave gaps of about 1/2 inch, which

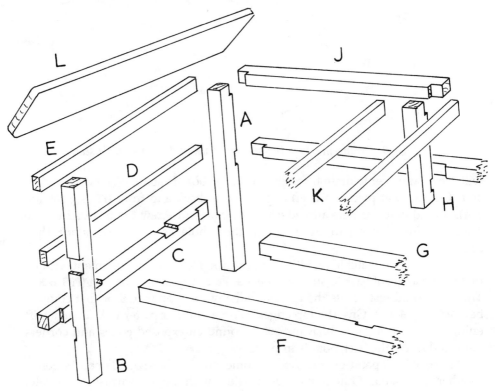

Fig. 6-29. Assembly details for the sociable seat.

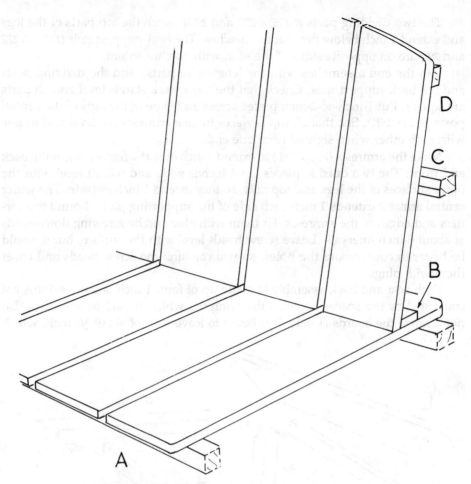

Fig. 6-30. Arrangements of the seat and back parts of a sociable seat.

will allow rainwater to drain through, so cut the boards about 4³/4 inches wide to suit. Cut the seat pieces to overhang 1 inch at back and front (FIGS. 6-26E and 30A). Round outer corners and edges; then glue and screw the boards in place. These boards play a part in stiffening the whole assembly, so attach them securely.

Use boards of matching widths for the back (FIG. 6-27F). Experiment with the height and angle of back to suit your needs. Fit a strip across the seat (FIG. 6-30B). The back could rest across the angular edge of its support rail or that could be beveled (FIG. 6-30C). Give the top edges a curve or other pattern. Arrange a stiffening piece across (FIGS. 6-26F and 30D). Round all exposed edges and corners. Glue and screw the back boards in place.

Finish will depend on the wood. Some durable hardwoods can be left to weather untreated. Others may be treated with oil or varnish. Untreated softwood needs plenty of paint.

7

Tables

The need for tables comes only second to the need for seats in outdoor furniture. They will vary from permanent structures attached to the ground and of sufficient size for many people to enjoy meals, to smaller tables that can be moved, to others that may be folded and stowed away. Folding tables are described in Chapter 9. Within the other categories exist a vast number of designs. The primary need is a flat top at a suitable height from the floor. It is in the means of support that designs vary.

Tabletops for use indoors are always without gaps. If boards have to make up a width, they are joined tightly edge-to-edge. Sometimes such a closed top is needed outdoors, but in many cases the top is made of many boards with gaps between. One advantage of this is in shedding rain water more easily. The gaps should not be too wide or there will be difficulty when a cloth is spread over and cutlery and other small items press the cloth into the gaps. For normal use, the gaps should not exceed $1/2$ inch (although there are many tables in use with wider spaces).

A table should stand firmly. The ideal arrangement for stability is three legs that will not wobble, no matter how uneven the ground. For most tables, it is preferable to have four legs to give support near each corner. The spread of legs on the floor is greater than the spread of most chair legs. This aids in finding a level stand. If the supports are not individual legs, but there are broad surfaces at the bottom, it is always advisable to thicken at the corners to provide feet (as in the first example).

Be careful to brace against diagonal or sideways loads, as well as those pressing directly downward. There must be enough stiffness in the joints. If the top and any shelf are firmly attached, they also serve as stiffeners. Lower rails act as stiffeners, but if it is a table where someone will be sitting on a chair with their legs underneath, the rails have to be kept out of their way. In the first example, the end rails support a shelf of slats far enough in so as not to interfere with a sitter's legs at the sides.

Light Table

Figures 7-1 and 7-2 show a rigid, small table with a shelf below. It is a height suitable for meals using a chair with seat height of 16 inches to 19 inches. The design is intended to match the chair shown in FIG. 5-1. Its construction is basically similar, so it will be advisable to refer to the instructions for the chair for some details.

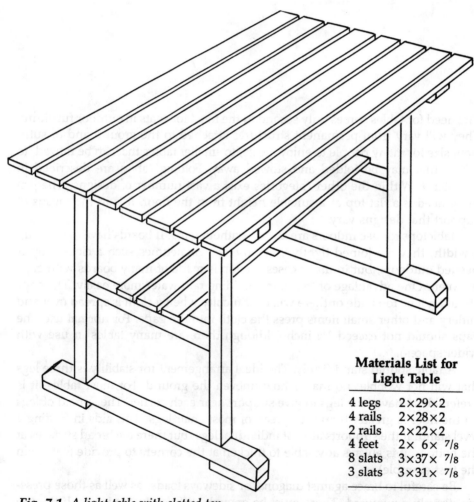

Materials List for Light Table	
4 legs	2×29×2
4 rails	2×28×2
2 rails	2×22×2
4 feet	2× 6× 7/8
8 slats	3×37× 7/8
3 slats	3×31× 7/8

Fig. 7-1. A light table with slatted top.

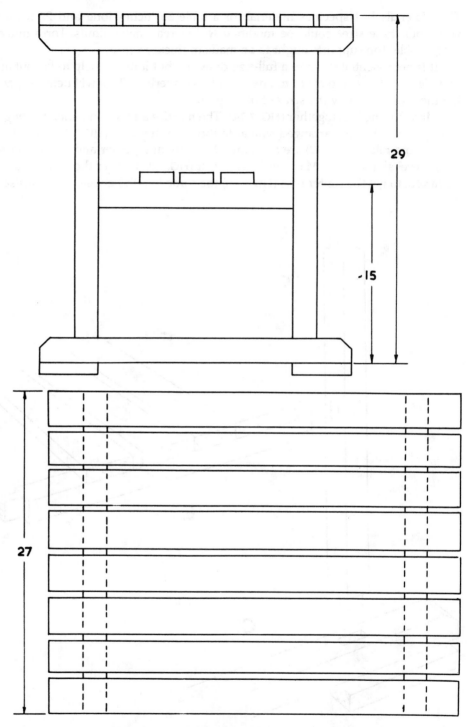

Fig. 7-2. Sizes for a light table with a slatted top.

The Materials List specifies material for a table 36 inches long and 27 inches wide, but these sizes could be modified within reasonable limits. For a much longer table, the supports ought to be made of thicker wood.

It is not essential to make a full-size drawing, but it might help to lay out an end view—either complete or to one side of its centerline. This will help in spacing the slats and show the sizes of other parts.

Mark out the legs together (FIG. 7-3A). The mortise and tenon joints do not go through, and they are arranged similar to those on the chair (FIG. 5-3A). The top and bottom rails (FIG. 7-3C) are the same. Mark them together and cut the mortises. Bevel all the ends. Make and attach feet (FIG. 7-3D) under the bottom rails. Be careful to get the center rails (FIG. 7-3E) the same length between the mortises

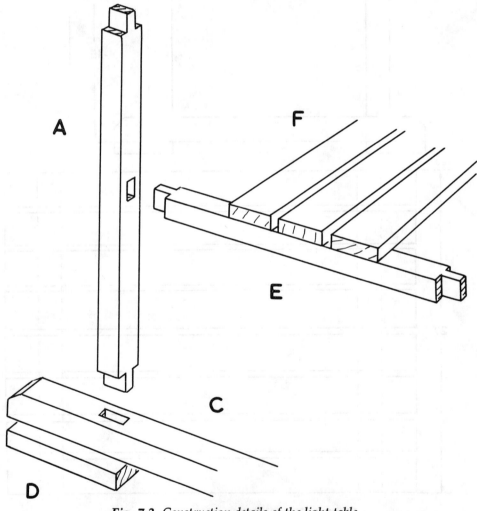

Fig. 7-3. Construction details of the light table.

on the top and bottom rails. In this way, the joints will pull tightly. Assemble both end frames. Measure diagonals to see that they are square. Check that they match each other.

It is important that all the top slats are flat and straight. Variations will be very apparent in differences of level or uneven gaps. If you have to use slats that are not quite perfect, keep them for the shelf. There they will not be so obvious. Take sharpness off the edges and ends of the slats, but otherwise concentrate on keeping them straight and parallel in width and thickness. The outer slats can have their corners cut off, but otherwise leave the ends square.

Attach the outside slats to the cross rails, and measure the top for squareness. Lay the other top slats in place, and adjust them to get even spacing (before attaching them). Use a straight piece of wood across an end to get all pieces level.

Check that the legs are square to the top. If there is any difficulty in making the table stand true, nail on temporary diagonal braces, while you fit the shelf slats (FIG. 7-3F). Arrange them centrally. They could carry through to the same lengths as the top ones, but they are shown cut off at the rails. The outer edges of the outside slats could be rounded, in case they are knocked by bare legs.

The table should be rigid enough. If you think extra stiffness is needed, put metal angle or shelf brackets between the tops of the legs and the adjoining top slats (where they will be inconspicuous).

Round Patio Table

A round tabletop can be supported with three or four legs. The table shown in FIG. 7-4 has four legs and is intended to stand on a deck or patio where the surface is reasonably flat. It would, of course, be suitable for any level ground. It could be used as a table only, but a shelf below and a hole through the center of this as well as through the top would take the upright of an umbrella. The distance between the top and the shelf is enough to support the umbrella without it wobbling.

The top is made of several boards, with gaps between, and held to shape with strips across underneath. These also serve as attachments to the under framing (which is made up as a straightforward square table). The sizes shown in FIG. 7-5 and the Materials List should suit most purposes. If the table is altered, arrange the top to an odd number of boards so that the central hole comes at the center of one and not at a gap.

The framework is best tenoned together, but you can use dowels. The legs (FIG. 7-6A) are all the same. Top rails (FIG. 7-6B) and bottom rails (FIG. 7-6C) are also in matching sets. The joints are on the same level. Allow for the tenons being mitered in the legs (FIG. 7-6D). The lower rail tenons can be the full depth of the rails, but at the top, cut down a little and divide the tenons (FIG. 7-6E).

Make up two opposite sides first, by carefully squaring and checking that the pair match. Pull the joints tight with clamps. If you do not have enough clamps, you can pull a joint tight and drive a nail from the inner surface of the leg

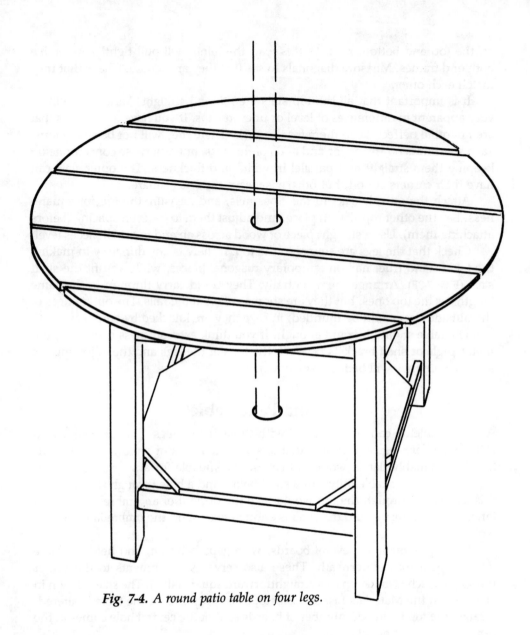

Fig. 7-4. *A round patio table on four legs.*

Materials List for Round Patio Table

4 legs	$1^3/4 \times 27 \times 1^3/4$
6 tops	$6^3/4 \times 37 \times \,^7/8$
2 tops	$3^3/4 \times 33 \times \,^7/8$
4 top rails	$3^3/4 \times 24 \times \,^7/8$
4 bottom rails	$3^3/4 \times 24 \times \,^7/8$
1 shelf	$24 \quad \times 24 \times \,^1/2$ plywood

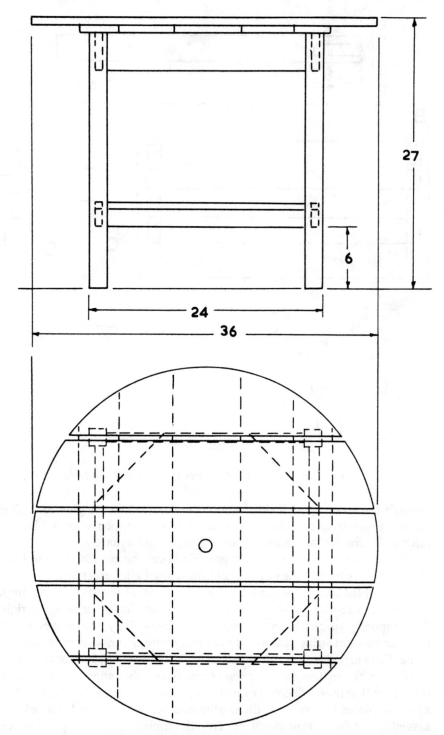

Fig. 7-5. *Sizes of the round patio table.*

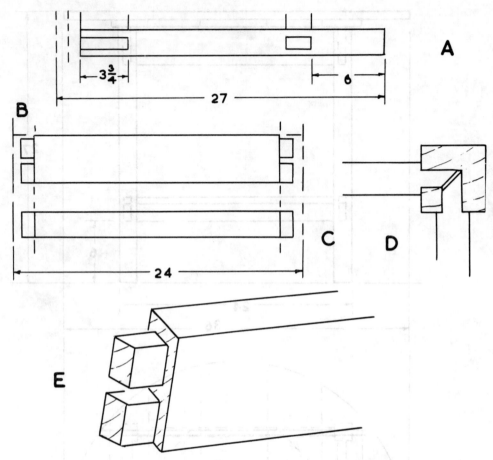

Fig. 7-6. Parts of the supports for a round patio table.

through the tenon at each side to hold the parts while the glue sets. Then you can move the clamp on to another position. Join the opposite assemblies with the other rails; check that the table stands upright and squarely.

The top assembly is in two stages. First, cut the boards close to their final sizes. Final curving of the edges is not done until after assembly.

Lay out the boards for the top; mark the center of the middle one. Improvise a compass of 18-inch radius (FIG. 7-7A), so you can draw a circle of the right size. Put temporary spacing pieces between the boards. They need not be full length; they can be short strips positioned near where the circumference of the circle will come. Cut fairly closely to the line, but leave a little for trimming after assembly.

One stiffening piece goes across centrally and the other two have to be positioned, so that they will come over the top rails of the framework (FIG. 7-7B). Let all these pieces be too long; then, glue and screw them on from below. After assembly, cut the ends to the curve. Trim the circle finally to shape, and bevel the cross pieces underneath (FIG. 7-7C).

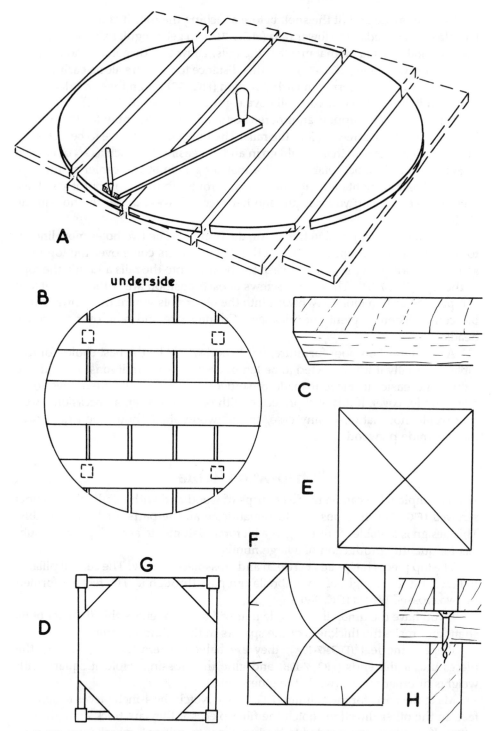

B underside

Fig. 7-7. Shaping and constructing the top and shelf of a round patio table.

Second, make and fit the shelf before attaching the top. It is made as a regular octagon screwed to the lower rails (FIG. 7-7D). To get a regular shape, mark out the plywood to a square that matches the rails. Draw two diagonals and measure half the length of one (FIG. 7-7E). Use this distance to measure along each edge of the square from each corner in each direction (FIG. 7-7F). Join these marks. If you have laid it out accurately, you will have eight equal sides (FIG. 7-7G).

If the table is to support an umbrella or shade, drill centrally for the upright in the shelf, before screwing it to the rails. The hole does not have to be a close fit on the upright because that should go in and out easily. As much as 1/4 of an inch clearance would be acceptable. Drill a matching hole at the center of the top. Most umbrella uprights are intended to go through to the floor, but if you have one that needs a stop you can put another piece of wood under the hole in the shelf.

Be careful as you position the top on the framing. The two holes must line up to hold the umbrella upright. Where the two crossbars come over the top rails, screw downward, in the gaps between top boards, into the rails and into the tops of the legs (FIG. 7-7H). Those four screws at each position are sufficient, but you can put one or two more downward into the other rails where the central crossbar comes. There is plenty of thickness. Counterbore and plug over the screw heads.

As with most outdoor furniture, hardwood would be the best choice for this table, especially if it is expected to be left outside in wet conditions. It would be lighter and easier to move if made of softwood, but it would then have to be stored under cover. If it is well protected with paint, however, an occasional wetting would not matter. In any case, the plywood shelf should be exterior- or marine-grade plywood.

Strip-wood Table

A very simple table can be made of strips of wood and with nearly all the joints screwed (FIG. 7-8). It is possible to prefabricate all the parts for later assembly. This design is suitable for offering as a kit for a customer to assemble, or as a subject for quantity production of a large number.

The top pieces have gaps between and crosspieces below. The central pillar is hollow, and the upright of an umbrella can pass through it. The feet are formed by two crossed pieces (FIG. 7-9).

If you have the umbrella or shade that will be used, check the diameter of its shaft, and make the thickness of the spacers in the column to suit.

Prepare the feet (FIG. 7-10A); they are halved where they cross. Add the pieces under the ends (FIG. 7-10B) and glue the crossing. Hold it square with weights or other means (while the glue sets).

Make the parts for the column (FIG. 7-10C). Notch the 4-inch pieces to suit the feet. In the other direction, notch the filler pieces if they are thick enough (FIG. 7-10D). If you have not needed to thicken them to suit an umbrella, they can be

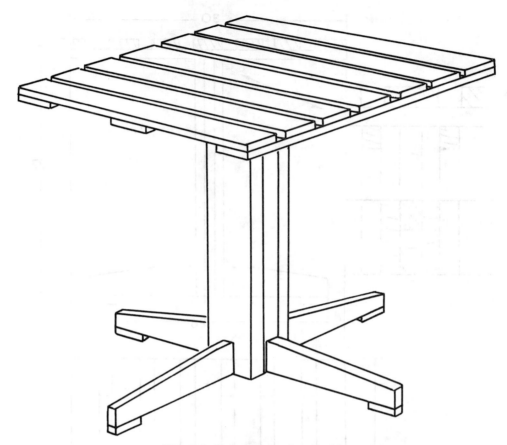

Fig. 7-8. Strip-wood pedestal table.

Materials List for Strip-wood Table

7 tops	3	$\times 31 \times 1$
3 tops	4	$\times 31 \times 1$
2 feet	3	$\times 27 \times 1^{1}/_{4}$
4 feet	1	$\times\ 4 \times 1^{1}/_{4}$
2 posts	4	$\times 27 \times 1$
2 posts	$1^{1}/_{2} \times 27 \times 1^{1}/_{4}$ or to suit umbrella	
2 cleats	1	$\times\ 5 \times 1$

cut short, and packings can be used on each side of the feet, if necessary (FIG. 7-10E). At the top, check that the parts are cut squarely because this will affect the level of the tabletop. Assemble the column parts with glue and screws. Add cleats on the 4-inch pieces (FIG. 7-10F) and make sure the whole top surface is flat, as well as square to the sides.

Assemble the tabletop after cutting or marking all pieces to length. Screws

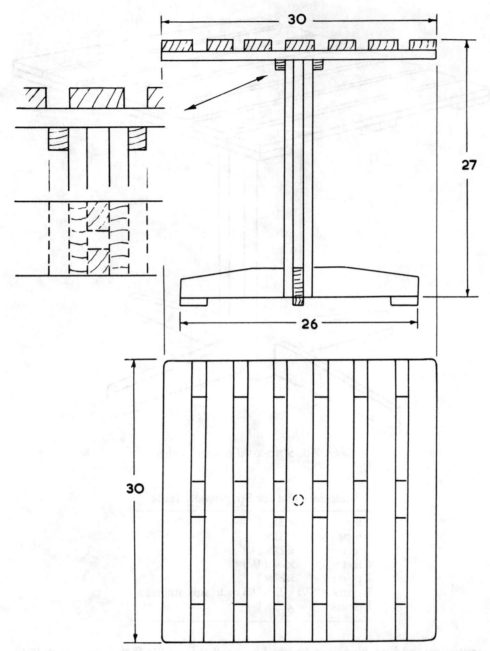

Fig. 7-9. Sizes of a strip-wood pedestal table.

can be driven upward, so that the exposed surface is not marked by screw heads. At this stage, leave out the center top piece (FIG. 7-11A), but have it ready. Screw and glue the parts together; then, level the edges and round the outer edges and corners.

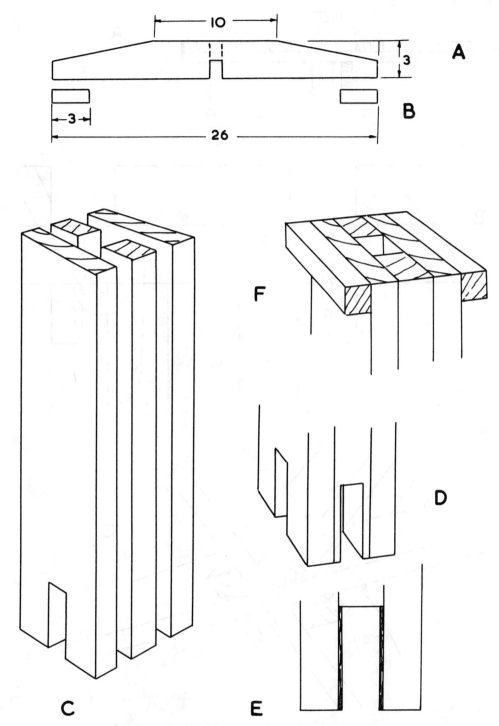

Fig. 7-10. Construction of the pedestal and feet.

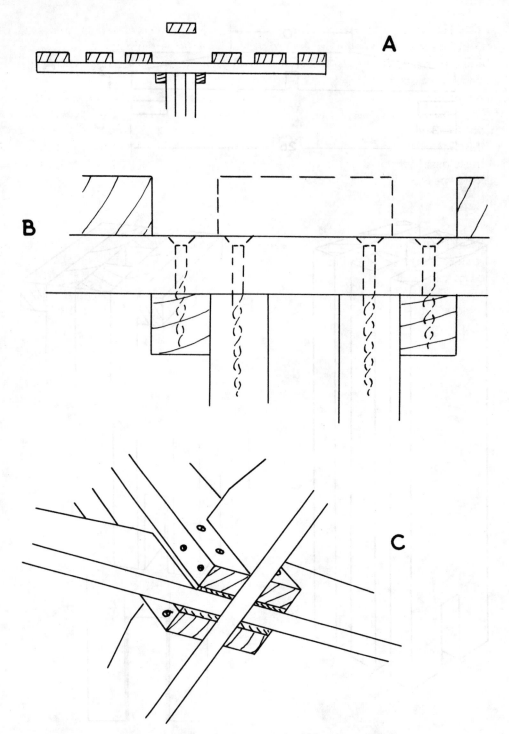

Fig. 7-11. Assembly of the top and feet to the pedestal.

Mark where the column comes under the top on the central cross member. Drill for screws downward into the column. Use 3-inch screws into the end grain, and 2-inch screws into the cleats (FIG. 7-11B). Add the central top strip; then, drill downward through the center to suit the umbrella.

Invert the table, and check that the pillar is perpendicular to the top. Bring the crossed feet into their slots. Check their fit. If that is satisfactory, drill for screws each way (FIG. 7-11C), and then glue and screw in the feet. While doing this, measure from the underside of the top to the ends of the feet to see that these parts are parallel and the table will stand level. Try it the right way up and leave for the glue to set. Finish with preservative and varnish or paint.

Simple Slab Table

Boards cut right across a large log suggest a simple table construction. Cut any roughness off the waney edges. Otherwise leave the natural shape. End supports can be made of similar material. Some lengthwise bracing completes a table. There is a limit to the size that should be made this way. It depends on the widths and thicknesses available; for 2-inch boards a top about 24×48 inches is reasonable.

The table shown in FIG. 7-12 uses the wood as it comes from the saw mill. You

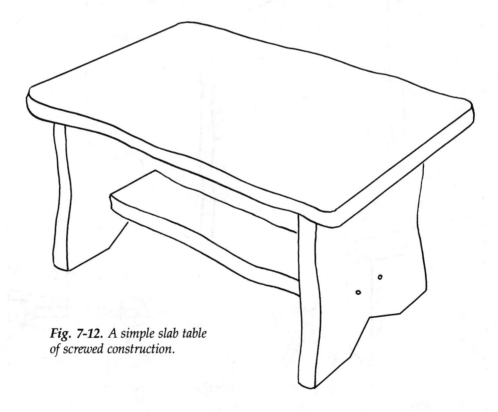

Fig. 7-12. A simple slab table of screwed construction.

might have to do some planing of the top surface to make it acceptable and flat. All of the parts are nailed or screwed. Construction is basic (FIG. 7-13A).

Although the long edges can be far from straight, the ends should be square to a mean line along an edge if the top is to look right. Draw a centerline and mark the ends square to that (FIG. 7-13B). At the same time, mark where the sup-

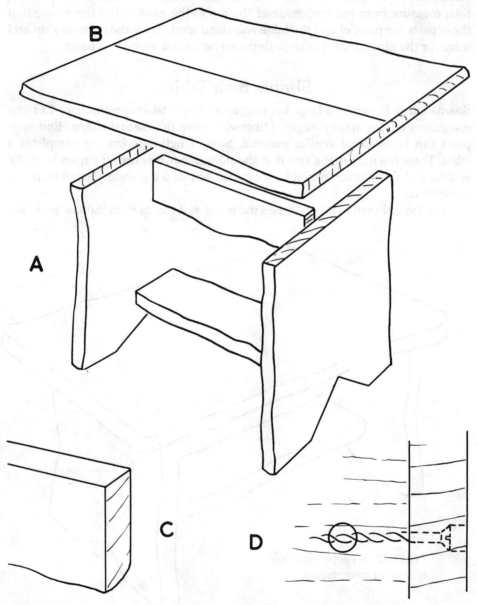

Fig. 7-13. *The separated parts of a simple slab table.*

ports will come underneath. The sharp corners of waney-edged boards are easily broken, so you should either bevel or round them.

Make the leg tops and bottoms parallel in the same way as the tabletop, and cut into the bottoms to make feet for steadier standing than the full width would provide. Two lengthwise rails are needed for stiffness. Get their lengths the same. Make a straightedge on the top one (FIG. 7-13C). The deeper this rail is, the more stiffness it will provide. The bottom rail can be narrow, it can either be parallel or have waney edges.

Assembly is with nails or screws. As they have to grip in the end grain, they should be fairly long. As a rough guide, with 2-inch wood, let the fastening go about 4 inches into the lower part.

In most woods, it is advisable to drill undersize holes for the nails; this helps to keep long nails straight and makes driving easier. It also reduces the risk of splitting. For screws, drill clearance holes in the top piece and undersize holes for most of the length of the screw in the lower piece. Leave the screw and nail heads level on the surface, but it would be better to sink them a little and cover with stopping. Screws are better counterbored and plugged. It will help to strengthen screwed joints if you drive dowels across the wood. Then the screw threads will bite into the cross grain of the dowel for increased hold compared with that of end grain (FIG. 7-13D).

Oval Tabletop

The tabletop that provides the most space within its size is rectangular. If you increase the number of sides or round the corners, within the same overall sizes, you must reduce the area. Shaping is often done for the sake of appearance. It can also be done to remove sharp corners. An attractive shape is an ellipse. This is often called an "oval," but that really means egg shaped, with one end larger than the other.

An elliptical top could be substituted for one of another shape on the under-framings already described. The example shown has shaped slab ends and a tenoned rail (FIG. 7-14). An elliptical top could be made from one wide board or several joined together. If boards are of different widths, avoid having narrow ones at the sides. Not much would be left when the curves are cut.

The special problem is drawing the ellipse. There is no easy way comparable to drawing a circle with a compass. There are geometric ways of finding a large number of points, on the circumference, that have to be joined. It is possible to use compass curves with two smaller radii at the ends joining two larger ones at the sides. This gives an approximation, but to the practiced eye it is not as good as a true ellipse.

One practical way, particularly suitable to the large ellipse needed for a tabletop, uses a pencil, loop of string and two awls or nails. Draw centerlines both ways on your wood (FIG. 7-15A). These are the axes of the ellipse. From where the minor axis touches an edge measure a distance equal to half the major axis to

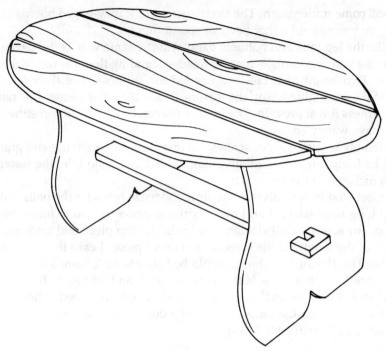

Fig. 7-14. A table with an oval top made from three boards.

mark a spot on the major axis (FIG. 7-15B). Mark the same distance in the other direction. These foci (plural of focus) give you positions for the awls. After a trial drawing you might have to move the awls slightly to suit the wood, as described in the next paragraph.

Push the awls or nails into these points and tie a loop of string around them long enough to reach the end of the long line (FIG. 7-15C). Put a pencil in the loop and pull it around; keep the string taut all the time (FIG. 7-15D). That will draw an ellipse. If you find the ellipse is finishing too narrow, bring the awls slightly closer together and adjust the size of the loop to reach the end again. If the ellipse is too wide, move the awls a little further apart. This can be done directly on the tabletop.

If you prefer to work from a template, use a scrap piece of plywood or hardboard that is half the width of the top, and experiment to get the curve you want. Then, cut it and mark around it on the tabletop. If you turn the template over on a marked line, check the accuracy of the setting out. You might have to make slight adjustments.

Table/Workbench

Light portable tables might have sufficient rigidity for meals and casual use, but if you want to do heavy cutting or hammering or support bulky items to work

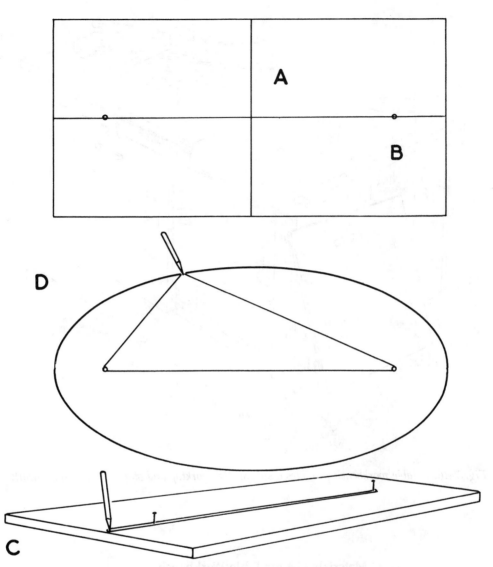

Fig. 7-15. Drawing an ellipse using nails, string, and a pencil.

on, you need something more substantial. A gardener might want to repair mechanical tools or deal with a large quantity of plants. Even for a barbecue for large numbers you will be glad of a large steady surface to use for preparations.

This table/workbench (FIG. 7-16) is intended to be mounted in one place and either fixed to a concrete base or have its legs let into the ground. There is a strong top and the space underneath is closed permanently at the ends, but at the front and back there can be lift-out doors. With the doors removed, this is a table at normal height for sitting beside. With the doors in place you can store things, so they are protected from the weather and curious animals.

Fig. 7-16. *A table/workbench provides a substantial worktop and storage space underneath.*

Materials List for Table/Workbench

4 legs	4	×31×	4
2 end rails	1	×22×	4
2 end rails	1	×22×	2
2 side rails	1	×40×	4
4 side rails	1	×40×	2
8 end boards	3/4×31×	7 or plywood	
3 top boards	11/2×56×	10	
4 doors	3/4×26×	24	
8 door rails	1	×20×	4
4 door catches	3/4×20×	3	
turnbuttons from	3/8×15×	2	

A height of about 30 inches is suggested, but length and width can be altered to suit your needs. Sections of wood listed should make a strong assembly, able to withstand rough work. Use a durable hardwood or softwood treated with preservative. If you want to keep the top clean, use a canvas or plastic cover. If you only need to open one side the other side could be permanently boarded. Instructions are for a table/workbench of the sizes shown (FIGS. 7-17 and 18) with lift-out doors on both sides and mounted on a concrete base. Suggestions are given for other ways of mounting.

Make the legs as two pairs. They are shown as being bracketed to the con-

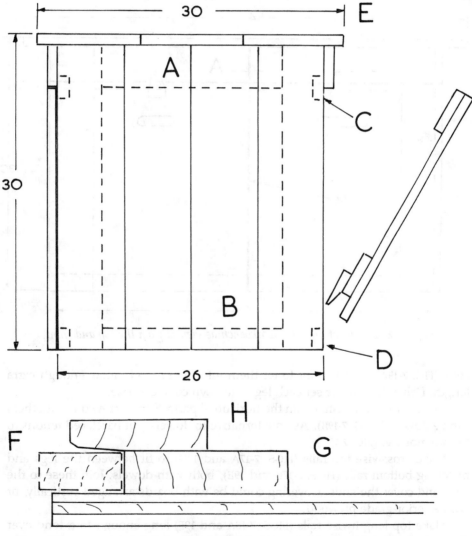

Fig. 7-17. An end of the table/workbench and details of door attachment.

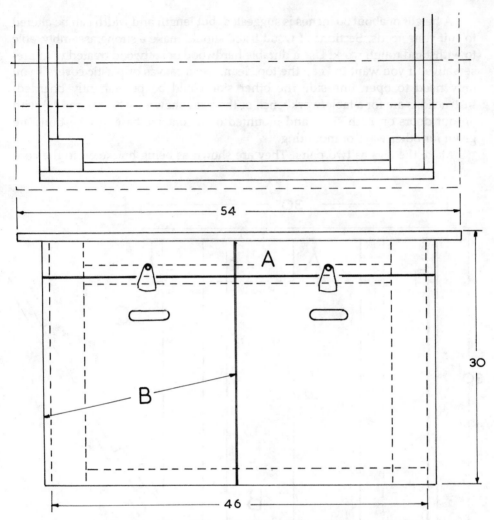

Fig. 7-18. Details of the table/workbench as viewed from the top and front.

crete (FIG. 7-19A). If you want to let them into the ground, allow enough extra length. Drive them in, or set each leg in its own concrete base.

Decide how you wish to join the horizontal parts. Some screw on, but others can be doweled (FIG. 7-19B). As an alternative to dowels, cut barefaced tenons to fit into mortises (FIG. 7-19C).

Make crosswise top rails (FIGS. 7-17A and 19D) to fit between the legs and matching bottom rails (FIGS. 7-17B and 19E), both with dowels. Join these to the legs, and cover the ends. Covering could be with boards arranged vertically, or with exterior-grade plywood.

Make top lengthwise rails (FIGS. 7-18A and 19F) long enough to extend over the end covering boards. Cut a strip to fit between the legs, to overhang the

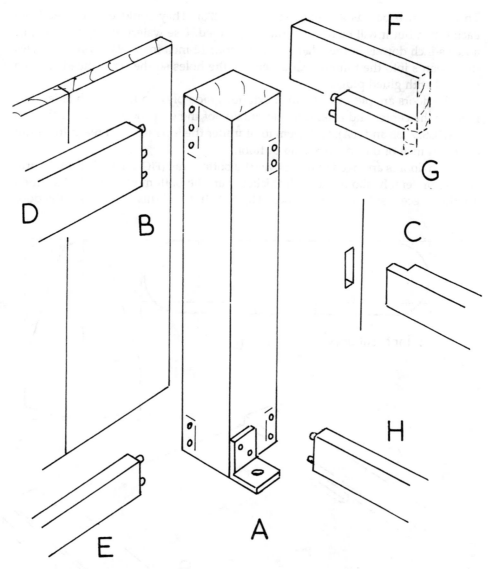

Fig. 7-19. Construction details of a corner of the table/workbench.

lower edge of the rail and act as a door stop (FIGS. 7-17C and 19G). Make a matching rail to fit across at the bottom of the legs (FIGS. 7-17D and 19H). Glue and screw the door stops to the top rails. This may be sufficient, but you can also secure with dowels to the legs. Fit brackets with holes for bolts into the concrete inside the bottoms of the legs. Join the lengthwise parts to the end assemblies.

Construction of the top will depend on the intended uses. Use 1-inch exterior-grade plywood, but solid wood will be better for heavier and rougher use. If the top has to withstand hammering, it should be at least 1¹/₂ inches thick.

Three, 10-inch boards are suggested (FIG. 7-17E). They could be laid free from each other, but it will be better if they are joined. Use waterproof glue alone, or add 5/8-inch dowels in the edge joints at about 12-inch intervals. Drill for screws downwards into the framing. Counterbore the holes so the screw heads can be covered with glued plugs.

The doors are pieces of 3/4-inch exterior-grade plywood. On each side, they meet at the center and extend to the outside of the end covering under the top rails (FIGS. 7-18B and 20A). Cut them to fit under the top rails, and reach to within about 1/4 inch of the concrete slab or floor.

Each door is arranged to hook over the bottom rail (FIG. 7-17F). Include a strip across, preferably about 1/16 inch thicker than the bottom rail (FIG. 7-17G); then another piece inside to act as a hook (FIG. 7-17H). Bevel this to allow for the door

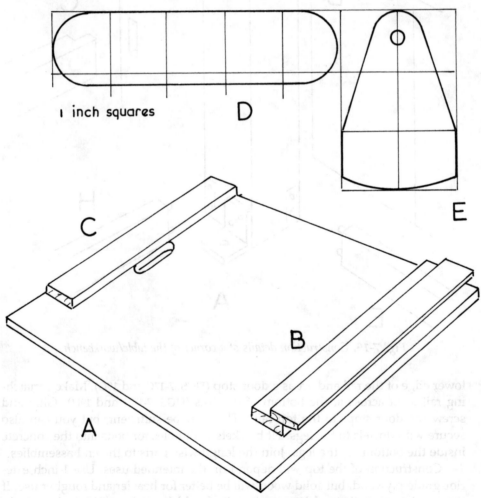

i inch squares   D

Fig. 7-20. Details of a door for the table/workbench.

tilting and being hooked on or off. Arrange this assembly to come close to the leg when the door is fitted (FIG. 7-20B), and arrange another strip of similar length across the top (FIG. 7-20C).

Put handles on the outsides of the top edges of the doors, or cut finger slots (FIG. 7-20D). Arrange them immediately below the top crossbars. Drill the ends and cut away between the holes; then round the edges.

Use some form of catch to hold each door in the closed position, or make turnbuttons by putting screws through the centers of strips of wood. The suggested fasteners are one-sided turnbuttons that are heavy enough to fall into the closed position when released. Cut the shapes from dense hardwood (FIG. 7-20E). Each turnbutton should swing easily on its screw. Put thin washers between the turnbutton and rail, and under the screw head.

The doors will lift away, leaving a free space underneath the table. Add shelves, or leave the inside uncluttered. Then, you can fit in a variety of things: a cultivator, plants and pots, or barbecue equipment.

The finish depends on the wood. A durable hardwood could be left untreated. It could be oiled. Softwood might be treated with preservative or paint or both. However, with food on the top, it will have to be covered. The doors each have one smooth side. A door could be used on top as a tray for something being prepared for the garden, then carried to where it is needed. Similarly, you could put food or plates and cups that have to be moved on a door. If the table/workbench is to have a regular use for a particular purpose, put racks for barbecue or other tools inside one or more doors. Install hooks or shelves outside the closed ends for things in frequent use.

8
Combination furniture

There are some situations where it may be better to have furniture performing two or more functions than to have separate items. Usually the combined piece is more compact, but the parts cannot be moved in relation to each other. There is also the value of mutual support. It is possible to design a combined item with fewer and lighter parts than two separate items, yet have adequate stability and strength. Each part will support the other. If a table and a seat, for instance, are combined you need have little fear of the table being inadvertently pushed over or a seat being tipped.

It is advisable not to devise some piece of furniture with multiple functions. You could arrive at something that is inconvenient to use and is not fully functional. There are some ingenious folding combination items that will soon break or fail to function. Always consider if the form fits the purpose. The combination item should do all that the separate items would do and, if possible, do them better.

The picnic table is probably the best-known example of a very functional combination piece of outdoor furniture. It is better in most situations than separate benches and a table. It stands up to exposure and neglect well; also it is very steady, with a simple and sturdy construction.

Picnic Table

The basic picnic table with attached benches is found in use all over the world in campgrounds, rest areas, and anywhere that people want to eat outdoors. It can be used in your yard, on a patio, or deck. You will probably want to give it a better finish than if it is to go into more rural surroundings.

The tabletop has to be level and of sufficient area; the seats must be compatible. Several methods have been used in the structure to hold these parts correctly, but a common and successful way uses splayed legs under the tabletop. Use crossbars to support the seats. The construction described here follows the most common form. As shown in FIG. 8-1, all of the assembly is made of 2-×-4-inch wood. If it is machine-planed, the sizes may be about 1/4 inch less. That must be allowed for when laying out the work.

The sizes shown in FIG. 8-2 are for a table that will seat up to eight people. The seats are longer than the tabletop, so the best use can be made of its ends. If the table is to be made much larger, the wood sections should be increased. In any case, make the top of fewer wider boards and the seats of single wide pieces (if they are available). The Materials List would have to be altered accordingly.

The important setting out is the splay of the ends. Draw a half view of the main lines of an end (FIG. 8-3A), preferably fullsize. That will give you the angles of crossing parts. Assemble nearly all of the construction by nailing, screwing, or bolting with the pieces merely resting against each other. The joints that get the most load are where the seat supports cross the legs; notch these parts together. There is no need to go very deeply into each piece; 1/2 inch should be enough (FIG. 8-3B).

Although the tips of the legs go out to a 48-inch spread in setting out, cut back squarely about 1 inch to remove the risk of the fine angle splitting (FIG. 8-2A). Nail or bolt the cross rails to the tops of the legs (FIG. 8-3C), and check one assembly over the other.

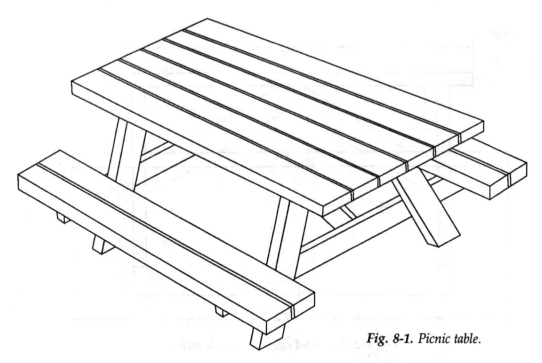

Fig. 8-1. Picnic table.

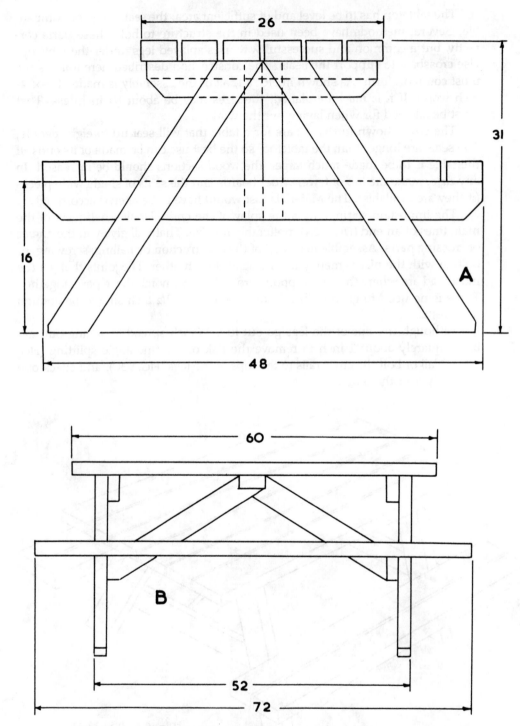

Fig. 8-2. Suggested sizes for a picnic table.

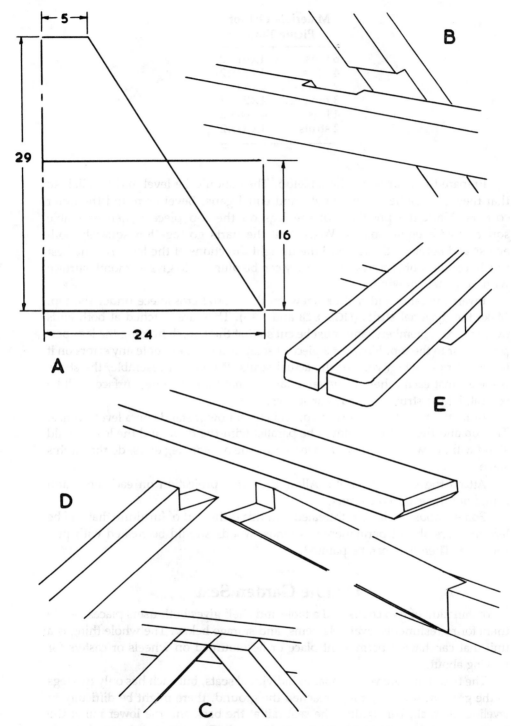

Fig. 8-3. Setting out and construction details for a picnic table.

Materials List for Picnic Table

6 tops	4×61×2
4 seats	4×73×2
2 seat rails	4×49×2
3 top rails	4×26×2
4 legs	4×60×2
2 struts	4×33×2

Prepare the boards for the tabletop. They should be level and parallel, so that they go together with straight and equal gaps. Bevel or round the outer corners. Mark the positions of the legs on the top pieces; then assemble squarely with equal spaces. Watch that the parts go together squarely both across and between the top and the upright directions of the legs. For the best finish, counterbore screws so that they can be plugged to give a smooth surface without metal showing.

Invert the table and nail or screw on the central crosspiece under the top. Make the diagonal struts (FIGS. 8-2B and 8-3D). They are notched at both ends over the cross members, and must be cut so that they finish holding the legs perpendicular to the top. First, cut a piece of scrap wood. Then, note any errors on it to be put right when you cut the actual struts. When you assemble, the struts come against each other on the table rail, so that their meeting surfaces will be central. Fit the struts with nails or screws.

Bring the table the right way up, and check how it stands on a level surface. The top and the seat rails should be parallel with the floor, and the legs should stand without wobbling. If you have to trim one or more leg ends, do that at this stage.

Attach the seats (FIG. 8-3E). Allow the same projection on each end, and round out the exposed corners.

Some woods can be left untreated, but this is the sort of furniture that will be left outdoors almost permanently, so most woods should be treated with preservative. Then they can be painted.

Double Garden Seat

A combination of two chairs and a table and shelf gives both users places beside them for refreshments, available items, and storage below. The whole thing is a unit that can have a permanent place or be mounted on wheels or casters for moving about.

The two chairs are very similar to individual seats, but each has only two legs to the ground. If all eight legs reached the ground, there might be difficulty in leveling them all. For rigidity, the seat rail at the back and the lower rail at the front are deep, and go through from end to end. The seats are shown flat with

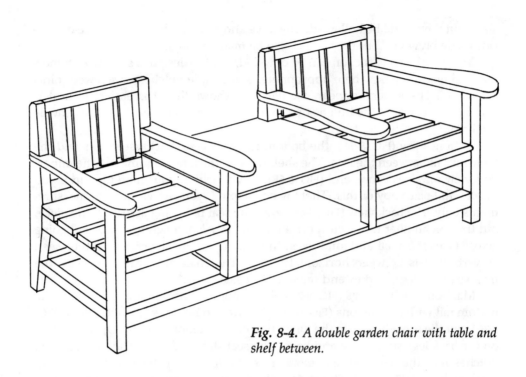

Fig. 8-4. *A double garden chair with table and shelf between.*

Materials List for Double Garden Seat

Legs
2 rear	3	×32×2
2 rear	3	×28×2
2 front	2	×25×2
2 front	2	×21×2

Long rails
1 seat	3	×72×2
1 front	3	×72×2
1 rear	2	×72×2

Chair parts
6 rails	2$^{1/2}$	×24×2
4 rails	2	×22×2
4 back rails	2	×24×1
8 back slats	3	×15×$^{1/2}$
4 arms	4	×25×1
8 seat slats	4	×25×1

Table and shelf
6 rails	2	×24×2
2 trays	23	×26×$^{1/2}$ plywood

slats, but they could be hollowed. The table and shelf as shown are made of exterior grade plywood, but they could also be made of slats.

Much of the construction can be doweled, but the design is shown with mortise and tenon joints, where appropriate, and simple notches or screwed joints elsewhere. The general appearance (FIG. 8-4) shows that it is easiest to understand if you consider the unit as two chairs with some parts extended to provide the links.

In front view (FIG. 8-5A), the bottom rail goes across. The seat rails and the table rails fit between the legs. The shelf rests on the long bottom rail. The important view for sizes is one end (FIG. 8-5B). It will help in your marking out if you make a full-size copy of this. There is no shaping; you can work from measurements only. The back view (FIG. 8-6) shows the seat rail going across in one piece, but there is another rail to support the tabletop. Also, a lighter, lower rail going across takes the shelf and inner legs. In both views, the chair backs can be seen as vertical slats between horizontal pieces. The chair arms are level with the insides of the legs, and extend outside the seats.

Mark out the back legs (FIG. 8-7A). The inner ones are similar, but stop at the bottom rail with stub tenons (FIG. 8-7B). The front outer legs reach the floor (FIG. 8-7C), but the inner ones join the long rail with stub tenons (FIG. 8-7D). The tapers on the back legs start above and below the seat slats and rails. The long seat rail notches into the legs, but cut more from the legs than the rail, so as not to weaken the rail (FIG. 8-7E). The ends of the rail can be tenoned into the outer legs (FIG. 8-7F).

The long front rail can also be tenoned into the outer legs. At the inner legs, make the stub mortises and tenons no more than 1 inch deep. During assembly, put a dowel through each joint (FIG. 8-7G).

Other rails that come within the individual seat construction are mortised and tenoned into the legs in the usual way (FIG. 8-8A). All surfaces finish flush, but at the seat level, add small cleats to support the ends of the front seat slats (FIG. 8-8B). Cut the lower side rails at an angle where they join the tapered rear legs.

Join the horizontal chair back rails to the legs with bareface tenons (FIG. 8-8C), or dowels. The slats can also have barefaced tenons into the rails. Space them so the gaps between them are the same as the gaps next to the legs (for a uniform appearance). Round the edges of the rails and slats before assembly.

The arms are 4-inches maximum width, but taper them or curve them as you prefer (FIG. 8-8D). The best joint at the front is a stub tenon or a pair of them (FIG. 8-6E). Use foxtail wedging if you think that is necessary. At the rear legs, the rear rail can notch to the legs, to take the load, and then be screwed from outside (FIG. 8-8F).

To support the shelf, there are two long rails running through. Rails back to front can be tenoned into them a short distance from the legs (FIG. 8-9A). That will be stronger than cutting the joint into the leg, where there is already a joint between a leg and a long rail. The shelf need not be cut until the framework is assembled. Then, you can make a close fit of it. Glue and screw it downward into

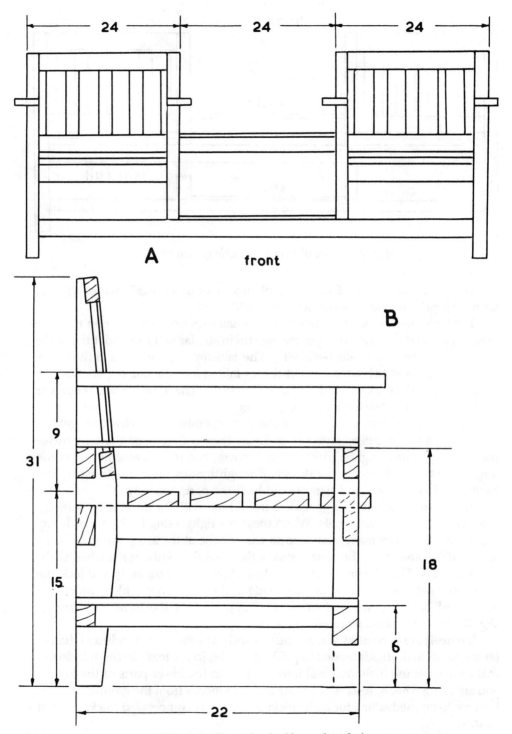

Fig. 8-5. *Sizes of a double garden chair.*

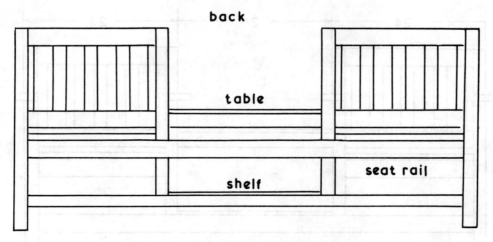

back

table

shelf

seat rail

Fig. 8-6. Back view of the double garden chair.

the rails. It is probably satisfactory as a plain surface that is easily wiped off. Put strips around with gaps for removing dirt (FIG. 8-9B).

The tabletop has rails tenoned into the chair legs (FIG. 8-9C). Tenon rails the other way into the legs as well, but arrange them similar to those under the shelf, into the front and back rails (FIG. 8-9D). The tabletop is plywood and fitted like the shelf. Strips at the sides prevent things falling into the chairs (FIG. 8-9E). A similar strip at the back will stop things falling there. The front can be left open or with partial strips—leaving a gap for cleaning.

Unlike most chairs, do not make the end assemblies first. Instead, get the front and back assemblies together as far as they will go. Use the lengthwise pieces to unite the uprights; check for squareness; and try one assembly over the other. Pull the joints tight; put dowels through tenons for extra strength. The back assemblies of rails and slats should hold the parts squarely.

Next, join in the rails that go back to front. Start with the lower rails; work up through the seat and table rails. When these are tight, bring in the arms. If any adjustment has to be made, that is most easily done at the arms. Assemble on a level surface, and check the squareness of the assembly without the table, shelf, and seat slats. The plywood table and shelf should go in squarely and lock the assembly to shape. The seat slats are made in the usual way, with rounded top edges and screws downward into their supports. Let the front slats project slightly and well round its outer edges.

If wheels are to be used, choose casters with wheels about 3 inches in diameter on the stem fittings intended to push into holes in the legs. Be careful; do not make the seats too high. You will have to shorten the lower parts of the legs, if you are using wheels, to keep the seats about 15 inches from the ground. If cushions are to be used, allow for their thickness. It is the compressed thickness that counts.

If the seat is to be painted, it will probably be given the same color all over. It

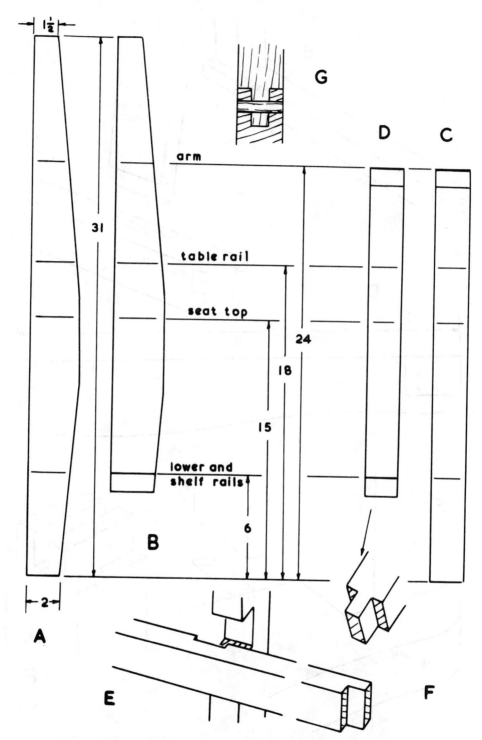

Fig. 8-7. *The upright parts and some joints of the double garden chair.*

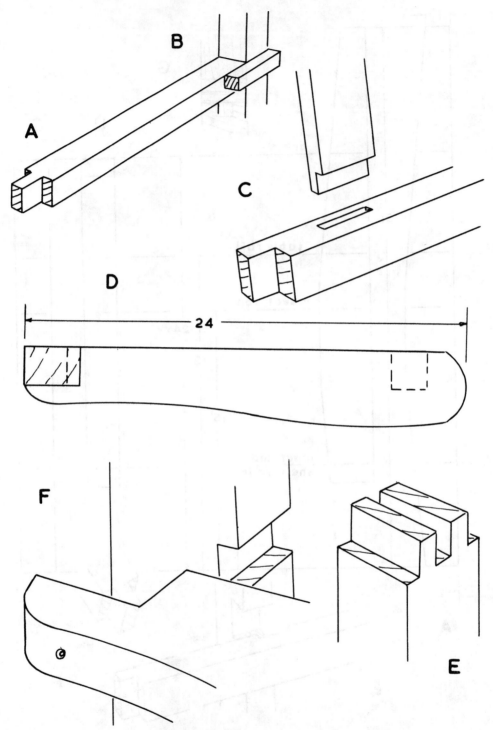

Fig. 8-8. Rail assembly and an arm for the double garden chair.

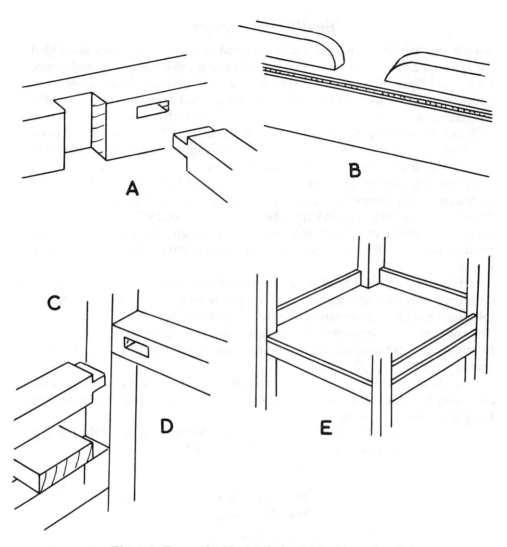

Fig. 8-9. Tray and table details for the double garden chair.

could be made distinctive by painting seat slats, the tabletop, and the shelf a different color than the rest of the woodwork.

Some modifications are possible. There could be shelves at table level extending outside the chairs. Build in supporting rails between the back and front legs. Make wooden brackets to come under the plywood shelves (which will serve as additional table space).

The space between the tabletop and the shelf can be enclosed to make a compartment for game materials or for anything that needs protection from animals. Make the sides and back of plywood. Make pair of doors to meet at the center. Hinge the doors at the bottom, to drop as a flap.

Seat/Bed/Lounger

Something that can be used as a seat, adapted as lounger and then assembled flat as a bed, has obvious attractions, particularly when it can be reduced in size for storage. Figure 8-10 shows a three-part piece of furniture of very simple construction. It can be used without padding, but it could become very comfortable with cushions linked together (as described for use with a lounger). The size is sufficient for use as a bed, indoors as well as outside, if fitted with the linked cushions or a separate mattress. Construction is substantial and the assembly should not suffer if left outdoors for long periods.

There is a main central part 30 inches long, and two similar end pieces 24 inches long. All of these parts are 24 inches wide. For a total length greater than 78 inches, make the end parts longer. Height is controlled by the capability of the legs in the central part to fold into it. For a greater height, the length of 30 inches must be increased. You can gain another inch of height for every extra 2 inches of length.

The parts are hinged together. The head end will fold on to the center section with their slats coming together. The foot end is hinged underneath, so that it folds under, with slats outward (FIG. 8-10A). The central part has two pairs of legs. The end parts have single sets at their ends. In all cases, the legs fold inside the framing (when not needed). When lowered, the legs rest against the ends of the framing.

As a lounger, the foot end is kept level, and the head end raised (FIG. 8-10B). As a seat, the foot end lowers (FIG. 8-10C). As a bed, all the legs are lowered to bring the assembly level (FIG. 8-10D).

Construction could all be by screws or nails. The corner joints of the framing could be tenoned. Make the central part first (FIG. 8-10E).

Materials List for Seat/Bed/Lounger

Center section

2 sides	$3 \times 31 \times 2$
2 ends	$3 \times 21 \times 2$
7 slats	$4 \times 25 \times 1$
4 legs	$3 \times 13 \times 2$

Two end sections

4 sides	$3 \times 25 \times 2$
2 ends	$3 \times 21 \times 2$
10 slats	$4 \times 25 \times 1$
4 legs	$3 \times 13 \times 2$
2 struts (optional)	$2 \times 30 \times 1$
4 leg rails (optional)	$4 \times 21 \times 1$

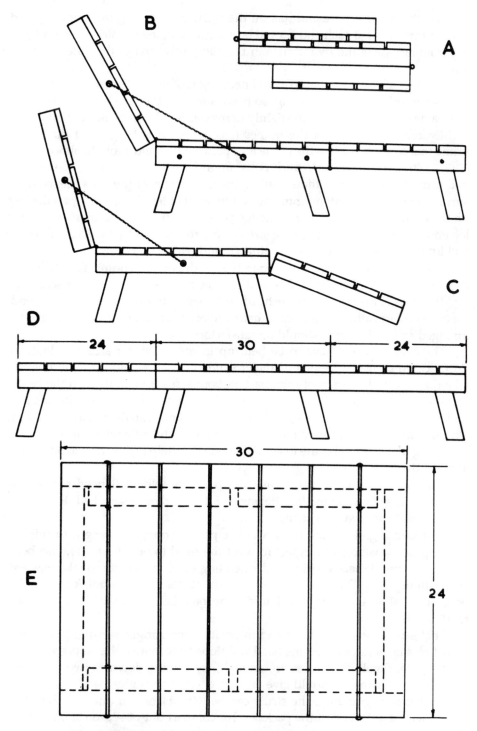

Fig. 8-10. *Several layouts are possible with this seat/bed/lounger.*

Get the frame square and nail on the slats, so that they are evenly spaced. Two or three nails at each end should be sufficient. Plane the slat ends level with the framing. Make the two frames in the same way, except they are 24 inches long.

The legs are all the same; you will need eight of them. They have to fold into the framework without projecting, so make sure that they are the same width as the frame sides, or plane them slightly narrower. Bolt holes come centrally and 4 inches from the corners of the frames (FIG. 8-11A). It is the size of the central frame that controls the lengths of the legs because they must fold to almost touch (FIG. 8-11B). Drill for $3/8$- or $1/2$-inch bolts. Round the tops of the legs, so that they will turn on their bolts without fouling the undersides of the slats. Leave some surplus wood at the bottom until you can try a set of legs in place. Open the legs on the center section; use a straightedge parallel with the top to mark across the leg ends. If you are working to the sizes given, the longest legs you can allow for will lift the section 12 inches above the ground (FIG. 8-11C).

The best hinges to use are the strap type with arms extending about 6 inches each way. They can be mounted near the edges of the sections, so that screws go into the sides of the frames. At the head end, they come on top. At the other end, they are underneath. If you want to use ordinary butt hinges, three, 4-inch ones arranged across the joints should be satisfactory.

The head end will have to be held up in some way for a seat or lounger. Ropes could be used; $3/8$-inch-diameter synthetic rope would do. Drill holes to take the rope at the center of each part on both sides (FIG. 8-11D). On the center section, the knot must not project inside. There it could interfere with the legs folding. Counterbore with a larger drill to sink the knot into the wood (FIG. 8-11E). Do the same on the head section, but if you locate the hole where it misses the folded leg, the knot will come inside. That will be a help if you want to adjust the angle of the two parts.

The rope can stay in place when the parts are folded. It need not be disturbed, unless you want to alter the angle of the head or make a bed. For a more rigid support, use wooden struts.

A strut can go from the centers of the parts. Arrange its length to suit the most upright position you expect to want the head to be (FIG. 8-11F). Use bolts with countersunk heads inside and extending enough outside to take washers and butterfly nuts. Do not cut the ends of the struts too short outside the holes because the short grain may break under the load. Leaving about 2 inches is better (FIG. 8-11G).

That setting holds the head end in position for upright seating. If you drill more holes in its sides lower, the head will slope back more if the bolts are moved at each side. Small differences are enough; try coming down in two, $1^{1}/2$-inch steps. That adjustment should give enough alternative angles.

For temporary folding, the struts can be left attached at one end, but they will project past the end of the package. For compact out-of-season storage, they should be removed.

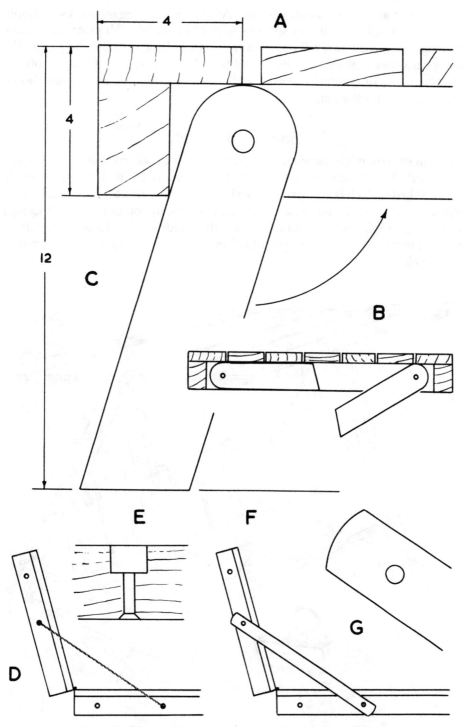

Fig. 8-11. Leg and back arrangements for the seat/bed/lounger.

The legs are shown as individuals. At the lengths suggested, they should hold without wobbling. If they seem loose or a larger and taller piece of furniture is being made, include a rail between each pair of legs. It cannot be put on the surface because that would interfere with folding; instead, it must be notched into the edges, or tenoned centrally to the legs. A section of 1×4 inches should be satisfactory for the rail.

Sheltered Bench

A seat in the sun might be what you want on some occasions, but shade is often welcomed. This bench seat (FIG. 8-12) offers comfort for two or three people under a shade which is adjustable. The shade may have narrow gaps and be suitable for keeping off the sun's rays and falling leaves, or you can make it enclosed so it is rainproof. This adjustment allows the shade roof to be at any position between horizontal and near upright behind the seat, where it could serve as a windbreak.

Fig. 8-12. *This sheltered bench seat can have the angle of its roof adjusted.*

The bench seat fits between two inverted "V" supports, which carry the roof. Adjustment to four positions is by handles at each end. Make the whole bench in three stages. The bench assembly can be made complete and its sizes will control some other measurements. The end supports are made and fitted to the bench; the roof assembly is finally made to fit.

Use hardwood or softwood, preferably treated with preservative. For the best appearance all wood should be planed, but there are a few parts that could be left from the saw. Many parts have to be joined, so they finish with their surfaces level. You have a choice of joints. The strongest joints are mortises and tenons (FIG. 8-16A). Halving joints (FIG. 8-16B) are a simpler alternative. Use dowels in some places, but they should be hardwood, about 1 inch in diameter. Use waterproof glue on all joints. If you have any doubts about fit and strength, add a screw across halving or tenoned joints.

The seat assembly is arranged at a comfortable angle between the end supports (FIG. 8-13); then the roof pivots at the top. In a front view (FIG. 8-14) the seat can be seen to provide rigidity to the whole sheltered bench. Suggested sizes are for a seat area about 4-feet long and near standing headroom under the canopy when it is horizontal. Alter the sizes to suit your needs, after you have compared the sizes and angles of other seats you have or measured the position this bench has to fit.

Make the two ends of the seat first (FIG. 8-15). Allow some excess on the ends of strips, as shown, for cutting to the angles of the support later. An angle of 80 degrees is suggested, but vary this if you think a different angle would be more comfortable. Join with halving (FIG. 8-16C) or tenoned joints. Mark the positions of lengthwise parts.

Cut the four lengthwise parts to matching sizes. Mark and cut the joints to the ends. Hardwood seat boards will probably be stiff enough, but these or softwood boards might sag under the weight of three people. This can be counteracted with a central support (FIG. 8-16D). To prevent weakening the lengthwise parts, use notched blocks inside (FIG. 8-16E).

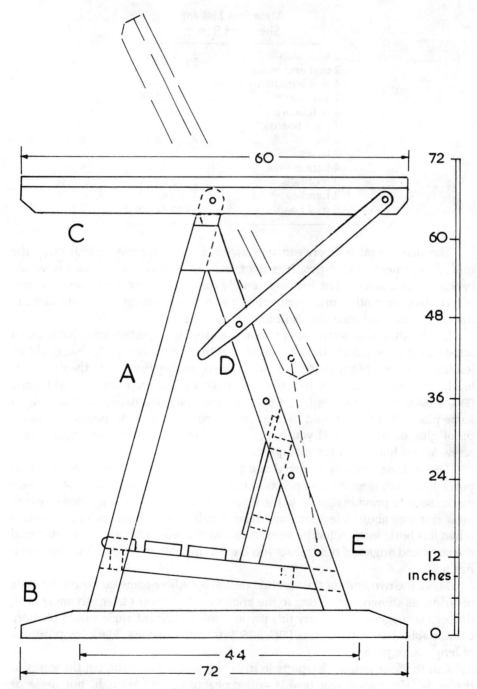

Fig. 8-13. An end view of the sheltered bench, showing the limits of angle of the roof.

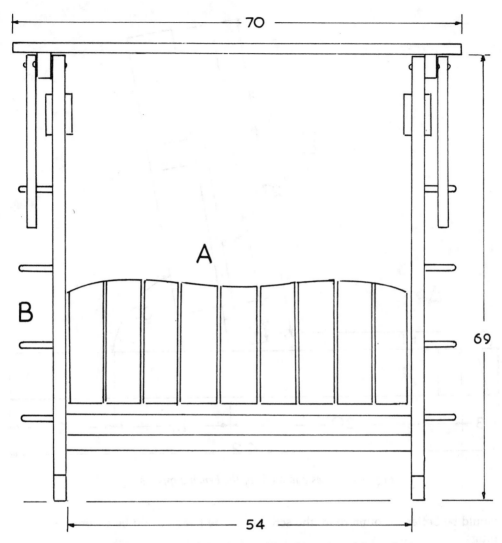

Fig. 8-14. Sizes of the sheltered bench as viewed from the front.

Assemble this framework squarely. Its accuracy controls the appearance of the finished project. Trim any projecting joint ends. Add seat and back boards now, or leave them until after assembly. Adding now will be easier, but the result will be rather heavy if you have to complete the job without helpers.

The seat is made of three boards (FIGS. 8-15A and 16F) about 6 inches wide with gaps up to 1 inch, to shed rainwater. Round the outer edge of the front one, and take the sharpness off the edges of the others. Screw in place with the ends level with the framework ends. Leave screw heads level on the surface, but it

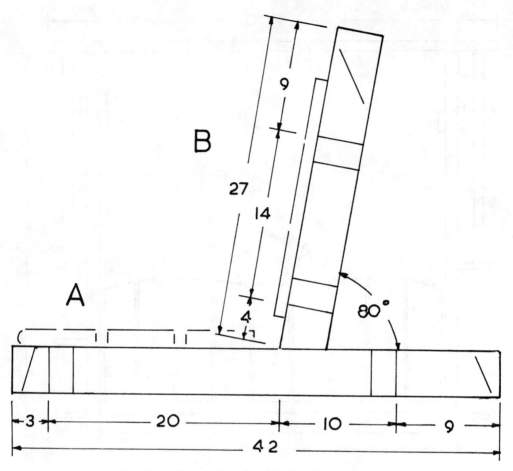

Fig. 8-15. Sizes and angle of the bench supports.

would be better to counterbore the screws, so the heads could be covered with plugs.

Boards 6 inches wide with 1-inch spacing are suggested for the seat back (FIG. 8-15B). Make the tops to any reasonable height, and either cut straight across or arrange a curved shape (FIG. 8-14A). Round all exposed edges and corners. Glue and screw the boards.

The end supports are the same (FIG. 8-13A), except for the pegs (FIG. 8-14B) arranged in opposite directions. Construction of the base depends on the situation. It might be possible to put a rail across at about seat level and bury the feet in the ground. As shown, (FIG. 8-13B) base strips spread the load on the surface. They could be pegged down, but there is plenty of weight in the whole bench, and movement is unlikely. Leaving the bench unattached to the ground allows you to move it, possibly only a short amount, if you want to give the grass a chance to grow. You might prefer a concrete base, with the wood bolted down.

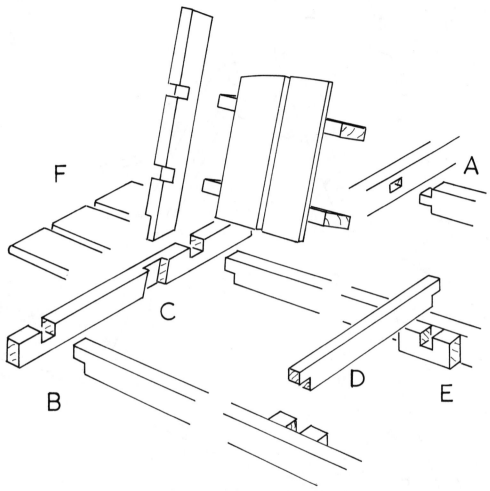

Fig. 8-16. *Assembly of main parts of the bench.*

If possible, set out the main lines of an end fullsize on the ground, to get sizes and angles. Alternatively, use the pieces of wood overlapping each other and mark their lengths and joints.

In each frame the top of the front leg extends to provide a pivot for the roof (FIG. 8-17A). The top of the other leg comes against this (FIG. 8-17B), and is joined with two cover pieces (FIG. 8-17C), glued and screwed on.

Join the bottoms of the legs to the base piece (FIG. 8-17D). Let the base piece extend enough to provide stability and bevel the ends. Holding-down bolts could go through the beveled ends, or you could arrange pegs to the ground outside the wood. Assemble the pair of ends, but do not mark or drill peg holes at this stage.

The roof could be made in several ways. It could be thick plywood. You could use close boards, preferably tongued-and-grooved. In either case, paint the

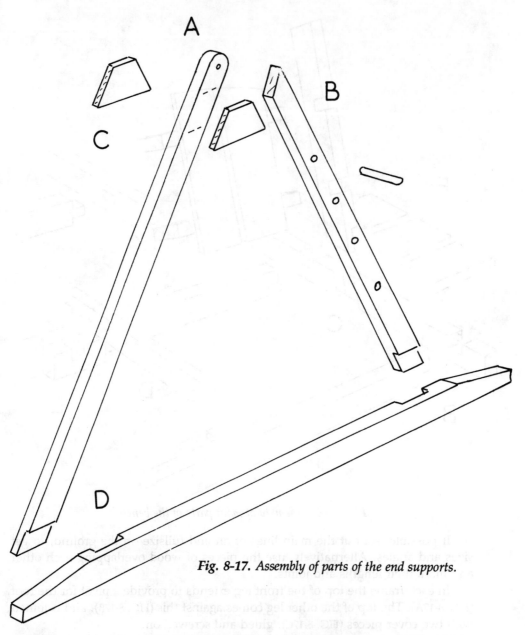

Fig. 8-17. Assembly of parts of the end supports.

wood or cover with roofing felt or similar material; this type of roof would be rainproof. If you are more concerned with providing shade from the sun, use boards with gaps between (FIG. 8-18A). This would keep off falling leaves as well as sunshine, but rain would leak through.

Before making the roof, cut one of the crossbars to size (FIG. 8-13C). Mark and drill for the pivot bolt and another for the handle (FIG. 8-18B). It should be satisfactory to use 1/2-inch bolts, but they could be up to 3/4 inch in diameter.

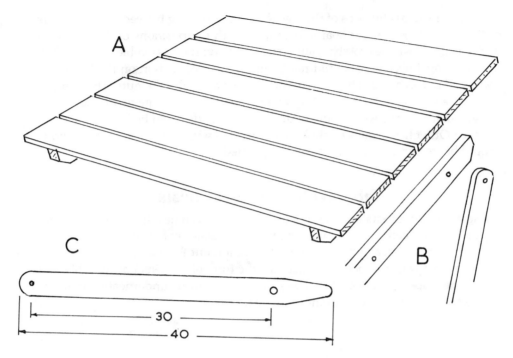

Fig. 8-18. Details of the roof of the sheltered bench.

Make a handle (FIG. 8-18C). The hole at the end will take a bolt, but the other hole has to fit easily over a 1 inch in diameter peg. Round the tapered end for a comfortable grip.

Temporarily bolt the crossbar to the top of a leg, and attach the handle. Arrange the crossbar parallel with the base, and mark on the rear leg where the peg hole comes (FIG. 8-13D). That is the position of the top peg. Pull the roof down, until it is almost at the angle of the rear leg. Extend the handle down to mark a new peg position (FIG. 8-13E). Two more positions equally spaced will probably be all you need.

The pegs are 1-inch hardwood dowels, taken right through holes in the legs and extending far enough to project about 1 inch outside the handles. Drill for them now, but wait until after the complete assembly before putting in the pegs.

Join the end frames to the seat. The extending pieces on the seat ends allow for some experimenting. You will want the front edge of the seat about 15 inches from the ground, but you can try different degrees of tilt while the parts are temporarily clamped together. Do all this on a flat surface, so there is no risk of a twist developing. Stand back and sight along to check that the two end assemblies are parallel. When you are satisfied glue and screw the assemblies together, but it will be safer to include a 1/2-inch bolt through the center of each joint. Cut off the protruding ends of the seat assembly. Take off all sharp edges and corners of these ends.

Measure across the tops of the legs to find the spacing between the crossbars of the roof. Mark the roof boards to length, with the positions of the crossbars underneath. Have the crossbars and handles ready; then assemble the roof. Bolt the parts together. There should not be much wear or friction on the bolts, but you could put washers between the wood parts and under the nuts. The handles have to be sprung outwards slightly when you wish to change to another peg.

Finish to suit the wood. Some durable hardwoods could be left untreated to weather. Other hardwoods might be better treated with oil or varnish. Softwoods should be treated with preservative and painted.

Table with Stow-away Seats

If a seat is left outdoors in all weather, the surface becomes dirty and often wet, so you have to clean it or cover it before use. If the seat can fold away, undercover, there should be a clean top every time you pull it out for use. This project (FIG. 8-19) is a table with two benches, that take the form of the usual picnic table and seats when open, but both benches can be tilted to fit underneath the table, where they are protected from the elements.

Fig. 8-19. This picnic table is arranged with seats that fold to fit underneath.

**Materials List for
Table with Stow-away Seats**

4 table legs	1¹/₂×34× 5
2 table rails	1¹/₂×36× 4
2 table rails	1¹/₂×44× 4
2 diagonal struts	1¹/₂×36× 4
2 joint covers	1¹/₂×18× 4
4 tabletops	1¹/₂×56× 9
4 bench legs	1¹/₂×15× 8
2 bench rails	1¹/₂×42× 4
2 bench tops	1¹/₂×44×10
4 pivot arms	1¹/₂×21× 6

The drawings (FIGS. 8-20 and 21) are for a table with a top 36 inches wide and 54 inches long, standing 30 inches off the ground. The legs spread to 44 inches. When the seats are stowed they are entirely within the table size, but they open to provide seats 10 inches wide and about 42 inches long, 15 inches from the ground. Sizes could be modified to suit your needs, but make sure the folding arrangement will still function. A seat pivots on bolts through the table legs (FIG. 8-20A). The bench will tilt, so it rests against the table rail (FIG. 8-20B) or the center struts.

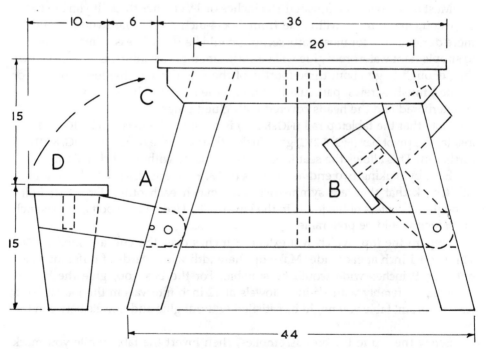

Fig. 8-20. End view of the table with stow-away seats, showing how the seats swing to fit underneath.

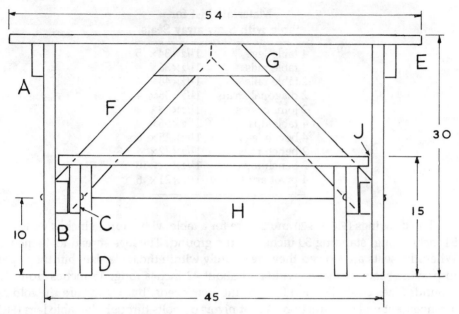

Fig. 8-21. Sizes of table and seat as viewed from the side.

Most of the parts are finished $1^1/2$ inches or $1^3/4$ inches thick. If you are using softwood, many parts will come from 2-×-4-inch stock. Hardwood would be more durable, and for most parts sections could be $1/4$ inch less. Simple screwing to supplement waterproof glue will be sufficient for most joints. Use stout screws long enough to go about three-fourths of the way through the lower parts. For the best finish, screws, particularly through the table and bench tops, should be counterbored and the heads covered with glued plugs.

Note that the tabletop rail (FIG. 8-21A) is outside; the lower rail (FIG. 8-21B) is inside; the pivot bar (FIG. 8-21C) goes inside that; and the bench leg (FIG. 8-21D) is further in. This allows the seat tops to swing inside without obstruction.

Start by making two end assemblies (FIGS. 8-20C and 22A), which are identical. Check that they are symmetrical and match each other. Drill bolt holes through the centers of the joints in the lower rails. Use $1/2$-inch bolts, but $5/8$ inch or $3/4$ inch would be preferable.

Prepare the top, which will extend 3 inches over the end assemblies (FIG. 8-21E) and 1 inch at each side. Make up the width with boards of different sizes, but four, 9 inches wide would be suitable. For the best top, glue the boards together, preferably with $1/2$-inch dowels at 12-inch intervals in the joints. For a less important table you might be satisfied without glue and dowels between the boards.

Screw the top to the end assemblies; then invert the table while you mark and cut the diagonal struts. Arrange them to meet at the middle (FIG. 8-21F), and notch over the lower rails (FIG. 8-23B). Make sure the legs are square to the top

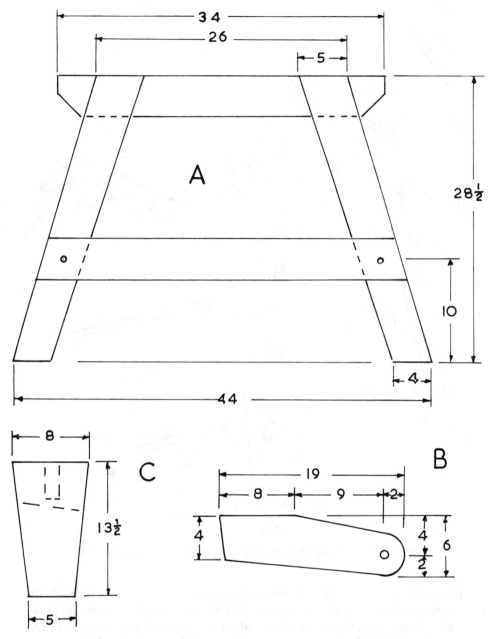

Fig. 8-22. Sizes of a table end frame and parts of the stow-away seats.

when you mark the lengths of the struts. Fit joint covers at the tops of the struts (FIGS. 8-21G and 23C). Screw downwards through the tabletop into the struts and their covers. Screw securely to the rails. Check that the table will stand firmly on a level surface. If necessary, trim the bottoms of one or more legs.

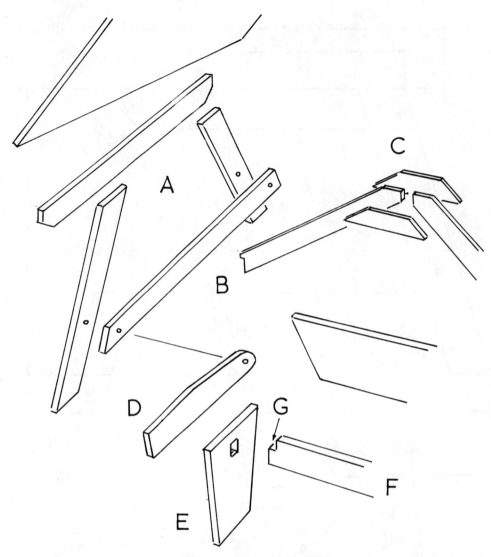

Fig. 8-23. Assembly details of the table with stow-away seats.

Each seat is a simple bench joined by two pivot arms to bolts through the ends of the table lower rails. Get sizes from the table. Variations between opposite sides do not matter, providing you allow for them. Make four pivot arms (FIGS. 8-22B and 23D). Trim the outer ends to match the bench legs later.

Make four bench legs (FIGS. 8-22C and 23E). The rails between them (FIGS. 8-21H and 23F) could have their ends screwed, or you could use dowels. Tenons will make it stronger (FIG. 8-23G).

Assemble the bench legs to the pivot arms; try these parts temporarily in their position on bolts through the legs. Allow for washers between the moving surfaces. Test for tilting action. Measure between the legs to get the lengths of bench rails.

Join the rails to the legs. Make the bench tops to overlap the legs (FIG. 8-20D) and of a length that will pass easily between the table legs (FIG. 8-21J). Join each bench top to its legs and rails with screws, preferably counterbored and plugged.

Put the bolts temporarily in place, and check the folding action. Disassemble the parts for finishing. Remove sharpness from the edges and corners. Softwood should be treated with preservative and/or paint. Some hardwoods can be left untreated, but others will be better if oiled, varnished or painted.

9
Folding furniture

Most outdoor furniture is used only occasionally. In some cases it will be convenient for the furniture to be rigid and permanently in shape, but for many things it is better if its size can be reduced. If furniture can be folded or disassembled, parts will occupy much less storage space. Care is needed with disassembled parts, so that you do not lose any of them. This is particularly true for nuts, bolts, and washers. Most folding furniture does not require loose parts, so there is nothing to lose.

Besides the convenience of reducing bulk for storage of furniture used in the vicinity of the home, folding furniture is useful for camping and other trips where you need to stow everything as compactly as possible.

It is important that a folding piece of furniture be strong enough during use and when folded. Some things are satisfactory when assembled, but a comparatively fragile part will be exposed to damage when folded. Guard against inadvertent folding when the item is in use. There must be a definite lock in some way, so that a chair does not collapse under a normal load.

Some folding furniture is designed most ingeniously and usually with rather complicated mechanisms. This type is more suitable for factory production because there are special parts that most individual craftsmen cannot make. In any case, a simple action is preferable to a complicated one.

Folding furniture manufactured in quantity is mostly metal, formed by machine. This technique is unsuitable for the home shop. Wood is the preferred material, but some simple metalwork is needed. This involves sawing, filing, drilling, and some simple bending. All of this can be done with hand tools, if necessary.

For the sake of lightness, wooden folding outdoor furniture is normally made with sections no thicker than necessary. Because of this, select straight-grained hardwood that is free from knots. Do not use softwood. If it is unavoidable, then sections should be increased and joints would have to be reinforced in many places with metal brackets or plywood gussets.

Folding furniture should be painted or varnished to prevent the wood from absorbing moisture, as well as for the sake of appearance. A boat varnish gives good protection, and it allows the grain to show through, resulting in a lighter appearance than a painted surface. Pay particular attention to any end grain that will rest on the ground because it is particularly prone to soak up moisture.

Folding Stool

This is a basic type of seat with a canvas top that is comfortable to use. Packing under 3 inches thick, it is suitable for camping and fishing, as well as in your yard. The parts are made as two frames pivoted near their centers (FIG. 9-1) with canvas across the top bars. The frames are the same, except that one is narrow enough to fit inside the other.

Mark out the two top bars (FIG. 9-2A), but do not round the edges until after the joints are cut. Mark out all four legs (FIG. 9-2B). Leave the cutting of the bottom angled ends until after assembly. The joints are simple mortise and tenons (FIG. 9-2C). They should be strong enough, but if you have any doubts add strip metal brackets inside each joint (FIG. 9-2D). Check that the legs of the narrower assembly fit inside the other ones.

The braces on the outer pair of legs should come below the pivot points (FIG. 9-1A). Otherwise, they will interfere with the action by hitting the inner legs when the stool is opened. This would not happen with the inner legs if the braces were higher, but it is standard to put both sets at the same height. As shown in FIG. 9-2E, the braces are put on through the marked positions on the legs and held at each place with one screw; then they are cut level. Where the braces cross they are sprung over each other. It would weaken them too much to cut halving joints there. Fit the legs into each other when you put on the braces, so that you see that they will be able to move.

The pivots can be carriage bolts. Let the square neck pull into the outer leg, include a thin rivet between the legs; then, have a washer and nut inside (FIG. 9-2F). Cut off the bolt end fairly close to the nut, and hammer over its edges all

Materials List for Folding Stool

2 tops	$1^1/8 \times 16 \times 1^1/8$
4 legs	$1^1/8 \times 24 \times {}^7/8$
4 braces	${}^7/8 \times 18 \times {}^1/4$

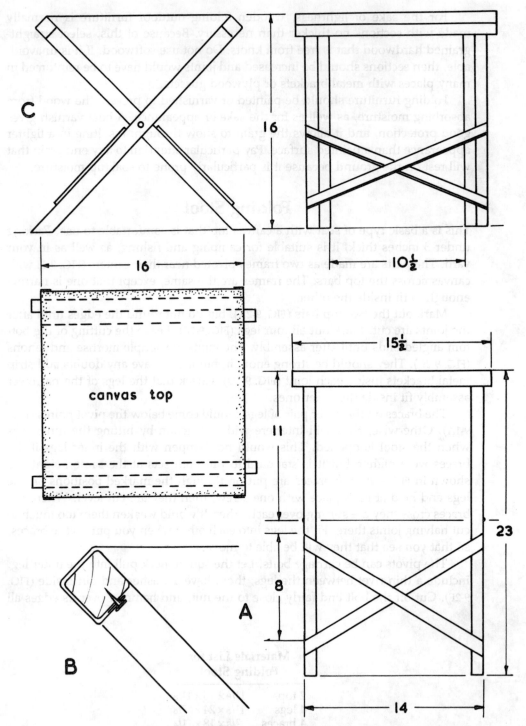

Fig. 9-1. A folding stool with a canvas top.

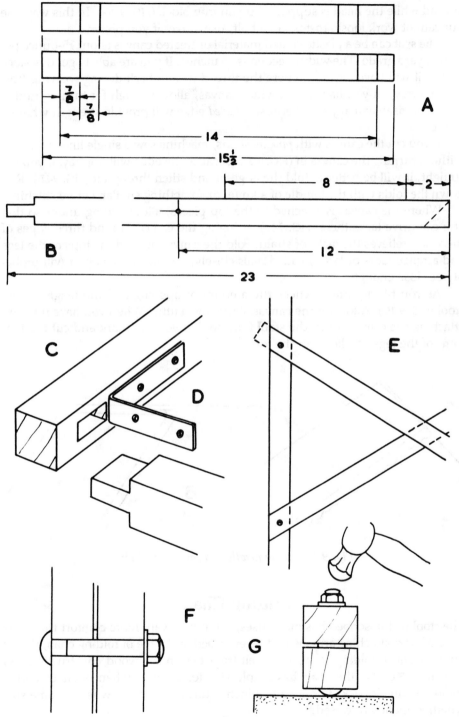

Fig. 9-2. Construction of the folding stool.

around while the head is supported on an iron block (FIG. 9-2G). In this way, the nut cannot work loose. Instead of a bolt, use a rivet if you prefer.

The seat can be a plastic-coated material or treated canvas about 15-ounce per square yard grade. The width needed is 15 inches. If you are able to get this stock width, it will have a *selvage* where the thread turned back during weaving (this will not fray). If you have to cut wider canvas, allow enough for turning under. This is advisable in any case because a *tabled* edge will provide strength where it is needed.

If you cut the canvas with *pinking shears*, machine sew a single line of stitches without turning the canvas in (FIG. 9-3A) because the edge will not fray. If you cut straight, it will be better to fold the edge in and stitch through it (FIG. 9-3B). Rub down the folds with the handle of a knife, or something similar, before stitching.

Where the canvas is attached to the top pieces, allow folding under so that you can drive tacks there (FIG. 9-1B). Bringing the canvas around three edges of the wood relieves the tacks of strain. Fold the canvas around the tops of the legs and arrange tacks or large-headed nails closely; spacing 1-inch apart will probably be close enough.

As you fit the canvas, check the amount of opening and the height of the stool (FIG. 9-1C). Allow for the canvas stretching a little. When you have finished attaching the canvas, open the stool fully so that you can mark and cut the bottoms of the legs parallel with the top.

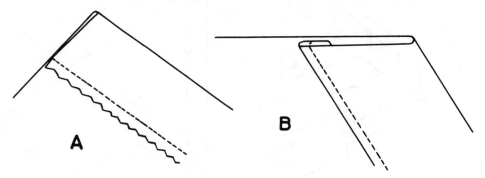

Fig. 9-3. Sewing details of a canvas stool top.

Folding Chair

The stool just described has many uses, but if you want more comfort there has to be a back; attaching arms would be even better. A type of folding chair, that is built around a folding stool, is a well-tried design for wood construction. As shown in FIG. 9-4, the chair has ample size for comfort when opened, and it stands rigidly. It packs to only a few inches thick; its side view is the same size whether opened or closed.

The framework, including the arms, is made of wood, but the seat and back

Fig. 9-4. A folding armchair.

Materials List for Folding Chair

4 stool legs	$1^1/4 \times 26 \times$ $^5/8$
2 stool crossbars	$1^1/4 \times 18 \times 1^1/4$
2 stool rods	$^5/8 \times 18$ round rods
4 side legs	$1^3/4 \times 26 \times$ $^7/8$
2 side rails	$3 \ \times 18 \times$ $^7/8$
2 side slats	$4 \ \times 15 \times$ $^1/2$
2 arms	$3 \ \times 22 \times$ $^7/8$
2 backs	$1^3/4 \times 26 \times$ $^7/8$

are canvas. This will conform to body shape and provide comfort. Make some simple metal links and spacers. The most attractive finish is boat varnish, with the metal parts painted. Paint the wood as well, if you prefer. Do not leave the wood bare because it would absorb moisture.

The general drawing (FIG. 9-5) shows that the seat is a stool. A pair of sides link to the stool and join with canvas to form the back. Make the stool first, and fit the sides to it. Get an accurate assembly by starting with the pair of sides. Then, adjust the spacings of the stool sides and legs to suit.

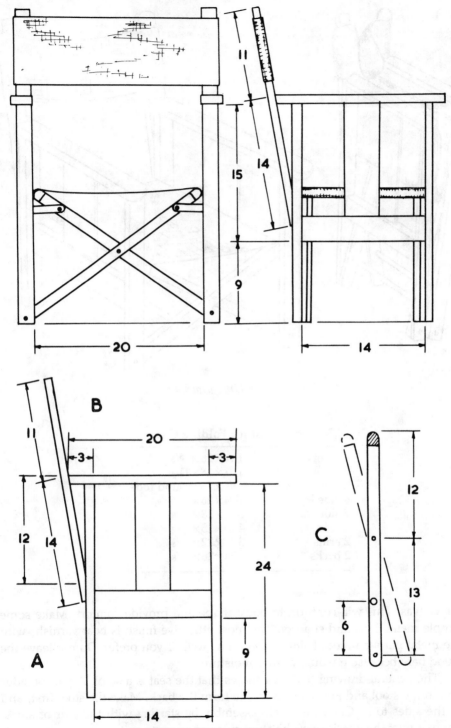

Fig. 9-5. Sizes of a folding armchair.

Set out the chair side full size (FIG. 9-5A). Make the parts with square edges. After cutting the joints and doing general shaping, round all edges that will be exposed (FIG. 9-6A). Most joints can be doweled. Use mortise and tenons if you prefer.

Mark out the four upright legs together (FIG. 9-6B). Drill 1/4-inch holes for bolts, 1 inch up from the bottom, to form stool pivots. The side rails dowel into the marked positions on the legs (FIG. 9-6C). The tops of the legs have dowels into the arms (FIG. 9-6D).

The arms are parallel except for rounding at the front and a taper at the back. The side slats are too thin for dowels; slot them into the arm and rail (FIG. 9-6E).

The back piece and the arm that attaches to it should be marked and cut to match. The back (FIG. 9-5B) has its bottom cut to an angle against the leg, but a feather edge would weaken it. Well round the top. The joint between the end of the arm and the back has to resist the thrust of a person sitting and leaning back. A joint that cuts too much out of the back can cause it to break there under pressure. So that there is enough wood left in the back, join the arm with a single 5/8-inch dowel. Drive a wedge from behind (FIG. 9-6F). Do not load the joint at the bottom of the back because thrust at the top tends to push that joint together. Use glue and one or two screws there. After you have prepared all parts and rounded where advisable, assemble to make a matching pair.

The stool is made up of two crossbars to take the canvas, with four crossed sides, held below the pivot with lengths of dowel rod (FIG. 9-7A). The sizes of the sides shown (FIG. 9-5C) will give a satisfactory spread when opened.

As you set out the stool, the crossbars are as long as the widths of the sides, but the joints between them and their legs have to be spaced to suit the spacing of the chair side legs. One pair of the stool legs, that come outside the others, has to fit between the chair side legs with just enough clearance for thin washers. Then, the inside stool legs must fit between them with similar clearance.

The legs might be joined to the crossbars with dowels, but it would be better to use tenons, either right through (as in the stool first described) or with stub tenons (FIG. 9-7B). Round the top edges of the crossbars (FIG. 9-7C). Drill for 1/4-inch pivot bolts 1 inch from the rounded bottoms of the stool legs and again at the pivot points.

Drill for the dowel rods that brace the lower parts of the stool legs. When you assemble, the rods can go right through and be held with glue and nails driven across.

The central pivot of the stool is a 1/4-inch bolt or rivet taken through the washers. The pivot of the outside stool legs to the bottom of the side rigid legs is the same (FIG. 9-7D). Carriage bolts, as described for the first stool, could be used (but rivets are shown). When you do the final assembly, have the prepared rivet head outside and hammer over on the washer on the inside.

At the other side, fill the gap between the stool leg and the side rigid leg. Use short pieces of tube on the rivets. Make the length to take up the thickness of the

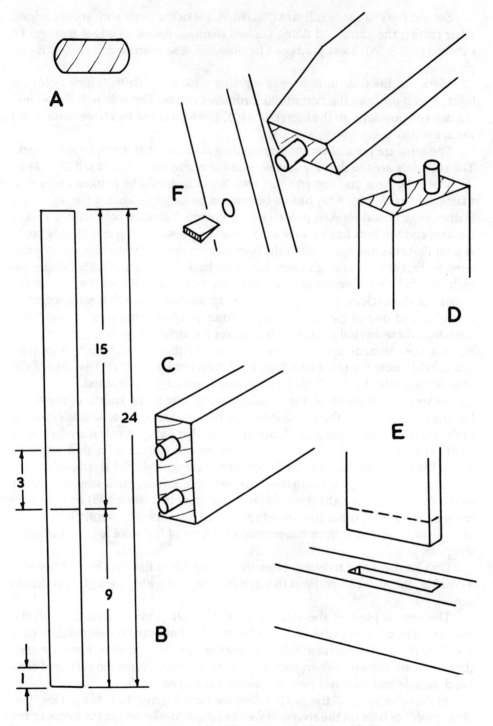

Fig. 9-6. Parts of the side frames of the folding armchair.

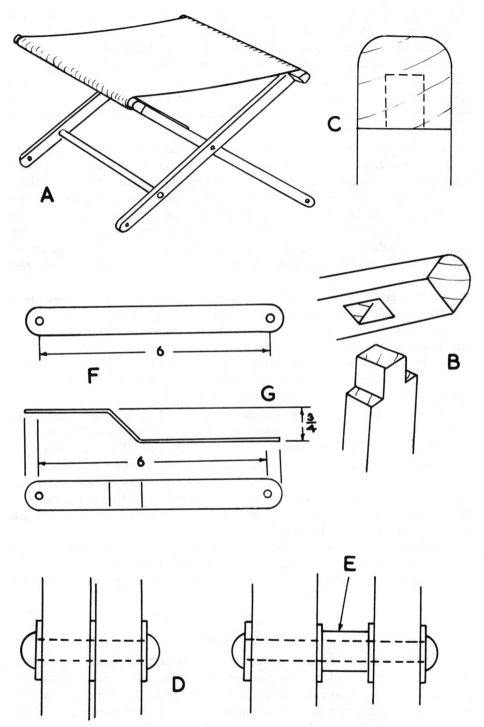

A

C

B

F

6

G

$\frac{3}{4}$

6

E

D

Fig. 9-7. *Details of the folding seat part of the armchair.*

outer stool leg (FIG. 9-7E). Make a trial assembly with the rivets or bolts loose, but do not tighten them until you have the canvas on and the metal links ready.

The links that join the stool to the sides and permit folding are pieces of strip metal about $5/8$ of an inch wide and under $1/8$ inch thick; $3/32$ inch would be ideal, but any strip about this section could be used. Iron is the obvious choice, but it rusts. Painting iron before assembly will give ample protection. Brass would resist corrosion and stainless steel would be a good choice. Some of it, however, is difficult to bend and drill.

The straight links that join the outside stool legs to the rigid side legs (FIG. 9-7F) are simple, straight pieces. Mark the centers of the holes with a center-punch, and use these dots as centers for drawing the end curves before drilling.

At the other side of the chair, the links should have the same distance between the holes, when finished, but the links have to be cranked to allow for the legs being in a different plane (FIG. 9-7G). Bending can be done while the strip projects above the vise jaws. Drill holes to suit the screws used; 10-gauge screws are suitable. Countersink the holes, so the heads will not project and interfere with folding.

The best positions for the links are found by a trial assembly. Loosely insert the rivets or bolts, and open the chair to the sitting position. Attach the links temporarily to the rear stool legs only, about 3 inches down from the crossbar. Put screws into the side legs when the links are about horizontal. Try the folding action. Then, alter the screw positions until the action is correct. Mark and drill similar positions for screws at the front. Measure across the top of the stool in the open position as a guide to the length of canvas to fit.

Do any finishing to the woodwork before attaching the canvas—including the parts that will be covered by canvas—for the sake of protection. The seat canvas is dealt with in the same way as described for the stool. A width of 15 inches or 16 inches would be suitable. Roll the canvas over the crossbars and tack closely underneath. In the first fitting of the seat canvas, aim to have it finish taut in the open position, to allow for some stretching. When the seat canvas has been fitted, assemble the pivot rivets or bolts together with the links. Then, have the seat standing with its sides upright.

The back strip of canvas should be 7 inches or 8 inches wide. Deal with the edges in the same way as the edges of the seat. Do not stretch it as tightly as the seat; it can start with a little slackness. Wrap the ends around the wood, and tack inside in the same way as the seat.

Deck Chair

The fold-flat deck chair is common in many forms in most parts of the world. There are versions with leg rests, canopies, arms, and other additions, but the basic pattern is the most common form. It serves as a simple and comfortable adjustable seat that can be stored in a minimum of space. The example shown in FIG. 9-8 is of straightforward construction with no extras. The sizes given will

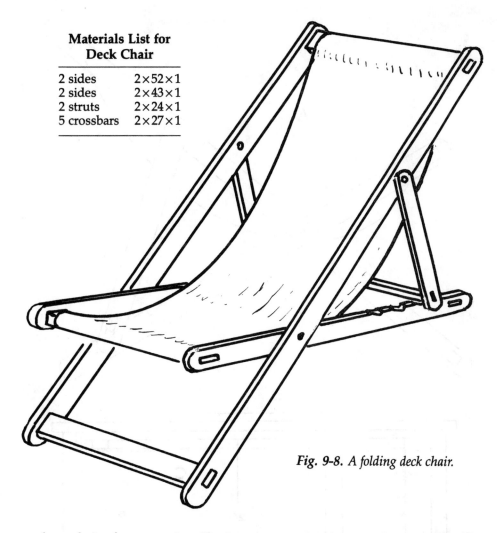

Materials List for Deck Chair

2 sides	$2 \times 52 \times 1$
2 sides	$2 \times 43 \times 1$
2 struts	$2 \times 24 \times 1$
5 crossbars	$2 \times 27 \times 1$

Fig. 9-8. A folding deck chair.

make a chair of average size. If other sizes are used, remember that the inner assembly has to fold inside the outer one and that the strut part must swing over the top of the outer frame for folding. If the canvas is flat and moderately taut when the chair is folded, it will curve into a comfortable shape when the chair is set up.

Two frames pivot together. A strut assembly allows the chair to be at any of three angles (FIG. 9-9A). When the frame is folded, the two four-sided parts close into line, and the strut part rests on them (FIG. 9-9B). This brings the assembly down to less than 4 inches thick.

All of the parts are 1-×-2-inch section and should be of straight-grained hardwood free from flaws. A heavy person using the chair puts considerable strain on some parts. The width shown is intended to take canvas 18 inches wide, but that can be adjusted if only canvas of another width is available.

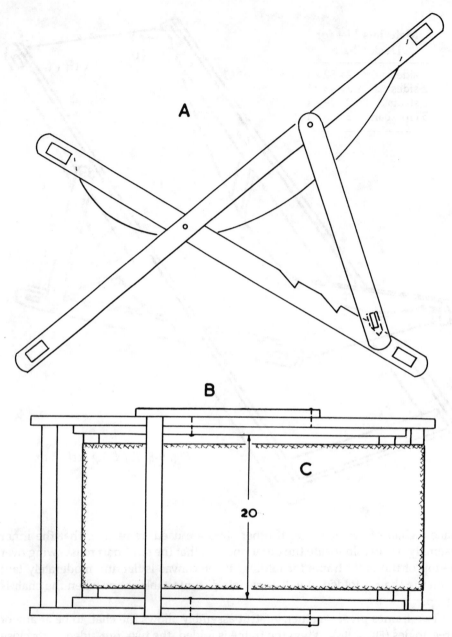

Fig. 9-9. The general arrangements of a folding deck chair.

Mark out the long sides (FIG. 9-10A). All of the ends with crossmembers tenoned in are made the same (FIG. 9-10B). The ends are rounded, using the edge of the crossmember as the center for the compass. Mark out the shorter sides (FIG. 9-10C). The notches for the strut are cut into a ³/₈-inch hole (FIG. 9-10D). It is possible to make all the notches the same and have the strut crossmember an

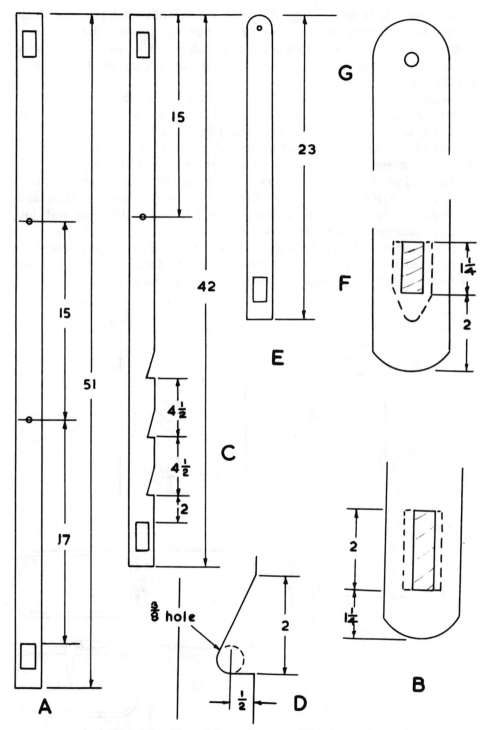

Fig. 9-10. *Sizes of the main parts of the deck chair.*

average shape. Because the angle at the side is different in each position, obtain the best fit by making the furthest notch as shown and having the strut cross-member match it. Alter the other positions to suit during a trial assembly. All of the notches will be cut into 3/8-inch holes, but the angles into them will be slightly different at the inner two positions.

Make the strut sides (FIG. 9-10E). The bottom joint is similar to the others, except that the tenon is cut back to allow the bevels on the crossmember (FIG. 9-10F). The top is cut semicircular and drilled for the bolt (FIG. 9-10G).

The joints are all tenons about 1/2 inch wide (FIG. 9-11A). Round the edges of the crossmembers of the four-sided frames (FIG. 9-11B). Cut the tenons slightly too long and put saw cuts across them, so that the joints can be tightened with wedges (FIG. 9-11C). They are planed level after the glue has set. Make sure assemblies are square; the inner frame should fit inside the other with just enough clearance for a washer on each side.

Pivots can be 1/4-inch or 5/16-inch carriage bolts. For the main pivots, position the heads *outside*. Set them *inside* for the strut pivots. Include washers between the parts and under the nuts (FIG. 9-11D). After the final assembly, cut off any

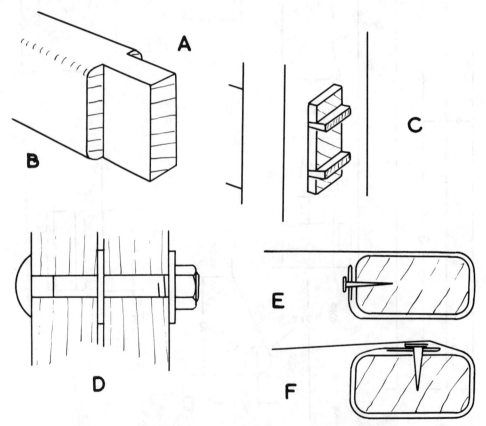

Fig. 9-11. Assembling, pivoting, and canvasing the deck chair.

surplus threaded bolt ends, and rivet the remainder by hammering on to the nut to lock it. If the notches for the strut are to be individually fitted, do that during a temporary assembly.

Take off the sharpness from the edges of the main parts. This is particularly important for anyone sitting in the chair. But do not reduce the cross-section much. Varnish the wood before final assembly, so that you can get at the parts that would otherwise be difficult to reach.

If the canvas is bought already at the right width, its selvages (fabric edges) can be used as they are because they will not fray. If you have to cut wider canvas, turn in the edges (as described for the folding chair).

Fold the frames so that they are in line. The canvas has to go from the front rail of the inner frame to the top rail of the outer frame (FIG. 9-9C). Allow enough to wrap around the rails and turn in to be tacked. Tack to the edges of the rails (FIG. 9-11E), but for the strongest joint the canvas should go around to the flat part (FIG. 9-11F). Tacking in this way is easy enough for the first end, but you can get enough slackness in the canvas to swing a hammer at the other end by folding the frames the wrong way (after you have settled on the canvas length). If fastened in that way, the canvas under load helps to keep the tacks in place.

Long Trestle Table

It is often useful to have one or more fairly light tables that can be folded flat when not needed. It is even more useful to have a folding arrangement that does not involve any special action or loose pieces.

The table shown in FIG. 9-12 has a framed plywood top and legs. The legs are held upright by struts, that are held in place by gravity; when folded upward toward the center, the legs come close to the top. The total thickness is only a few inches. The folding of the legs controls the length of the table. It would not be impossible to let the leg ends overlap, but that would increase the folded thickness. Otherwise, the length must be enough to keep the legs clear of each other. If the table is to stand 30 inches high, the length of the top cannot be fewer than about 65 inches. The example shown is 72 inches. The main parts are shown $1^{1}/4$ inches thick for rigidity. They could be increased to $1^{1}/2$ inches, but it would be unwise to reduce them much, unless lightness is the most important requirement. Width can be anything you want to make it, but it is shown as 27 inches. The leg assemblies and the top are the same width.

Materials List for
Long Trestle Table

1 top	$27 \times 72 \times {}^{1}/2$ plywood
2 top frames	$3 \times 74 \times 1^{1}/4$
4 top frames	$3 \times 28 \times 1^{1}/4$
4 legs	$3 \times 30 \times 1^{1}/4$
4 leg rails	$3 \times 27 \times 1^{1}/4$
4 struts	$3 \times 16 \times 1$

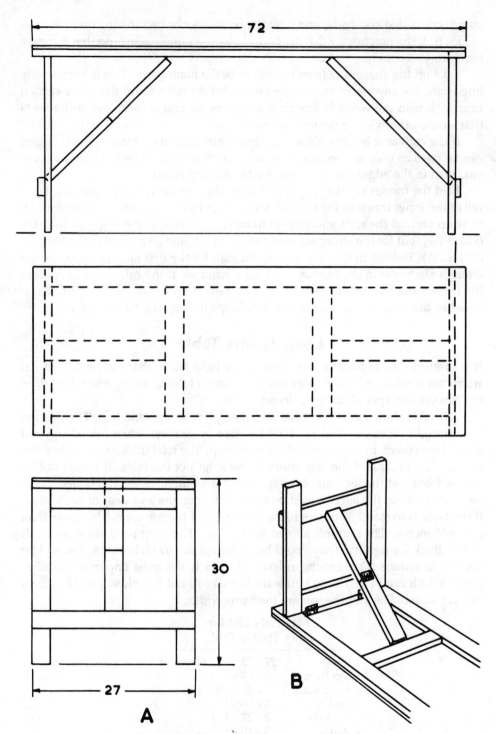

Fig. 9-12. A long table with legs to fold under.

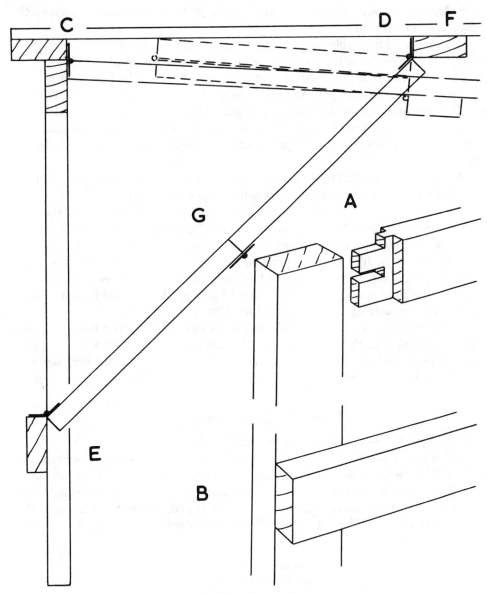

Fig. 9-13. End details of the long folding table.

The plywood supports the top framing, so there is little need for joints between the top parts. Corners could be mitered or the flat pieces could be halved. Use glue and plenty of nails through the plywood. Finish with the strips framing the plywood, but do not attach the other cross pieces yet.

Make up two leg assemblies (FIG. 9-12A). At the top, tenon the rail into the legs (FIG. 9-13A). For a simpler construction, screw to their inner surfaces. The lower rail comes 6 inches from the ground, and it is screwed and glued to the outer surfaces of the legs (FIG. 9-13B). Except for seeing that the parts are square and match each other, assembly is simple.

For neatly folding table legs, you must get certain distances correct. The distance from the center of the hinge between the legs and table (FIG. 9-13C) to the center of the hinge at the top of the strut (FIG. 9-13D), must be the same as the distance from the first hinge to the hinge on the lower leg rail (FIG. 9-13E). With a leg in place, measure the distance between the hinges when the leg is square to the top. Then, measure the same distance along the top—that is where you put another piece across (FIG. 9-13F). Put another one across the same distance from the other end.

Measure the overall length of a strut when the leg assembly is square to the top. Make each strut divided into two equal parts (FIG. 9-13G).

All of the parts can be joined with 3-inch hinges. Hinge the tops of the leg assemblies to the ends of the top framing (FIG. 9-12B). Hinge the ends of each pair of struts together so that they meet closely when laid out straight. Any space between the ends will cause the struts to sag in use. Join the struts to the rails with hinges on top; leave the central hinges underneath. When the table is standing the right way up, the struts should stay in place. To fold, push them toward the top, and lay the legs against the top.

This plain table can have a cloth over it for outdoor use. The edges can be framed around with thin wood to cover the plywood edges. The top can have Formica or a similar laminated plastic on it. If you prefer a solid top, several boards can be used, with battens across underneath used for hinging the legs.

Fold-flat Sun Lounger

This lounger (FIG. 9-14) can be wheeled and will fold flat.

All of the parts can be softwood, except that the two struts are better made of hardwood to reduce the risk of breakage at the ends. The general drawing (FIG. 9-15) shows the wheel arms inside the main frame, and the wheels inside them (FIG. 9-15A). This is necessary for the other parts to fold, without interfering with the wheels stowing. The legs are also arranged inside (FIG. 9-15B). The struts

Materials List for
Fold-flat Sun Lounger

2 sides	4×88×2
2 ends	4×24×2
2 legs	4×18×2
2 wheel arms	4×14×2
2 rails	3×24×1
20 battens	3×28×1
2 uprights	2×34×1
2 packings	2× 8×1
2 struts	2×24×1

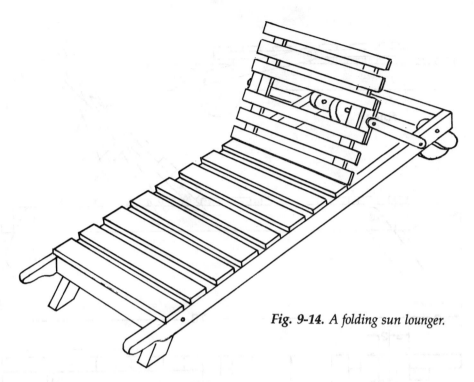

Fig. 9-14. A folding sun lounger.

pivot outside the main frame (FIG. 9-15C). The backrest is as wide as the main frame, but its uprights are arranged to come inside the main frame sides (FIG. 9-15D), so as to slip between battens in three positions.

The main frame is made with pieces across the ends (FIG. 9-15E). The corners can be tenoned or just nailed. Shape the handle extensions the same way as the other lounger. Drill the sides for bolts. The legs and wheel arms can be on $3/8$-inch bolts, but $1/4$-inch or $5/16$-inch bolts will be thick enough for the strut and backrest. All of the battens across the main frame are a 1-×-3-inch section, and at the foot end they are about 2 inches apart. Get the spacing even, after you have located the special positions near the other end. So the backrest will fit without excessive looseness in three positions, the battens across where it goes must have gaps of varying widths (FIG. 9-16A). With those located, space the others evenly for the rest of the length. Two nails or screws at each end of a batten should secure it and help to prevent the framework from twisting.

The wheel arms are simple pieces with rounded ends (FIG. 9-16B). The axle need not go right through, but set it deep enough to be secure. Wheels of 7 inches in diameter are suggested, but others can be used. The wheel arms bear against the cross member at the end of the main frame, but there is also a rail across them resting there to increase the bearing area and reduce any tendency to wobble when the lounger is moved.

The legs pivot on bolts in the same way as the wheel arms. They bear against the end cross member of the main frame and have a rail similarly arranged (FIG.

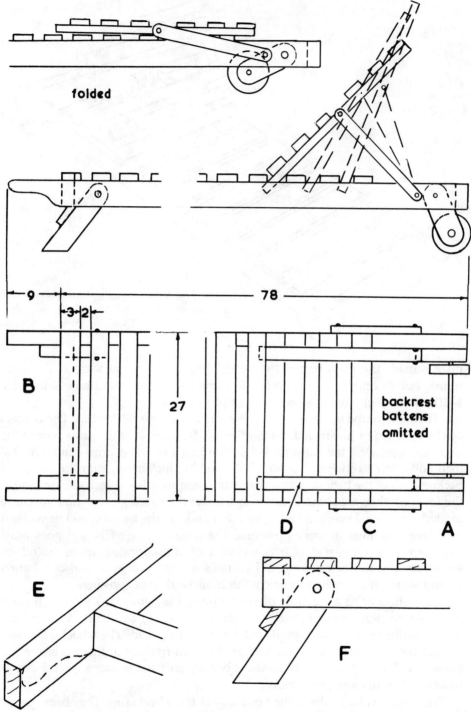

folded

backrest
battens
omitted

Fig. 9-15. Sizes of a folding sun lounger.

9-15F). Leave the legs too long until after the assembly. Then, they can be cut to hold the lounger level when the wheels are fully extended. The legs will fold fully inside the frame, but the wheel arms are restricted by the wheel sizes from going right in.

The backrest is made up with battens across uprights with their 2 inch side toward them (FIG. 9-16C). Make the uprights to extend about 3 inches below the lowest batten, and round the ends so that they will fit easily between the main frame battens. Make the lengths of the battens the same as those on the main frame, but set back the uprights to a width that will drop easily between the main frame sides. Note that there is a wide gap near the center of the assembly; that is to give clearance for the ends of the struts. This is particularly true when the assembly is folded flat.

Make the struts (FIG. 9-16D). They go outside the main frame sides, but the backrest they support has its uprights inside. To allow for this, put packing pieces outside the uprights at the hole positions (FIG. 9-16E), so that long bolts can go through.

Try the action of the backrest and its struts with a temporary assembly, going into all three positions. Also, make sure that the legs and wheel arms will fold and extend properly. If all is satisfactory, separate the parts for final cleaning up—particularly the removal of sharp edges and corners—before painting and final assembly. Similar cushions to those for the previous lounger can be made and fitted.

Ground-level Recliner

You may enjoy relaxing on the ground, but if you want to sit for more than a short period, you will welcome a back support. This recliner (FIG. 9-17) is intended to provide back support at several angles for anyone sitting directly on the ground, or on cushions or other fairly thin padding. It is rigid in use, but it can be closed flat for carrying or storage.

The back support is about 24 inches square, and the base occupies about the same area. When folded, this reduces to $2^1/2$ inches thick. For strength and durability, use a close-grained hardwood, although for a carefully used and lighter recliner, use softwood.

The back support is made with two strips holding pieces across (FIG. 9-18A). The base (FIG. 9-18B) fits inside this, and it has notches to give three positions for the struts. The pair of struts (FIG. 9-18C) are outside, and they are joined with a rod to drop fit into the notches. The design allows for three angles of the support (FIG. 9-18D), from near upright to as far as you are likely to want to go. Space notches differently for other angles, if you wish. Pivots are $1/4$-inch countersunk stove bolts, $2^1/2$ inches long, with washers under the nuts and between the parts (FIG. 9-18E). If possible, get locking or stiff nuts, so there is little risk of them working loose.

Make the back support first because this controls some sizes of other parts.

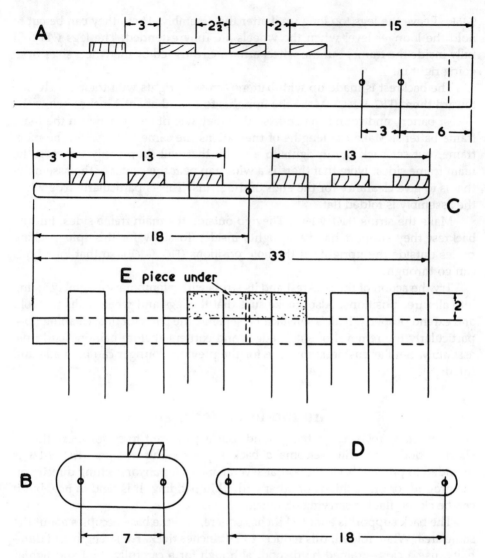

Fig. 9-16. *Sizes of parts of the folding sun lounger.*

Make two matching sides (FIG. 9-19A), drilled for bolts and rounded as shown. Cut four pieces to fit across (FIG. 9-19B), with the outer corners rounded. Assemble these parts with glue and screws. For smooth action, this assembly must be square, and the sides must be parallel.

Mark out the two base sides (FIG. 9-19C). The slots are made by drilling 1-inch holes centrally and sawing into them. To locate the strut rod easily, taper the cuts. Exact angles are not essential, but the drawing (FIG. 9-18) will serve as a guide. Drill for the pivot bolts, and round corners as shown. A crossbar joins the base sides (FIG. 9-19D). Finger joints are suggested, or use dovetails or other cor-

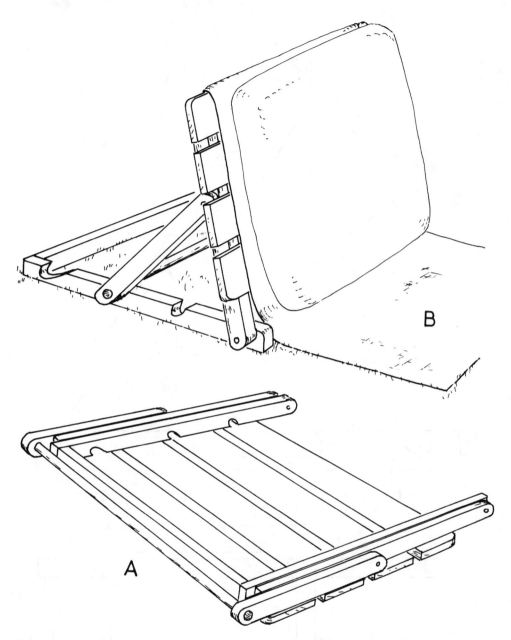

Fig. 9-17. *A ground-level recliner folds flat and can be used to provide back support when sitting on the ground.*

ner joints. The base has to fit between the sides of the back support, allowing for washers, so make the length of the crossbar to suit this.

The rod that fits into the slots should be a hardwood dowel rod. It should fit in each slot reasonably tightly, for security, but you should not need to use force.

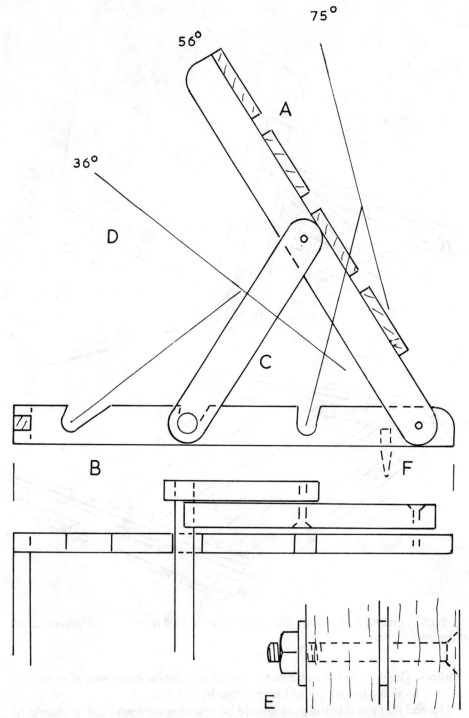

Fig. 9-18. *Action of the ground-level recliner, showing possible angles.*

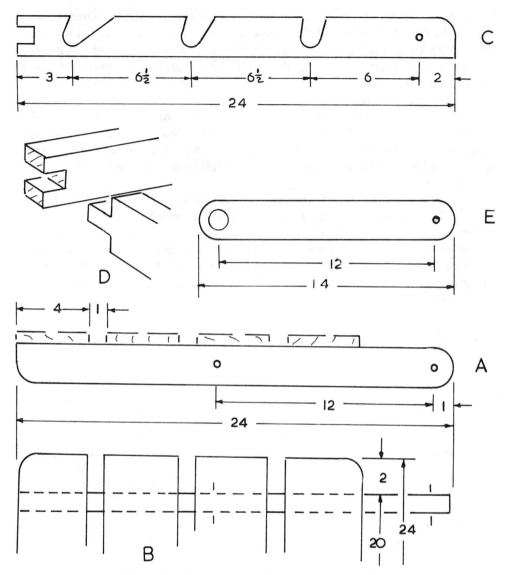

Fig. 9-19. Sizes of parts of the ground-level recliner.

**Materials List for
Ground-level Recliner**

2 backrest sides	1	×25×2
4 backrests		1/2×25×4
2 base sides	1	×25×2
1 base end	1	×20×2
2 struts	1	×15×2
1 rod	25	× 1 diameter

Make the two struts (FIG. 9-19E), drilled for bolts and the rod. When a strut is pivoted on its bolt the rod should clear the end of the support side for flat storage (FIG. 9-17A); check that this is so before completing the struts. To get this clearance, increase the length of the struts slightly. The struts have to go outside the support sides with washers between. Arrange the length of the rod to allow this, and glue it into the struts.

Countersink for the bolt heads, arranging the nuts to come on the sides of joints away from any adjoining piece when folded. Make a trial assembly to check action in all positions, including folded. Finish the wood with paint or varnish. If you have used a good hardwood, the recliner will look best if treated with an exterior varnish.

That completes the project. However, you might wish to prevent the recliner slipping in use. One way is to attach a length of canvas to extend some way under your body on the ground (FIG. 9-17B). Your weight will prevent the recliner pushing backwards. Another way is to make pegs to press into the ground. They could be 1/2-inch dowel rods under the base sides (FIG. 9-18F), extending with rounded points about 2 inches. They suit soil, but would be no use, and a nuisance, on a wood or stone surface.

10

Rustic furniture

Some outdoor furniture can be made from natural poles and logs, just as it is cut in the forests. Even if you cannot cut the wood yourself, get suitable material where trees are being felled or undergrowth is being cleared. Poles in the sizes you want usually are burned, and workers probably will be glad to have you take the wood away. You need poles up to 3 inches in diameter. Although you need straight pieces for many projects, they do not have to be very long. What is curved or twisted over a long length could yield the 3 feet or so that you want straight. Much of the attractiveness of this type of furniture is in the natural shaping of the wood. The curve can be included as a feature, or a slight variation from the precision of planed wood, and it can be regarded as characteristic of the material.

Obviously, poles recently felled will contain sap, but in the sizes you will be using, drying out will be unlikely to affect the wood enough to matter. Lengthwise shakes could open up, but they do not usually affect strength. Whether to leave the bark on or not is something you have to decide according to the wood. If the bark is firmly attached, as it is with some of the smooth-barked hardwoods, you can leave it. But if the bark can be lifted, the final furniture will be better if you peel off the bark before use. Otherwise, it might come away of its own accord after the furniture has been made; this could leave a patchy and unsatisfactory appearance.

Cut off branches and twigs, but be careful not to tear along the grain of the pole. If you use a hatchet, cut from the under side (FIG. 10-1A). It is better to use a saw, and then plane the remaining knots level (FIG. 10-1B). A useful alternative to a plane is a Surform tool or a rasp. Both of these can follow the curve easily. One

207

problem with some rustic furniture is the roughness that can be uncomfortable or snag clothing. Level off knots and other extending pieces before building the wood into furniture. Do not go so far as to plane the smooth parts of the wood. It should still look as natural as possible.

Sort your spars into sizes. Cut off parts that are not needed. Do not throw a piece away because of its shape. It might fit into a construction or give you ideas for using it as decoration. If the wood tapers much, it is not usually worthwhile using anything under 2 inches in diameter in furniture. For legs and other load-bearing parts, 3 inches is the diameter to choose. Cut away ends that are under-sized. Cut away part of the thick end of a pole. In felling, that end could have been bent and split if all the worker was doing was clearing quickly and expecting the wood to be burned.

Most of the wood will be used in the full, round section. However, you can get flat surfaces by cutting a log or a pole along its center. With a suitable circular saw available, you can cut the log that way, but it is possible to cleave, or split, a log with hand tools. One way is to start a split with an ax or by driving in a steel wedge (FIG. 10-1C). If the wood still has plenty of sap in it, it will cleave easily; and you can actually watch the split progress. Drive a wedge in the side (FIG. 10-1D). That will release the end wedge and force the split further. Use the wedge from the end to drive in further along (FIG. 10-1E); to lengthen the split and release the first wedge; to be entered in the split again; and so on in turn along the log.

The wood must have a reasonably straight grain; you cannot continue a split through knots. The split will follow the grain. Level bumps, but allow free-flowing, large undulations. They can be considered a feature of rustic furniture.

A traditional tool for cleaving poles of moderate size is a *froe* (FIG. 10-1F). A new froe might be difficult to find, but if you can find one, it is first hit into the log. Then, widen the split by wobbling the handle from side to side (FIG. 10-1G). Direct the split more one way than the other, within limited amounts, by using uneven levering strokes.

Joints

Rustic furniture can be described derogatorily as "hammer and nail" carpentry. Much assembly is done with nails, but in better work the nails are usually supplementing fitting joints. Nails should be protected by galvanizing or other means. This is particularly true for unseasoned wood where the moisture in the wood will attack steel. You can get away with driving a nail without a preliminary hole in many places, but near an end or where the direction the nail takes is important, provide a pilot hole, drilled undersize for most of the depth the nail has to go, or right through if it is to be clenched. Clenching is advisable in many assemblies. The nail point need not project much, but you should be able to turn back enough to give a rivet effect to the fastening.

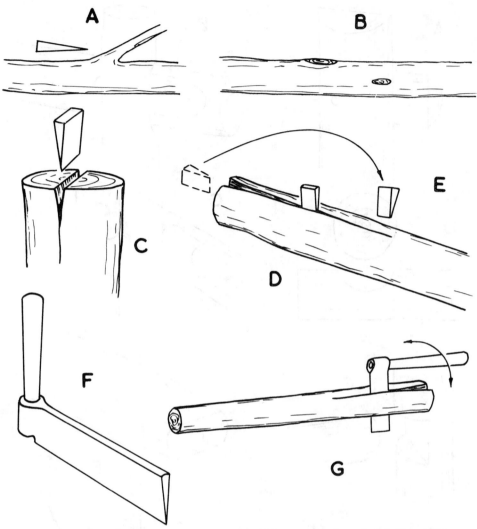

Fig. 10-1. Natural wood for furniture should be cut cleanly and cleft if possible.

Cleft wood can be joined face to face with clenched nails—possibly one from each side arranged diagonally—so as to come in different lines of grain (FIG. 10-2A). Sometimes round pieces crossing have to be nailed in the same way, but it is better to put some flats on the meeting surfaces. Scoop hollows (FIG. 10-2B), or saw more like halving joints (FIG. 10-2C).

Unless the parts have to cross in the same plane, there is no need to cut very deeply. Another way of getting a good bearing surface in that sort of crossing is to hollow one piece to match the curve of the other (FIG. 10-2D). There you only have space to drive one central nail (if it is to be effective).

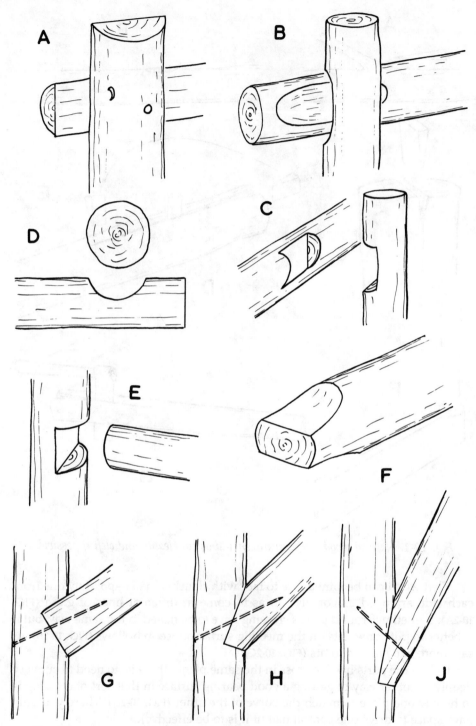

Fig. 10-2. Rustic wood can be joined by nailing and notching in various ways.

If two parts make a T-joint, one may be cut out and the round end driven in, possibly with a nail from the far side (FIG. 10-2E). A closer fit will come from thinning the piece that goes into the slot (FIG. 10-2F). If the meeting is diagonal, you can do something similar with a V cut (FIG. 10-2G). Let the full round of the other piece fit in. A nail comes through from the far side. Get a neater effect by trimming the end to fit the V cut (FIG. 10-2H). The two circumferences then more nearly match each other. There can be a nail through, but in some situations it is better across the inserted end (FIG. 10-2J).

If you are working with dry wood, use glue and nails in these joints, but nearly all waterproof adhesives are ineffective between damp surfaces. If the wood has not been fully seasoned, you must rely on nails only. The nail is there to keep one part in another; the load is taken by the way the parts are fitted together.

A different, interesting construction uses an auger or a large bit in a brace, and a draw knife. Work with a draw knife, a broad chisel and mallet, or a hatchet. The basic joint is then very similar to doweling. The dowel is formed like a round tenon on one piece (FIG. 10-3A). Drill a hole for testing in a thin piece of wood that can be slipped over the end being tapered, to test that it is to size as far back as needed. With a little practice, you can get the end round and accurate by estimation and very little testing. Shape the end so that it goes far enough into the hole to provide a good bearing surface.

In some things, the peg can go right through. That might be tight enough in itself, but it helps if you spread the end of the peg. Make a saw cut across it

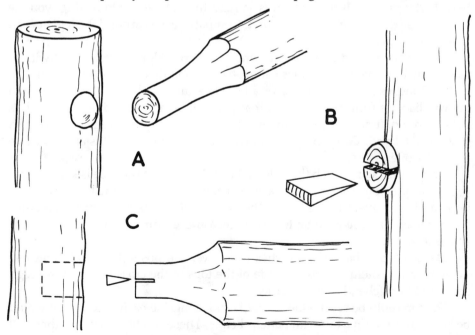

Fig. 10-3. Tavered ends can be driven into holes and tightened with wedges.

before driving it. Arrange that so it comes across the direction of the grain of the other part (FIG. 10-3B). Then, drive a wedge into the cut. Even if the parts are softwood, use a hardwood for the wedge. This should be long enough to be trimmed after driving as far as possible.

If it is a hole that does not go through, wedge the end by *fox wedging*, as is sometimes done with stub tenons. Make a saw cut in the end. Then, make a short wedge to fit. Estimate how much it can be expected to go into the cut. When it hits the bottom of the hole, it will spread the wood (FIG. 10-3C).

It is possible to use nuts and bolts instead of nails and screws, particularly in large assemblies or where several thicknesses are involved. With bolts, use those with square or hexagonal heads; this way a wrench can be used. The square neck of a carriage bolt does not grip well in unseasoned wood; this is even less so if it is only in bark. Tightening fully will be difficult, and loosening a rusted nut will be next to impossible.

Table Frame

A complete table could be left outdoors in all weather, but it is convenient to be able to remove the top to a sheltered place when it is not in use. The table shown in FIG. 10-4A has a pair of end supports driven into the ground and a lift-off top of planed boards.

When you drive posts into the ground, the actual amount of penetration is always doubtful. Have the upright poles too long and cut them to the same height after driving. If the ground is so hard that a hole has to be dug, you are able to settle the amount of penetration. Compact the soil around the leg, or even case it in concrete.

Do not sharpen to a fine point (which will crumble). A square end with at least 1/2 inch left flat (FIG. 10-4B) is better able to stand driving. Each leg should go about 12 inches into soft ground or a little less into hard soil. Put a mark on a known distance from the point, so that you will be able to judge how much is below ground. If possible, soak the wood in a bucket of preservative for a day, so that rot is delayed. Carry the preservative above ground level. It is at the surface that rot is often worst.

Have an assistant watch the pole as it is driven so that the pole is kept as near upright as possible. Mark where each post is to come; adjust the top to fit whatever spacing results. Cut the tops of the posts level. It is better to use a level on a straight board (FIG. 10-4C) than to rely on measuring from the ground that might not be level.

Make the crossbars. Cut notches to go over the posts (FIG. 10-4D) and nail downward into them. Check the state of the tops of the crossbars. Remove high spots with a hatchet, knife, or plane.

The top could be several loose boards laid alongside each other, but it would be better to make up a top with battens below. These can be spaced, so they will stop the top sliding on the supporting crossbars (FIG. 10-4E).

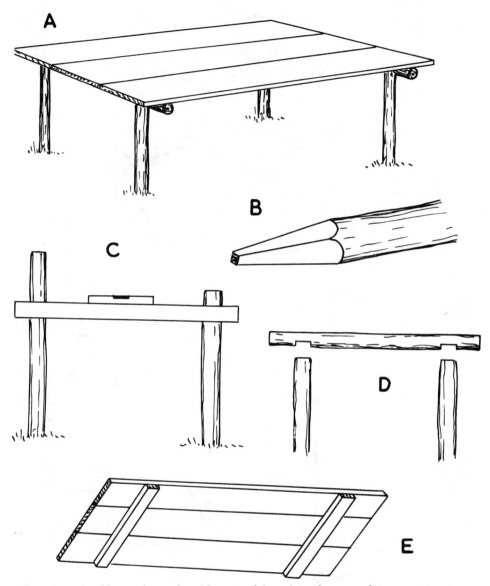

Fig. 10-4. *A table can be made with posts driven into the ground to support a top on crossbars.*

Portable Table

This is a rustic table that is not attached to the ground. It can be moved, even though it is not intended to be a lightweight assembly. There is a frame at each end with the parts notched together. Lengthwise parts are pegged into holes; the top is made from cleaved wood or sawn boards (FIG. 10-5A).

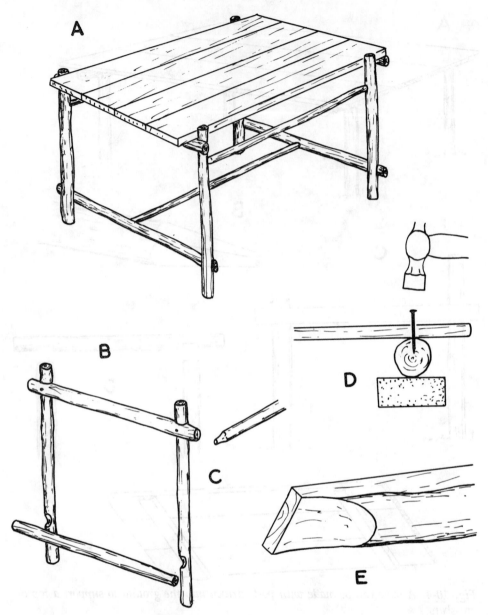

Fig. 10-5. A light, portable table can have a plank top over a framework of rods.

Choose four similar posts for the legs and four pieces that match for the crossbars. If thicknesses vary, the lower rails can be thinner. Join the crossbars and legs with notches cut in each, or make rounded hollows in the legs for the rails (FIG. 10-2). Mark the legs together. It does not matter if the crossbars are too long at this stage. Nail these joints (FIG. 10-5B). Square the assemblies; see that they match in a similar way to that for tables made of planed wood. The horizontal parts come on the outsides of the legs.

Two lengthwise rails fit into the legs, and a central stretcher into the lower end rails. The most convenient joints in those positions are pegged ends into holes. The ends could go right through, but part way with fox wedges will do (FIG. 10-5C).

If boards are to be used for the top, space them parallel with narrow gaps, and nail into the end crossbars. Use an iron block or another hammer under the rail to support it while hammering (FIG. 10-5D). If you use cleft pieces, trim adjoining edges, so the gaps are approximately parallel. At the ends, scoop away the rounded undersides, so the pieces will bed down level (FIG. 10-5E). Then, nail in place.

Milking Stool

You might not want to milk a cow or goat, but this stool can have many other purposes. Its top is a piece cut across a log, and there are three legs let in (FIG. 10-6A). Three legs will stand firm on any surface no matter how uneven it is.

Sizes are governed by the wood used for the top; this should be about 12 inches across. A smaller piece would still be useful. The legs have to be evenly spaced, and slope outward at the same angle. Extreme precision will not be needed, but it is best if the legs are not too far from geometric accuracy.

Draw a pitch circle for the leg holes; then, step off the radius around it. The holes will come on alternate marks (FIG. 10-6B). Decide on the angle you want the legs to slope outward; their feet should come just outside the area covered by the top. The exact angle is not important, but all three legs should have the same slope. Cut a piece of scrap wood to the angle to serve as a guide (FIG. 10-6C). The size of the hole depends on the size of the stool, but it will be between 3/4 of an inch and 1 inch. Drill from the top downward. Provide a piece of scrap wood below for the drill to run into as it goes through, but as you are drilling into the end grain, there is little fear of breaking out.

Make the legs slightly too long. Taper the tops to go into the holes. Drive them through and wedge them (FIG. 10-6D). Invert the stool, and measure the lengths of the legs by using a rule straight up from the table surface to the same height on each leg. Then cut them across to match. Remove the sharp edges around the feet, once you have tried the stool for level the right way up.

Chair

A full chair made entirely of round poles does not offer the comfort of one made from planed wood, but you could always add cushions. It would be improved by making the seat and back with cleaved wood having its flat sides to the body (FIG. 10-7A).

The general layout is very similar to armchairs made from squared wood.

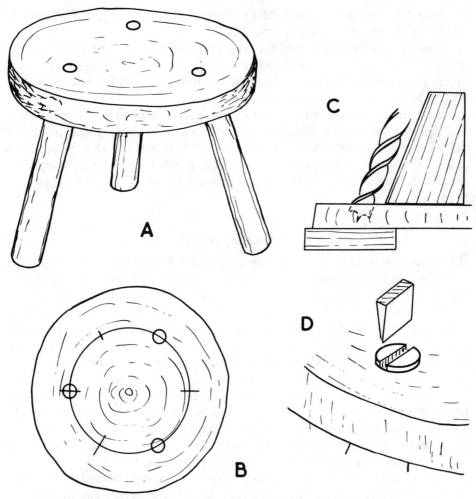

Fig. 10-6. A stool can be made with a section of log and three legs.

Two long back legs and two front ones go above the seat to hold the arms. If you have any bent poles, a pair will make the back with some slope. Notch the rails that support the seat into the legs on the inner surfaces. The bottom rails could be notched similarly or they can be pegged into holes (FIG. 10-7B). The arm will peg into the back legs, and notch or peg over the front legs (FIG. 10-7C). Make up the two ends as pairs, with matching pieces of wood, as far as possible.

The back has upright pieces on curved rails. The sizes are governed by available pieces of wood. The rails need not have much curve, but that should be about the same in the two rails. Cut pegged joints into the legs. Before assembling them, use their sizes as a guide to the lengths of the other rails going across. The front rail will be notched into the legs below the seat rails and the

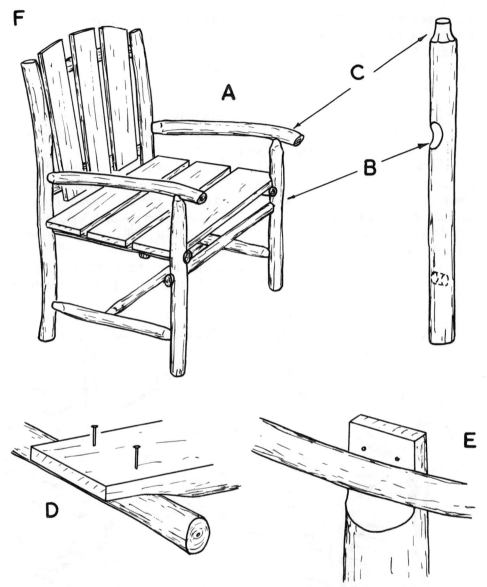

Fig. 10-7. The parts of a rustic armchair are notched and plugged together.

bottom rails peg into the side rails. Assemble all these parts and check that the whole thing is reasonably square.

The seat is made of cleaved, 3-inch poles notched over the seat rails (FIG. 10-7D), and nailed in place. Round the front edge, but otherwise the pieces can be as they come (except remove any lumps that would prevent a close fit or a level top). Make the back pieces in a similar way (FIG. 10-7E). Cut their tops to a curve after assembly (FIG 10-7F). Use a Surform tool to remove any sharpness that will come toward a sitter, but otherwise retain the natural rustic appearance of the wood.

Bench

A bench is made like a long chair, but there has to be some stiffening lengthwise to keep it in shape (FIG. 10-8A). The suggestion is for a bench about 60-inches long, with a seat 15-inches high and wide.

The two ends are very similar to those for the chair (FIG. 10-8B). An extra rail goes across the ends. Back and front lengthwise stretchers are joined to the legs and not the bottom rails. This allows notched joints to the legs instead of pegs to the rails. A similar rail goes above the seat level between the back legs, and the top of the back notches over the legs (FIG. 10-8C). The top rail could have a curve up to its center.

For lengthwise stiffness, arrange two diagonals in the back (FIG. 10-8D), going into notches in the rails. Besides stiffness, they help to fill the back as something

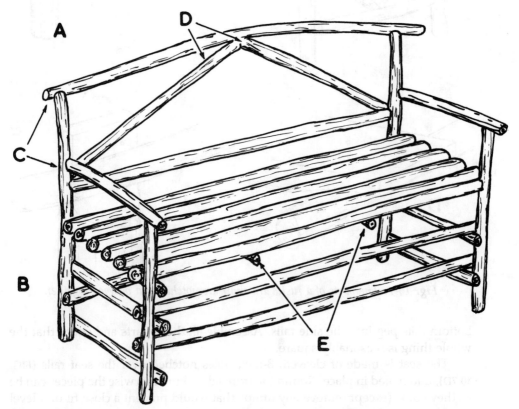

Fig. 10-8. The construction of a bench is a development of the previously described chairs and tables.

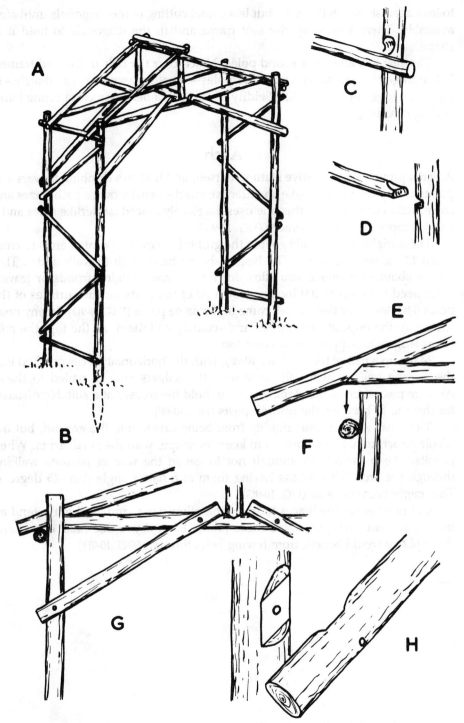

Fig. 10-9. A rustic arch has the parts notched and nailed together.

to lean against. Notch the rails, but leave final cutting of the diagonals until after assembly. Then, square up the seat frame and fit the diagonals to hold it in shape.

The seat is made up of round poles. Notch over the rails in the end frames, but arrange two crossbars under the poles—equally spaced intermediately—to link them together (FIG. 10-8E). Rigidity of the seat depends on close fitting joints and tight nailing.

Arch

An arch provides a decorative feature in itself, and it allows climbing flowers and plants to interweave and make an attractive effect—usually over a path. Sizes and construction can vary, but this one uses diagonally braced ladderlike sides and a trussed top with diagonal braces (FIG. 10-9A).

The uprights will usually go into the ground. Allow for pointed ends to enter about 12 inches (FIG. 10-9B). The height should be enough to walk under. That means about 84 inches if you allow for trailing and hanging fronds or leaves. Poles need to be up to 100 inches. Notch all of the parts on the surfaces of the poles (FIG. 10-9C), or they can all come in the same plane (FIG. 10-9D). In any case, square up the opposite assemblies and securely nail them. At the top, the rails act as ledgers to support the trussed top.

Make up a pair of trusses (FIG. 10-9E), with the horizontal pieces notched into the sloping ones, which will come over the ledgers and be nailed to them. Arrange pieces across the sloping parts to hold the trusses at a suitable distance for them to fit between the upright posts (FIG. 10-9F).

The posts will get some rigidity from being driven into the ground, but the whole structure has to be braced to keep its shape, with diagonal struts. When possible, keep them high enough not to get in the way of persons walking through the arch. This means having them at a flatter angle than 45 degrees. That might seem obvious (FIG. 10-9G).

Cut notches for the braces to fit on the other parts, and let them extend an inch or so past each joint. Nail these joints. Even if you use nails elsewhere, these places would benefit from having bolts through (FIG. 10-9H).

11

Outdoor cooking

Outdoor furniture is often associated with eating and drinking. Tables and chairs are regularly used for open-air meals, but there are some things particularly used for food—either its preparation or transport.

Some of the items described in this chapter are portable and might not be left out in the same way as other furniture. They do not have to be as weatherproof but there is always the possibility of them being left out in dew or rain. It is best to prepare them in the same way as the heavier furniture that is intended to stay outside. Exceptions are things that could have uses indoors as well. For instance, a food trolley might be used indoors. It would be given a better finish, for the sake of its appearance alongside other indoor furniture, than something that will only be used with rustic things outdoors.

Table/Trolley

It is convenient to have a means of carrying food, crockery, and cutlery to where you need them outdoors; it can also be used as a table. Figure 11-1 shows a trolley with a flat top and a shelf underneath. It has handles at one end and wheels at the other. The sizes suggested in FIG. 11-2A and the Materials List are for a moderate-sized assembly that could be taken indoors for loading. It will pass through doorways on its way to the patio, yard, or garden. It could be made much bigger if it is intended for large numbers of people.

Get the wheels and axle first; then, it may be easy to modify other sizes to suit. Wheels with 6-inch diameters are drawn, but any convenient size can be used. They should be metal with rubber tires for most situations, but you might

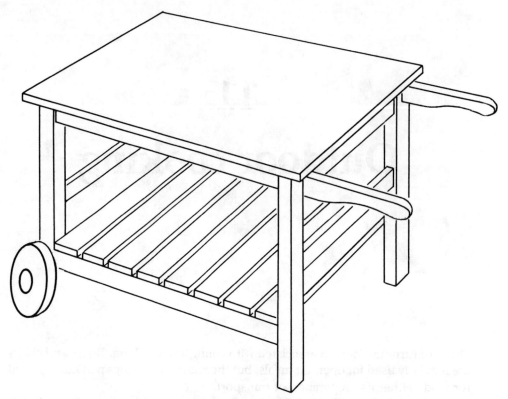

Fig. 11-1. A table/trolley is useful for transporting and preparing food outdoors.

use wide, solid-rubber wheels for soft surfaces. Also, you could turn wooden ones. The axle goes through the front legs; choose a size with just over 18 inches between the wheels.

Start by marking out the legs (FIG. 11-3A). The front pair of legs are kept 1 inch short for ground clearance. The lengthwise lower rails are kept low, but the crosswise ones are higher, so that they will prevent things being carried from slipping off (FIG. 11-2B). Most joints should be doweled, but you could use tenons.

Materials List for Table/Trolley		
4 legs		$1^1/2 \times 27 \times 1^1/2$
2 top rails	3	$\times 45 \times 1$
2 top rails	3	$\times 18 \times 1$
2 lower rails	2	$\times 32 \times 1$
2 lower rails	2	$\times 18 \times 1$
1 top	20	$\times 36 \times {}^3/4$
8 shelf slats	3	$\times 19 \times {}^3/4$

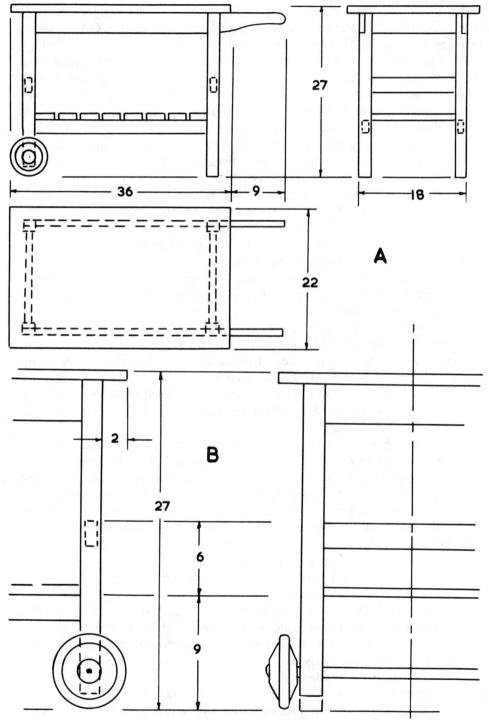

Fig. 11-2. Suggested sizes for a table/trolley.

The four lower rails are central at the legs (FIG. 11-3B), but the long top rails have to be treated differently because of their extending handles. One way is to tenon or dowel centrally to the front legs (FIG. 11-3C); then, notch them through the rear legs (FIG. 11-3D). Do not cut too much from the rails, or that will weaken them where they take the load when the table is moved. Notching 1/8 of an inch on each side is enough; therefore, 3/4 of an inch is cut from the leg. Alternatively, make the rails level with the outsides of both legs. At the front, use dowels. At the rear, notch the rails around the tops of the legs in a form of halving joint. Do not cut too much away from the rails (FIG. 11-3E). When these joints are assembled (whichever method is chosen), the dowels from the crosswise rails can go right through to strengthen those joints.

Shape the handles so that the grip part is about 1^1/2 inches deep. Then, round its section and ends (FIG. 11-3F). Make up the other rails and assemble the framework in two stages. Put the opposite long sides together first; check that they match and that they are square. When the glue has set, add the crosswise members and again leave for the glue to set.

Arrange the shelf slats to come to the edges of their rails, and space them evenly. Attach them with two screws or nails at each crossing. This is more easily done before you add the top.

There are several possible ways to make the top. It could be made of wider slats put across in a similar way to those on the shelf. Allow for a 2-inch overlap all around. You could use solid wood by gluing two or more pieces to make up the width, with the grain the long way. An interesting variation of this is to use a butcher-block top. Many fairly narrow strips can be glued together to make up the width. Also, use a few dowels between adjoining boards. In any case, the glue should be fully waterproof.

A simpler top can be made from a single piece of plywood or particleboard. Edges can be left true and rounded, but a better edge has a strip around it (FIG. 11-4A). The best edge, if you have the equipment to work it, uses a tongue and groove joint (FIG. 11-4B). For the preparation of food, use a Formica surface or a similar surface as a facing; put a lip around the edges. If you do not expect to cut on or treat the surface roughly, use softer, plastic-faced particleboards that you can buy as stock-sized panels. The edges will already be treated in the same way.

Attach the top with screws driven down through into the rails, counterbored and plugged (FIG. 11-4C). The plugs form a decorative treatment on a wood top, but they do not look right on other surfaces. One way to avoid top surface marks is to screw strips inside the top rails, and screw upward through them (FIG. 11-4D). Pocket screwing is often used in furniture (11-4E); a hole is opened below for the head. The screw pulls up and the head goes below the surface (FIG. 11-4F). Instead of chiseling, use a large drill at an angle to make the recess for the head (FIG. 11-4G). In most assemblies, you will not need many screws to hold the top: two at each end and three at each side should be sufficient.

The top is shown with a flat surface; that is what is needed for a table. If the transport of a load of food or equipment is more important, the edging of the top

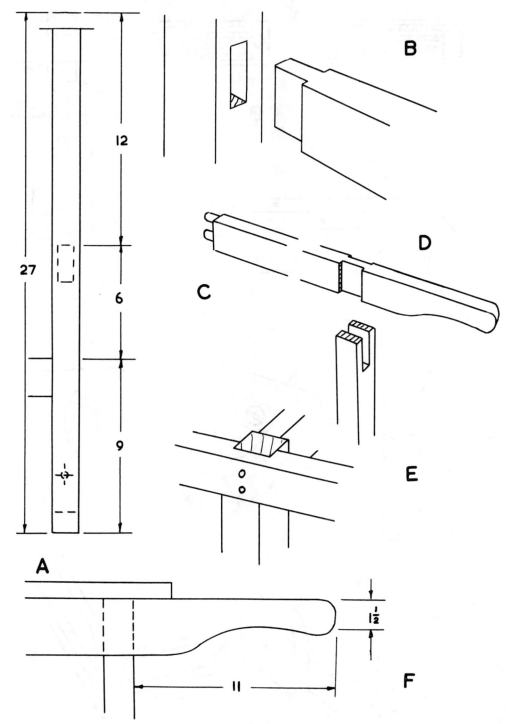

Fig. 11-3. Construction details of the table/trolley.

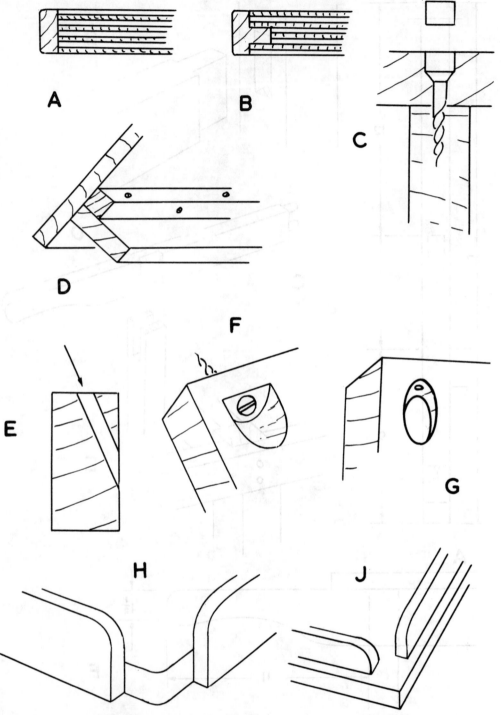

Fig. 11-4. Methods of making and attaching the tabletop.

could be carried upward to fully frame the top or to be cut back at the corners for ease in cleaning (FIG. 11-4H). It may be simpler, with some top materials, to put the border strips on top with screws up through (FIG. 11-4J).

Food Trolley

This trolley has similar uses to the previous one, but not for use as a table. The top has sides to keep things in place; it can have compartments for cutlery and other small items. The lower shelf is arranged as a tray that will slide in; it can be removed completely. This can be open to take a variety of things or it can be given storage compartments. Also, it could be arranged to take glasses or cups in individual positions.

The general assembly (FIG. 11-5) has sloping legs; it is arranged with wheels at one end, and handles at the other. This is another piece of portable furniture that could be made of an attractive hardwood, with a varnished finish, so it would also be suitable for use indoors. If it is only for outdoor use, painted softwood might be satisfactory. Nevertheless, the strength of hardwoods would be an advantage. The sizes shown in FIG. 11-6 and the Materials List would suit hard or soft woods, but sections could be reduced slightly for an indoor trolley. The construction suggested is nearly all nailed. For another option, dovetail the corners and cut other joints for what amounts to a piece of cabinetwork for use indoors and only occasionally for use outdoors.

The wheels and axles should be obtained first. Those shown are 7 inches in diameter, but the exact size is not crucial. Adjust the axle height on the legs to suit. Use a lathe, to turn wooden wheels, but metal wheels with rubber tires provide some slight cushioning and reduce vibration of the load.

Materials List for Food Trolley

4 legs	2	×30×1
2 sides	3	×38× 3/4
2 ends	3	×20× 3/4
2 top bases	2	×30×1
2 top bases	2	×20×1
1 top base	20	×30× 1/4 plywood
2 shelf rails	2	×30×1
5 cross rails	2	×20×1
2 tray sides	2	×27× 3/4
2 tray ends	2	×17× 3/4
or		
2 tray bottoms	17	×27× 1/4 plywood
1 top partition		1¹/2×20× 1/2
3 top partitions		1¹/2×12× 1/2
1 tray divider	17	×27× 1/4 plywood
2 tray dividers		3/4×27× 3/4
2 tray dividers		3/4×17× 3/4

Fig. 11-5. *A food trolley with compartments and a tray.*

The slopes of both pairs of legs are the same. If you are using power tools that can have their angles adjusted, the legs are at 15-degrees vertical. In any case, set out a full-size side view (FIG. 11-7A), using just the centerlines of the legs. Determine the lengths of the legs from this. Notice that the location of the legs on the sides are different at each end, but their angles are the same.

Make the pair of sides for the top (FIG. 11-7B). Locate the positions of the ends; this includes the bases that go under the plywood (FIG. 11-7C). Between these are lengthwise base pieces (FIG. 11-7D) that have to be notched to take the legs. Get their angles correct from your full-size drawing, and make them a close

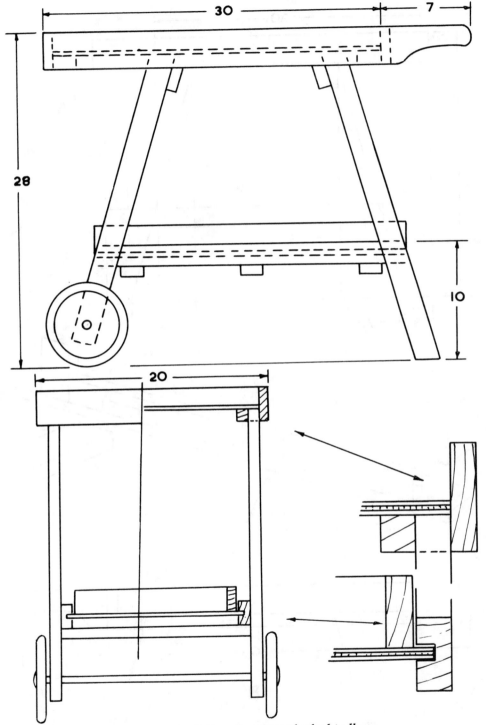

Fig. 11-6. Sizes and sections of a food trolley.

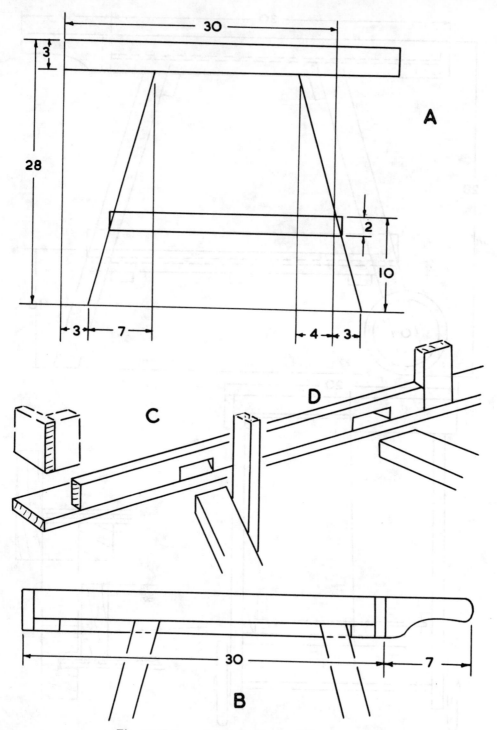

Fig. 11-7. *Layout and details of a trolley top.*

fit on the wood that will be used for the legs. Shape the handles before going further.

Cut the plywood for the base of the top part. Then, glue and nail it to the four strips that go under it and inside the framing. Plane the edges true; fit the sides and ends around it to complete the top.

Make the legs and mark on them the location of the shelf rails. The legs are paired; drill the ones that take the wheels to suit the axle. Cut them off to clear the ground, but do not make them too short, or you might split the end grain below the axle.

The tray has a plywood base that extends at the sides to run in the grooved shelf rails (FIG. 11-8A). Plow the grooves about halfway through the rails, and make them an easy fit on the plywood. Allow for the thickness of paint, but you should be able to slide the tray in and out without trouble. It should not be so loose that there is a risk of it slipping out when the trolley is being wheeled. If the ends of grooves are widened a little, positioning the tray when replacing it will be easier. Assemble the tray as a box on its base. Keep the sides a short distance in from the shelf rails.

Fit the legs into the sockets in the top framing, and screw the shelf rails to them. Sight across to check that they are parallel. Getting a twist in the relative positions of the grooves will cause the tray to stick when you try to move it. In the end view, the legs should be upright. Have the tray in position to keep the legs at the correct distance apart. Then, fit the cross rails to the legs under the top, and fit three more under the shelf rails. They keep the sides at the correct distance apart and stiffen the whole trolley. Round and sand the edges of the plywood that fit the grooves. Later, if there is too much stiffness there, rub the edges with wax or candle fat.

Temporarily fit the wheels and axle to check that the whole assembly is satisfactory. Then, remove the wheels and tray so that the wood can be painted or varnished.

There are a few possible modifications or improvements that you can incorporate during construction. If the trolley gets rained on or liquids are spilled on it, draining and cleaning can be difficult. Drill holes (3/8-inch holes will do) near each corner of the top and tray; liquids will drain away.

The tray is shown with straight ends, but it will help in lifting if metal or plastic tray handles are added to them. Another way of providing handles without projections is to make the ends from wider wood and shape hand holes (FIG. 11-8B). The holes do not have to follow a curve, but they look better shaped that way. Draw the shapes—a half template ensures accuracy—and then drill the ends of the openings. Cut the waste out with a fine jigsaw. Thoroughly round the edges of the wood and the holes.

Divide the tray and top into compartments. Divide across or lengthwise, but too many divisions could interfere with changes in the load. Divisions at the end of the top will separate cutlery and other small items (FIG. 11-8C). Keep the pieces just below the top edges and round them. They can be held in with fine nails.

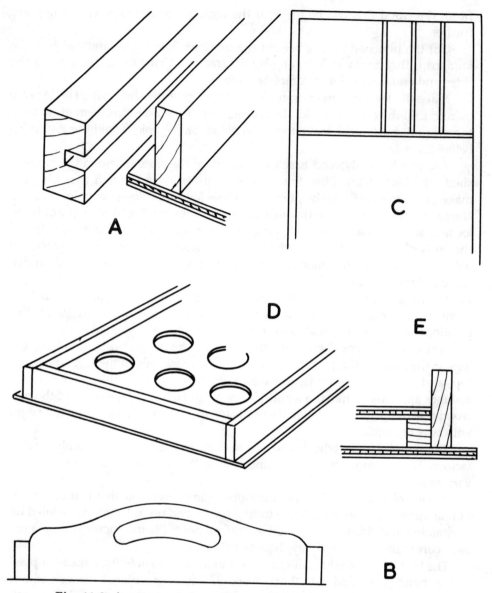

Fig. 11-8. Arrangements for a sliding tray and the top compartments.

If you want to carry glasses or cups, possibly with liquid already in them, give the top or tray a second piece of plywood—pierced with holes (FIG. 11-8D). Let this piece rest on strips around the inside of the tray (FIG. 11-8E), either all over, or only part of it. If this plywood is loose, put your hand through a glass hole to remove it when not needed.

Take-down Trolley

A food trolley that is always full size can sometimes be difficult to store. There is an attraction in one that folds or can be disassembled. This trolley is about the same size as the two previous ones, when prepared for use, but it can be partially disassembled and partially folded, so that it reduces to about the thickness of the two trays (while keeping the same length and width). The flatter package can be stored in a space about 7 inches deep, or hung on a wall until it is needed again.

The trolley shown in FIG. 11-9 consists of two trays joined by crossed legs, held in place with nuts and bolts. There are wheels on one pair of legs, and handles on the top tray at the other end. The sizes suggested in FIG. 11-10 and the Materials List can be altered to suit your needs. The main parts are 1-×-3-inch wood—strong enough for a larger trolley if you want to increase sizes. Recommended wheels have a 7-inch diameter. They should be obtained, with their axle, before deciding on the width of trolley. The stock axle length will determine the width to make this.

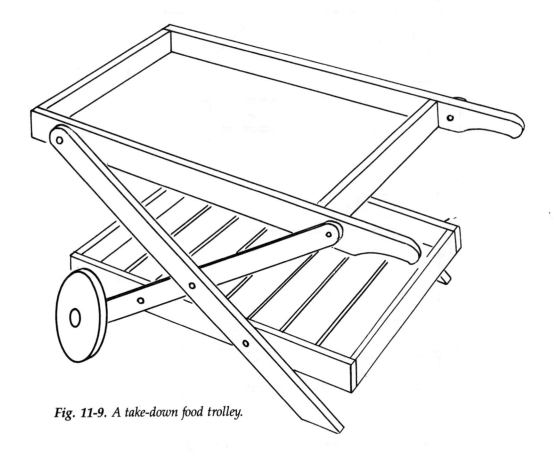

Fig. 11-9. A take-down food trolley.

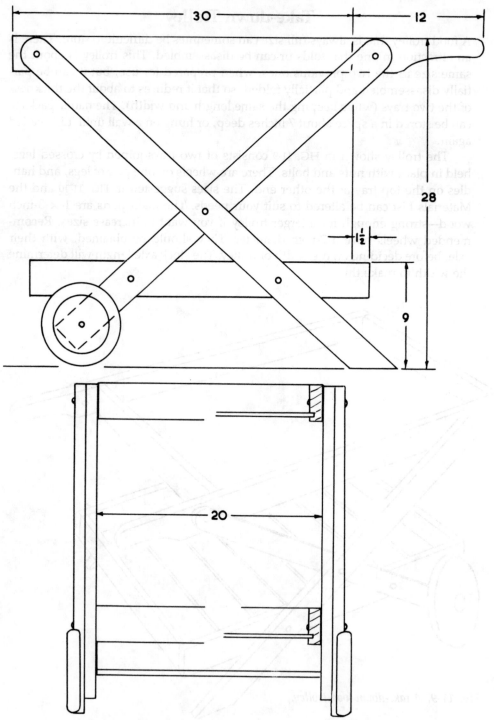

Fig. 11-10. Suitable sizes for a take-down food trolley.

Materials List for
Take-down Trolley

4 legs	$3 \times 42 \times 1$
2 tray sides	$3 \times 43 \times 1$
2 tray sides	$3 \times 31 \times 1$
4 tray ends	$3 \times 20 \times 1$
2 tray bottoms	$20 \times 30 \times$ $1/4$ plywood
or	
16 slats	$3 \times 20 \times$ $1/2$

Except for the handle extensions, make the two trays almost the same (FIG. 11-11A). The legs bolt on at different places. Make a full-size drawing, showing the trays in full, but with only the center lines of the legs (FIG. 11-11B). This will show you the sizes of the legs and the positions of the bolt holes on them and on the trays.

Make the sides of the trays; mark on the positions of the bolt holes. Also, mark out the pairs of legs. Mark where the axle holes will come, but it is best to leave cutting the other legs to length until after a trial assembly. Then, trim that pair of legs to bring the trays level with the legs on level ground.

Drill small holes at each bolt position of a size that will allow nails to be pushed through. Using nails, assemble one side to check that the two trays are parallel. Also, check that the feet will bring them level when the wheels and axle are in position.

The bolts can be $5/16$ of an inch in diameter, but it would not matter if you went up to $3/8$-inch bolts or down to $1/4$-inch bolts. With the bolts there should be enough washers and nuts. Use butterfly nuts if you expect to be unscrewing frequently. If the parts are only to be taken down at the end of a season, plain nuts are less obtrusive. Drill to suit the bolts in all positions.

Make up the trays. The simplest method would be nailed or screwed corners, with plywood nailed underneath (FIG. 11-11C), but the exposed edges of plywood do not look good. Moisture, entering the end grain of plywood, can cause damage even if it is exterior or marine grade. It is better to have the plywood inside. The best way of arranging this is to plow grooves in the sides (FIG. 11-11D), but then you have to choose corner joints that hide the groove ends. You could leave them exposed and glue in filler pieces. A simple nailed or screwed corner to hide the grooves can be made by rabbeting one piece (FIG. 11-11E).

Another way of enclosing the bottom is to put strips around and nail into them (FIG. 11-11F). Instead of plywood, attach slats to the strips, with narrow spaces between (FIG. 11-11G). Shape the handles that the two trays match.

Arrange the pair of inner legs to be the ones with the axle through. Their bolts into the trays have washers between and under the nuts (FIG. 11-12A). The other legs cross with similar bolt arrangements at the leg crossings, but at the other joints there must be packings. These can be pieces of 1-inch dowel rod

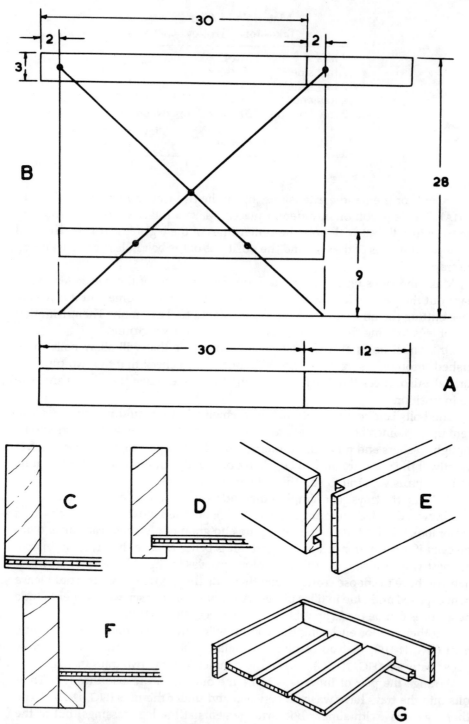

Fig. 11-11. Layout and tray construction for a take-down trolley.

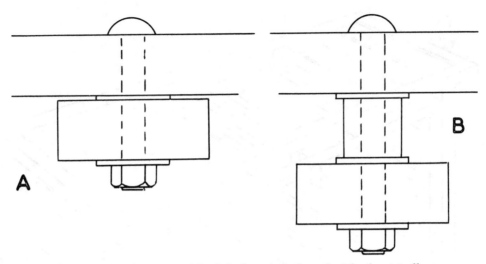

Fig. 11-12. Two parts of the bolted construction of a take-down trolley.

drilled through (FIG. 11-12B). Use metal washers at each end of the dowel rod, and make the total length to suit the leg clearance.

Take the pieces apart for painting; then reassemble. For storage, do not take out all the bolts. Leave the tops of the wheel legs bolted to the top tray, and the other legs bolted to the lower tray. In both cases, they will swing into line. To avoid losing the other nuts, bolts, and washers, put them in a bag tied to the woodwork, or replace them in vacant holes. Tie the parts together and hang the bundle from the axle.

Barbecue Bench

The bench shown in FIG. 11-13 is intended to be a substantial working place for a barbecue. It has a support for a barbecue grill at the center; a spacious shelf underneath; a rack for your tools and equipment at one side; and a strong

**Materials List for
Barbecue Bench**

4 legs	2×31×2
2 top frames	2×49×2
4 top frames	2×19×2
5 butcher blocks	2×19×2
3 top slats	3×15×1
2 slat supports	1×12×1
4 long rails	2×40×2
4 short rails	2×18×2
8 grill slats	1×19×1
7 shelf slats	4×19×1

Fig. 11-13. A barbecue bench.

butcher-block chopping area at the other side. Add hooks at the ends or sides for hanging many cooking implements.

The central recess is sunk slightly; it is provided with a number of square strips across, with plenty of air space between. How this part is planned and used depends on the type of barbecue grill fitted. In the bench shown in FIG. 11-14, there is a space 18 inches wide and 14 inches from front to back. Most grills need an air space around them. They should not fit tightly. Some grills need mounting on a metal plate or a sheet of asbestos. Check on the grill you intend to use, and work out the dimensions of the bench around it.

Nearly all the main parts are 2-inch square wood. For an outdoor bench, the wood should be a durable hardwood. If there is some shelter, many parts could be softwood, but the working surfaces—particularly the butcher block—should be a close-grained, clean-looking hardwood that will not splinter if you use a cleaver or hatchet over it.

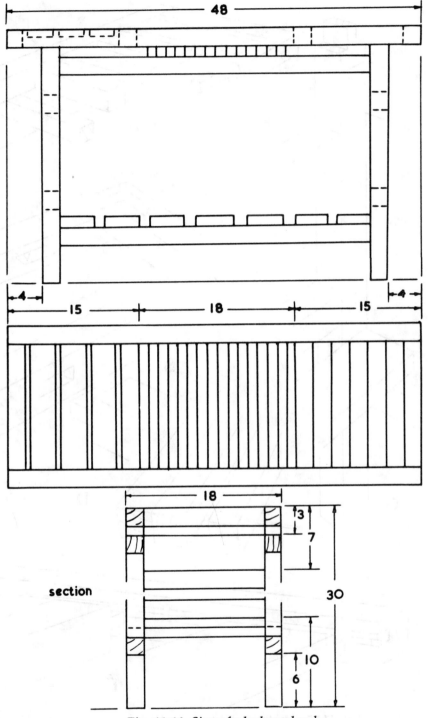

Fig. 11-14. Sizes of a barbecue bench.

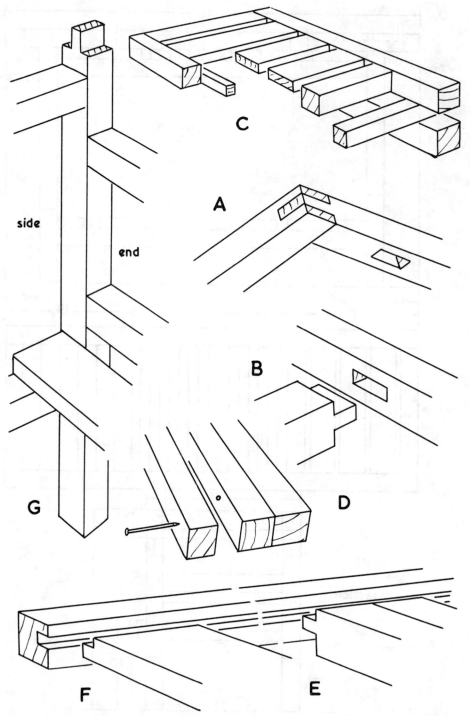

side

end

A

B

C

D

E

F

G

Fig. 11-15. Construction details of parts of a barbecue bench.

Although the general form is the same as many tables, double rails round the top, and the legs are set in from the corners. It will be best to make the top as a unit; then, build the supporting framework to match it. Join the framework forming the outside at the corners, with bridle joints (FIG. 11-15A). If necessary, put dowels through them when you glue the top. Mark and cut the joints now, but there are other things to do to the top before assembly. The intermediate crosswise pieces can be tenoned or doweled to the long sides (FIG. 11-15B). At the side where the slats come (shown on the left, but they could be either side), nail in strips for the slats to be nailed or screwed to (FIG. 11-15C).

There is another possible method of fitting the slats. It depends on how the butcher block is fitted. For the butcher block, join enough pieces to make up the width (keeping them overlong at this stage). Glue exclusively, or include dowels between meeting surfaces. A simple way of holding the joints close is to nail each piece to the next as you glue it (FIG. 11-15D). Cover each pair of nails by the next piece.

The butcher block assembly should have its top trued. The simplest way to fit it is to enclose it in the framing; nail through the sides. A better way, if you have the facilities for cutting the joints, is to groove the sides and cut the butcher block ends to fit (FIG. 11-15E). If you use a 1/2-inch groove, 1/2-inch down from the top, take to the full length of each side, and join the ends of the slats at the other end in a similar way (FIG. 11-15F).

The positions of other parts at the legs are shown on the general drawing (FIG. 11-14). To the side, there are two long rails: one supporting the grill strips, and the other supporting the shelf. At the ends there are two rails to provide stiffening. The shelf slats add strength in that direction (FIG. 11-15G). Dowel the tops of the legs, but use stub tenons into the long parts of the top (FIG. 11-15B).

Use the assembled top as a guide to sizes of the supporting framework, so that the legs will stand upright when they meet their joints in the top. You could use dowels between most of the framework parts, but tenons will be stronger. When marking the legs, position the mortises for the second top rail, just far enough below the top to take the 1-inch square strips (FIG. 11-15C).

Assemble the framing like a table (preferably in two stages). Get the two ends squared and clamped tightly, so that they match. Let their glue set. Then, add the long parts (FIG. 11-16A), and introduce the leg tenons into their mortises in the top before the glue in the other joints has started to set.

Put the grill strips between the top rails; space them evenly. Glue, or put long thin nails upward into them from below.

The shelf is shown in FIG. 11-16B with slats across. Screw them to their rails to provide strength as well as a place to store things. Arrange other forms of shelving. It is a fairly large storage area. Part of it can be boxed in to keep some items in place. Make fitted compartments to secure frequently used equipment. Install a bin to hold charcoal. Include a ledge or rail at the back to prevent things from falling. You might prefer a shelf without gaps. Use enough slats to fit closely, or substitute a piece of exterior plywood.

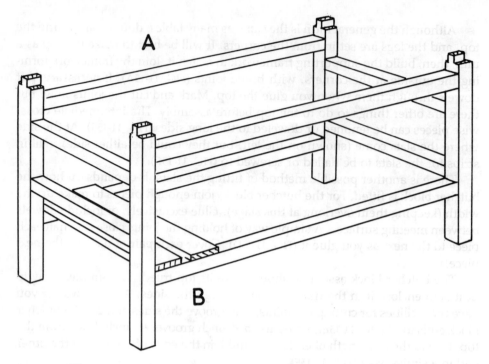

Fig. 11-16. *Assembly of the supporting framework for a barbecue bench.*

With an outdoors bench enclose a part underneath, with a door, so that animals cannot reach inside. The best place is under the butcher block (which will act as a top).

Drive metal hooks into the ends or sides of the top, for hanging tools on, but experiment with the bench before settling on hook positions. Hooks must be accessible, yet not likely to snag clothing. Any metal should be corrosion resistant. Alternatively, use pieces of dowel rod driven into holes that make them slope upward slightly.

In a windy climate, hinge a piece of plywood as long as the bench and about 18 inches wide to the back of the top, so it normally hangs down behind. To prevent drafts, swing up and hold with hooks. Arrange similar pieces at the ends.

Although paint is the usual finish for outdoor furniture, paint will blister in a hot position. Keep painted parts away from the grill. Leave the wood there and the butcher block bare; occasionally scrub it clean.

12

Butcher-block furniture

The traditional block on which a butcher chops meat is made up of many pieces of wood joined together with their end grain upwards. The name is given to an assembly of pieces laid with their grains parallel to the surface, and built up to the area required in much the same way as a wall is built by whatever number of layers of bricks are required.

Some furniture for indoor use is made in this way. The method is also suitable for outdoor furniture that can be made of softwood or hardwood. The effect is of a substantial and massive assembly. A complete piece of furniture is usually fairly heavy. This can be an advantage in outdoor seats and tables that have to be left out and will need to resist knocks or loads that might move them or turn them over. Nevertheless, they are not always as massive as they appear because some inner parts are not as thick as outer ones.

For indoor furniture, the parts are glued only. Outdoor furniture can be glued, but for many things—it will be enough to use nails. For softwoods of fairly large sections, nails alone are all that are needed. Each layer is nailed to the next (FIG. 12-1A). A zigzag arrangement of nails that go well into the lower piece will make a strong joint. For instance, 2-inch planed wood finishes about 1³/₄ inches thick. A 3-inch nail then goes 1¹/₄ inches into the lower wood, which is adequate, but a nail much shorter would not be adequate. Of course, nail heads will show on the last piece in a series, but you can usually arrange for that to be at the back or be hidden by another part. Waterproof glue in a nailed joint would strengthen it further and prevent water seepage between boards.

If the wood has been completely seasoned, rely on glue only, particularly with hardwoods, but unseasoned wood or softwood still containing much mois-

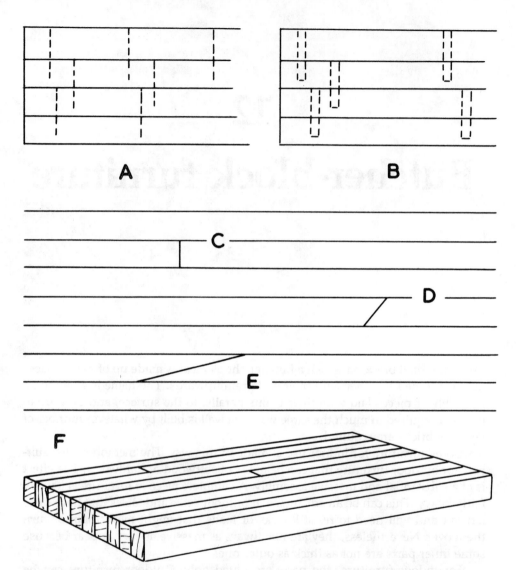

Fig. 12-1. In butcher-block construction, the parts can be glued, doweled, or nailed and can be assembled with occasional lengthwise joints.

ture will not take glue reliably. In any case, strengthen a glued joint by using dowels (FIG. 12-1B). How many depends on the joint, but a dowel near each end will resist any tendency for the joint to open.

Joints in the length would be inappropriate in a small assembly, but in a long bench or similar thing include an occasional joint to use up shorter pieces. It could even be considered a design feature. The simplest joint is a plain butt (FIG. 12-1C). Make sure the meeting ends are square and forced close together. The meeting angle need not be square, so long as both pieces are the same (FIG.

12-1D). If you cut them to a long angle, it becomes possible to nail through during assembly (FIG. 12-1E). Even with a wider angle, drive a nail diagonally across the joint. Most nailing of softwoods can be direct without drilling. Near the ends and in places where accuracy is important, drill undersize, almost as far as the nail is to go.

Do not have many joints in the length; always arrange short pieces between others going full length. Even then it looks better and is stronger if you stagger the joints (FIG. 12-1F).

Use stock sizes of softwood; 2-×-4 inch is the obvious selection. What quality depends on the project, but occasional knots can be regarded as decoration. The method of construction provides mutual support. You can sometimes include a piece with flaws that might not be suitable for an assembly where it has to form a part unaided. Straight wood is usually the best choice, but a curved piece could be cut for shorter parts, or it could be cut and butted between other layers that would flatten it.

Hardwoods need not be as massive as softwoods; 2-×-2-inch sizes would suit many things. Much depends on the wood. Use one wood throughout, or get an interesting effect by mixing two or more of different colors. Alternate strips of dark and light colors, or some other arrangement give an unusual effect.

Softwood Bench

A simple bench, sometimes called a *parson's bench*, can be made with the legs included in butcher-block layers (FIG. 12-2A). A short bench is shown, but this method can be used to build up any length bench when you want to provide seating all around the edge of a patio. You need intermediate supports for a length upwards of 8 feet.

For a simple bench, prepare the pieces to make up the width you want, and mark across the ends of all of them to get matching lengths. Cut them squarely. You might have to plane the ends after assembly. If you get them fairly accurate first, not much will have to be removed to level them. Alternatively, leave the wood too long and trim all the ends together after nailing. Whichever method is used, there have to be two pieces cut short, by the width of the legs (FIG. 12-2B). Squareness in both directions is important at the ends because it affects the squareness of the legs.

Nail the strips together; include the legs as you progress (FIG. 12-2C). Make up the thickness of the legs with pieces on the outsides (FIG. 12-2D). The tops of the legs are best left slightly too long, so that you can plane them level. Cleanly planed end grain looks good between adjoining long grain.

If the bench is to remain in one place, or against something else, legs nailed only should be strong enough. If the bench will be moved about or subject to rough usage, provide brackets. They can be simple iron angle or shelf brackets that extend both ways underneath (FIG. 12-3A). For an all-wood construction, nail or screw in wood brackets (FIG. 12-3B).

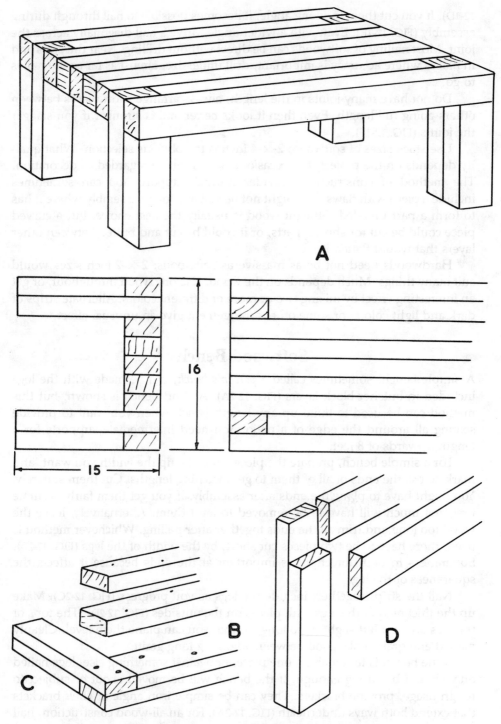

Fig. 12-2. This bench is built up from standard sections of lumber.

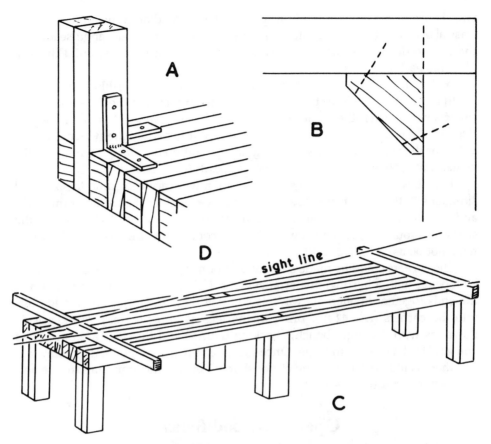

Fig. 12-3. Legs can be bracketed, and a long assembly should be tested for twist.

If the bench is long enough to need intermediate legs, include them during assembly (FIG. 12-3C) at back and front. Thickening pieces should be the same as at the ends.

During the assembly of any bench, watch that it is going together with the top flat and without twist. When possible, assemble the top downward on a flat surface, but tilt the work sideways for convenience in nailing. Bring it back to the inverted position after each series of nails, and see that the top still rests close to the flat surface. Also, check by standing the bench on its legs and sighting along. This check for twist can be helped by having long straight strips across the ends to exaggerate any twist (FIG. 12-3D). An old-time carpenter called these "winding strips," and a twisted assembly was "in winding."

Corner Softwood Bench

If you want to arrange bench seating around the edge of a patio, or if you need to angle the seats for any reason, make separate seats and bring them together. If you choose to join them, provide strips of metal or wood underneath (FIG. 12-4A). That allows you to disassemble them later if you want to rearrange seating. If there is no doubt that the seating will remain where it is made, build the seat tops into each other.

Make a frame against which you can assemble the butcher-block strips. This could be made from pieces that will be later cut and used in the assembly. Make that frame to match the angle of the intended seat. Even if it is apparently 90 degrees, there is no point in carefully getting your bench square, when the deck below or the corner of a house is a degree or so different. Make the frame to the actual shape; then, brace it with a diagonal strut (FIG. 12-4B).

Decide where you need legs; their location will vary according to sizes and situations. If the seat fits inside a corner, put one leg near the corner at the back, and two front legs a short distance each way from the angle (FIG. 12-4C). If the seat goes around an outside angle, a leg can come right at the corner. Back legs need not be as close (FIG. 12-4D).

The corners could be made straight and butted, with straps below, but they look better with a herringbone arrangement. Using the frame as a guide, bring the ends together in alternate ways as you nail them in layers. Then, add nails into the corners (FIG. 12-4E). Bring in the legs as you progress. Work upside down, as with a straight bench, checking flatness and that legs are upright as you go. Use brackets at the legs. Once the assembly has progressed to many layers, there is little risk of it going out of shape. Remove the temporary frame and use its parts in further assembly work.

Open Softwood Bench

The solid benches have smooth, level tops and an attractive, massive appearance. Also, they are heavy and rain water can settle on top. Provide gaps between the strips. In a given width, that would be lighter than a solid top and water would be able to run through. In the simplest construction, alternate pieces can be cut short. That would leave rather wide gaps that would be uncomfortable to sit on, and even cushions would become caught in the spaces. It would be better to have thinner spaces (1- × 4-inch is a suitable stock section).

The small bench shown in FIG. 12-5A has full-length, 2-inch widths, alternating with short sections of 1-inch width. The legs are made up to 5 inches thick. Ends could be left showing the end grain (FIG. 12-5B), or a strip could be put across between the outer sections of the legs (FIG. 12-5C).

Decide on the lengths of filler pieces. They should be shorter than the spaces between them (FIG. 12-5D). Plan the layout to suit the size bench you are making, but fillers between 6 inches and 12 inches will do. Make enough fillers for the whole bench, so that you get them the same length.

Legs have the inner and filler pieces the full depth of the bench, but the outer piece is cut back (FIG. 12-5E). Nail the parts of the legs together. Make all the legs,

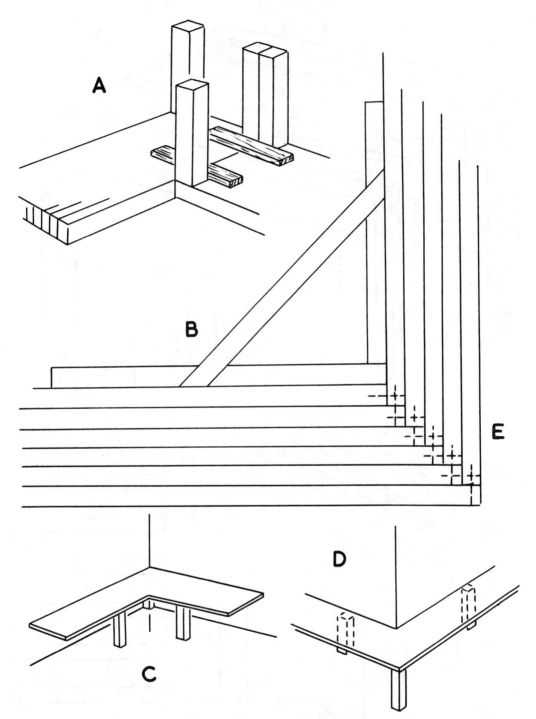

Fig. 12-4. *At a corner, parts can be butted, or they can be joined in a herringbone fashion.*

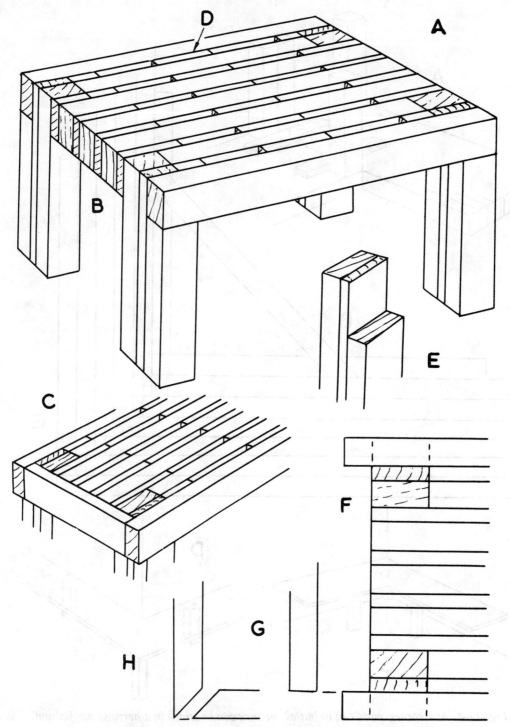

Fig. 12-5. An open butcher-block assembly will shed water.

so they are ready for fitting to the other parts as you come to them. Set back the tops (FIG. 12-5F) if there is to be a strip across the end of the bench.

Mark on the first outside piece where the legs and spacers will come. Join this to the legs and the first set of spacers. As you add more strips, use a try square to mark across, so that all the spacers are fitted level. Also watch the squareness of the ends if there is to be a strip across them. If the end grain is to be exposed, it would not matter if you left some excess length to be trimmed after complete assembly.

The simplest, closed end has the strip square between the outer pieces (FIG. 12-5G), but you can make a neater corner by mitering (FIG. 12-5H). Although all the parts are shown with sharp angles, the outer edges and corners should be rounded. Round the lengthwise strips and arrange the spacers a short distance below the top level.

For an angled corner of an open bench, there are several ways of arranging a herringbone effect. Treat each layer, whether a full length piece or a spacer, separately (FIG. 12-6A), and alternate the laps. Regard a long piece and its spacer as a unit; alternate these pairs (FIG. 12-6B). Whichever way you do it, the spacers should be all the same length, forming a diagonal line with the inner ones getting closer to the next spacers (FIG. 12-6C). Alternately, arrange their lengths so that they come square across (FIG. 12-6D). Keep spaces along the bench the same.

If you want to put a leg at a corner, whether inside or outside the angle, cutting its top away to allow the outer seat pieces to go right through takes a lot from the leg. It could be strengthened to allow for this by increasing the wood section to 2×6 inches. In any case, include wood or metal brackets underneath. Another way would be to cut off the leg below the seat—allowing the top assembly to go right through to the corner—and then secure the leg with angle brackets in both directions to as many top pieces as can be included.

Hardwood Bench

Any of the softwood bench designs could be made in hardwood, but that would result in great weight, increased costs, and a construction far stronger than required. A reasonable section for most benches built solidly is 2 inches square. This finishes after planing to about $1^7/8$ inches square. The tops can be of that size throughout and legs can be the same or larger section.

In the simple bench shown in FIG. 12-7A, the top is made up in the usual way. It could be of different woods for an unusual appearance. The exposed end grain adds to the effect (although it would be possible to frame across there). The legs are set in from the ends, and they are braced with framing (all have their joints to the top hidden). It is possible to do some assembly with nails, but cut joints are more appropriate to good hardwoods. Joints to build up the laminations could be nailed, but elsewhere glued cut joints are better.

Start by making the two assemblies; they each consist of a lengthwise piece with legs attached (FIG. 12-7B). Set out the shapes at one leg. For a short bench,

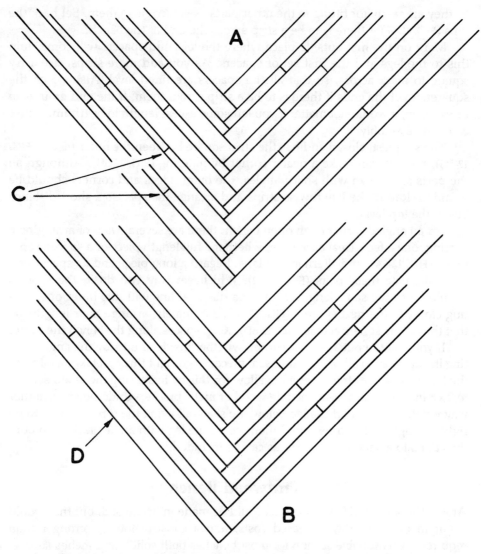

Fig. 12-6. An open-topped corner can have equal or graduated fillers.

the bracing strut can be at 45 degrees. If the bench is long, take the strut further along (FIG. 12-7C).

Use a mortise and tenon joint at the top of a leg (FIG. 12-8A), but do not take it through the top piece (1 inch or slightly more will be long enough for a tenon). Tenon the strut into the leg (FIG. 12-8B). Make a tenon at the other end of the strut, but it is easier to halve it—either straight (FIG. 12-8C), or dovetailed (FIG. 12-8D). Add a rail between each pair of legs. Don't make the rail yet, but cut its mortise in readiness (FIG. 12-8E).

With these two assemblies made up, further assembly is just a case of start-

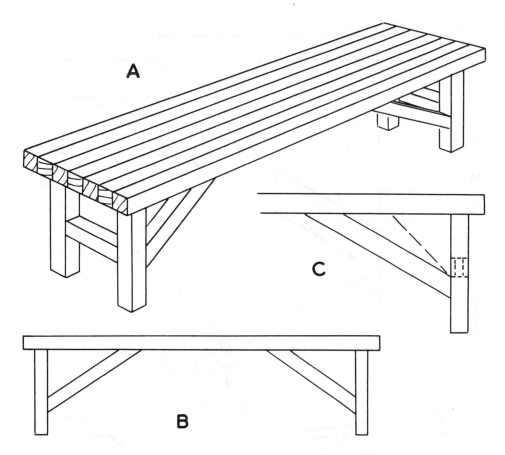

Fig. 12-7. A butcher-block top to a bench can have braced legs.

ing at one side with a plain strip outside one legged piece, and adding more layers until you are ready to take in the other legged piece. Glue each joint; then, nail it to its neighbor. Doweling is easy. Clamp the glued joint. Then, drill through it at about 10-inch intervals, so that you can drive in glued dowels (FIG. 12-8F). If you keep the dowels short, they will hold just as well. However, you will not have to level their tops after driving. Stagger the dowel positions as you progress.

When you reach the stage of bringing in the second long piece with legs attached, measure the length between shoulders of the lower crosswise rails. Make these rails; glue them in at the same time you build in the legged piece.

If you want to close the ends of the top with strips, make the outer strips long enough to enclose the end pieces (FIG. 12-8G). These can merely fit between or be mitered (FIG. 12-8H). If the size of the bench would be better with thicker legs, make them in any reasonable section. All that is necessary is to cut a suitable tenon at the top, and arrange the rail and strut joints centrally in the leg.

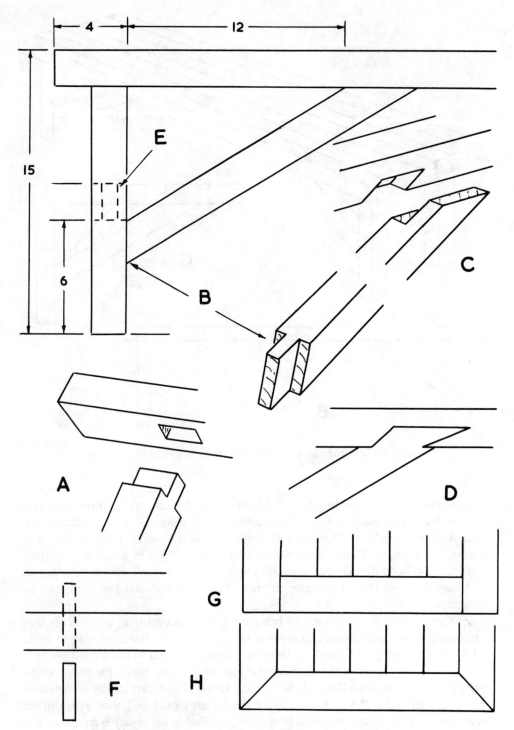

Fig. 12-8. *Different methods of constructing a bench.*

Butcher-block Table

A tabletop in the butcher style could be made of thick pieces as described for the benches. The result would be quite heavy; this might be an advantage in a permanent situation. If the table is to be used for outdoor hobbies, then a stiff solid top would be an advantage. For the more common outdoor use of a table, lighten construction—while retaining the typical butcher-block appearance—so it could complement forms or chairs made in this manner.

The table shown in FIG. 12-9 is of moderate size, with the usual sturdy butcher-block appearance, but with a top that is not as heavy as it appears. The sizes given in FIG. 12-10 and the Materials List are suggestions. They can be varied according to needs and available wood. Most of the parts are 2-inch square and 1-×-2-inch sections. They are shown without allowance for planing, but the wood should be planed all around. The final sizes will be less than shown.

It is the central area of the top that controls other sizes. Make this part first. If you work the other way and need to fit the top into a frame, alter the width of one strip. Join enough strips together (FIG. 12-11A). Glue alone might be sufficient. Assemble all the parts of the top face downward, on a flat surface covered with paper to prevent glue sticking to it. Pull them together with bar clamps.

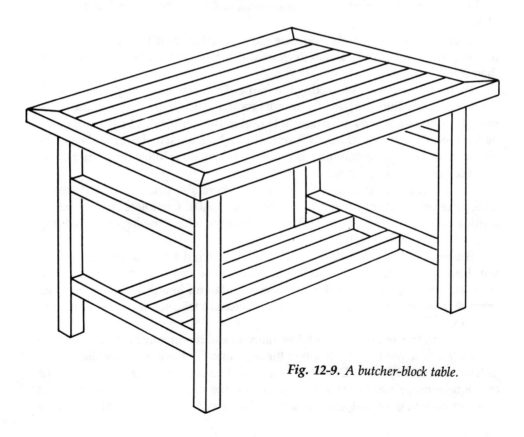

Fig. 12-9. A butcher-block table.

Materials List for
Butcher-block Table

10 tops	2×24×1
2 tops	2×28×2
2 tops	2×21×2
1 top stiffener	2×21×1
4 legs	2×27×2
4 rails	2×20×2
4 rails	2×24×2
2 rails	2×20×1

Also, put weights on the assembly to prevent it from buckling. A safer way of keeping it flat is to assemble the strips, in groups of two or three that have their tops planed true, before joining them to other groups.

Use nails between the parts in predrilled holes or dowels across in a similar way (three along each joint should be enough). Prepare the pieces too long at this stage, so that you can trim the whole assembly as if it is a single board. How the ends are dealt with depends on your equipment. The best way is to rabbet across so that a tongue goes into a plowed groove in the frame (FIG. 12-11B). This could be done with a router, two passes on a table saw, or with a hand fillester plane.

Alternatively, use dowels in square-cut ends (FIG. 12-11C). At the sides, glue or dowel the joints. In the 1-inch thickness, the dowels could be 3/4 of an inch in diameter.

There are three ways of making the frame. The ends can go right across with the sides taken into the same plowed grooves (FIG. 12-12A). Carry the sides through, so that the ends are covered. Dowel in the joint (FIG. 12-12B); they could be only partly into the sides, or taken through. Exposed dowel ends can be regarded as a design feature in this type of construction. Miter the corners, and take the dowels through diagonally (FIG. 12-12C).

The top could be stiff enough as it is, but there also could be a piece across under the center, tenoned into the sides (FIG. 12-11D). Complete the top before starting on the framing. Clean off the surplus glue where the legs and their top bars will come underneath.

The legs and rails are all square, in order to match the solid appearance of the top. Four rails go around the table a short distance down from the top. Then, there are two rails between the legs at the ends and lengthwise rails between them. At the tops of the legs, there are rails across to take screws upward into the tabletop.

Mark out the legs (FIG. 12-11E). Use mortise and tenon joints for the rails. The tenons can go about halfway through the legs, and the lower ones will have to be mitered where they meet. Doweled joints could be used if you prefer, but tenons are more appropriate. The thinner top rails to take screws could be tenoned, but they are better dovetailed into the tops of the legs (FIG. 12-11F). Drill for screws

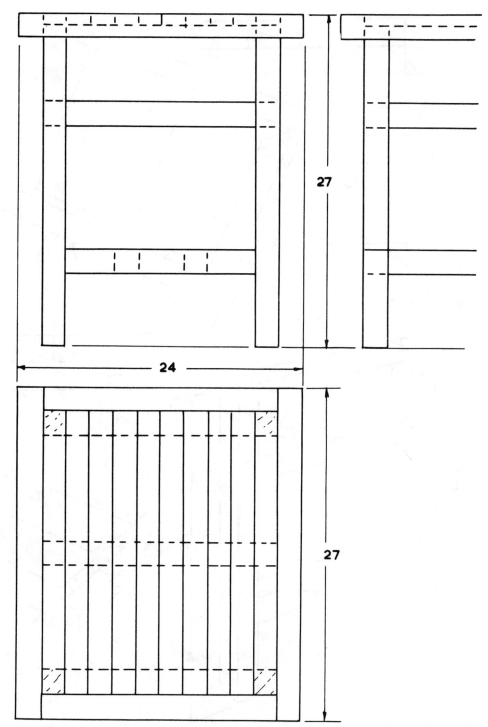

Fig. 12-10. Sizes for a butcher-block table.

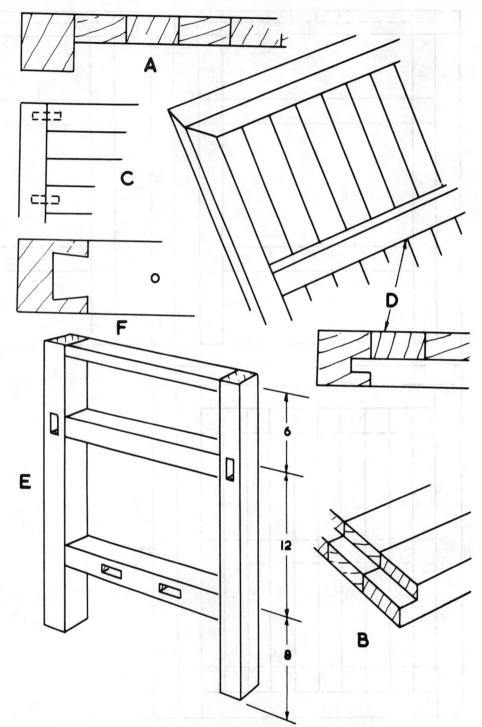

Fig. 12-11. Assembly details of the top and leg construction.

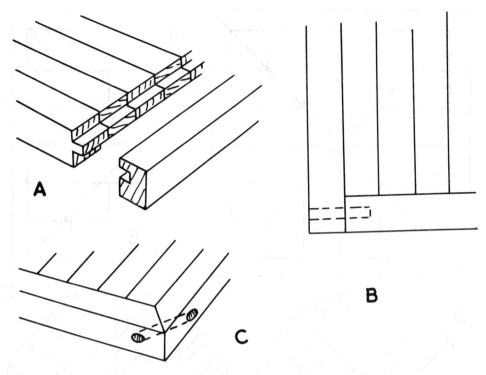

Fig. 12-12. Construction details for the tabletop.

before assembly, but angle them slightly, so that there is clearance for your screwdriver past the main rail. Get the lengths of the rails, so that the legs will come closely inside the top frame.

Make up the two end leg and rail assemblies. Check that they are square, flat, and match as a pair. Join them with the rails the other way; fit the framework to the tabletop.

Radial Tabletops

Butcher-block tops do not have to be only parallel strips. You can make interesting tables with the tops divided into segments that are all in the same wood or in different woods, so that the colors alternate. Make tops using narrow strips and a large number of segments; that gives you an opportunity to show your skills. For the usual purposes of an outdoor table, a more simple arrangement would be appreciated just as much. Usually, you can divide the top into four segments.

An example is a square top with or without a border (FIG. 12-13A). This is shown with 2-×4-inch pieces with the greater width on the top, but 2-inch-square pieces, or even narrower ones, could be used. Join enough pieces to make up the width of a side, with the outside edge cut squarely, but enough extended to mark the miter (FIG. 12-13B). The safest way to get an accurate shape is to set

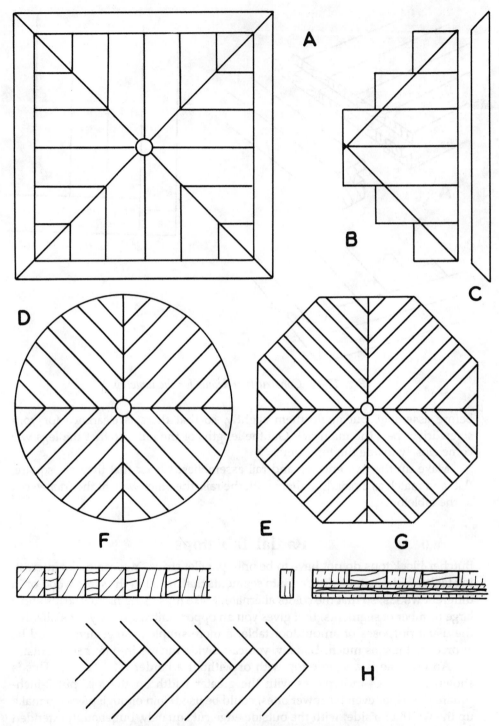

Fig. 12-13. Suggestions for radial butcher-block tabletops.

out the final square full size on a piece of scrap plywood or hardboard, with diagonals drawn; then, cut and plane the miter edges to that. In any case, you will have to do some careful planing for final close fitting. Mark adjoining surfaces, so that they go back in the same place. Then drill for a few dowels.

Exposed ends of hardwood look attractive with their different grain patterns. This is particularly true if woods are mixed and the ends are sealed with varnish. Softwoods are better covered; make a border (FIG. 12-13C) with mitered or lapped corners. Attach the top to the legs and framing; make it in the way described for the previous table.

A very similar top is easily converted to round (FIG. 12-13D). This is shown with square strips. The best plan to get a good shape is to start with the outline of a square table; draw the circle when the parts are joined. Draw curves on each segment, but cut oversize, so there can be a final trimming to a true circle later.

The strips used do not all have to be the same widths. An interesting effect can be obtained by using random widths. This is a way of using up scraps left over from other work. Alternate wide and narrow pieces. Dark narrow pieces between lighter colored ones can be very attractive. An example is shown with an octagonal outline (FIG. 12-13E), but the design could be used in other shapes.

Any top with straight edges can be bordered with strips glued and nailed or screwed on. An alternative to a square unbordered edge is to make it semicircular, or to bevel around the top and bottom edges.

The usual assembly is with pieces to the full thickness of the top (FIG. 12-13F), but there is an alternative way of getting a similar top appearance using thinner wood. The base is a piece of stout exterior grade plywood that is marked or cut to the shape of the intended table. Provide thinner strips of wood to make up any pattern you prefer (FIG. 12-13G). Any of the patterns suitable for solid wood could be used, but in this case you can put the pieces in place over a penciled pattern on the plywood. The parts can be glued only, or drive screws from below as well. Use glue because it seals the gaps and prevents water becoming trapped between and under the strips.

A variation in pattern that would be difficult with solid pieces is easier to do on a plywood base. An example is to arrange the meeting pieces in a herringbone pattern (FIG. 12-13H) instead of straight miters. Add a border, bedded in glue, to prevent moisture being absorbed by the exposed end grain of the plywood veneers.

Flat-seat Chair

Chairs to match other butcher-block furniture can have their seats and backs made in the typical manner, but otherwise they follow the usual construction. This is a plain chair with a flat sloping seat and a similar back (FIG. 12-14). The butcher-block parts are made up from strips $1^3/8$ inches square (FIG. 12-15). The design is intended for hardwood that will match a table. Like other assemblies, use a mixture of woods that will look good when varnished.

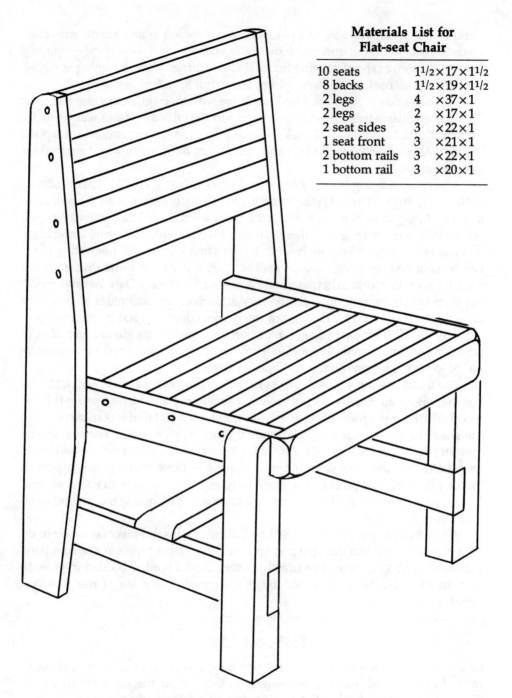

Materials List for Flat-seat Chair

10 seats	$1^1/_2 \times 17 \times 1^1/_2$
8 backs	$1^1/_2 \times 19 \times 1^1/_2$
2 legs	$4 \times 37 \times 1$
2 legs	$2 \times 17 \times 1$
2 seat sides	$3 \times 22 \times 1$
1 seat front	$3 \times 21 \times 1$
2 bottom rails	$3 \times 22 \times 1$
1 bottom rail	$3 \times 20 \times 1$

Fig. 12-14. A flat-seated, butcher-block chair.

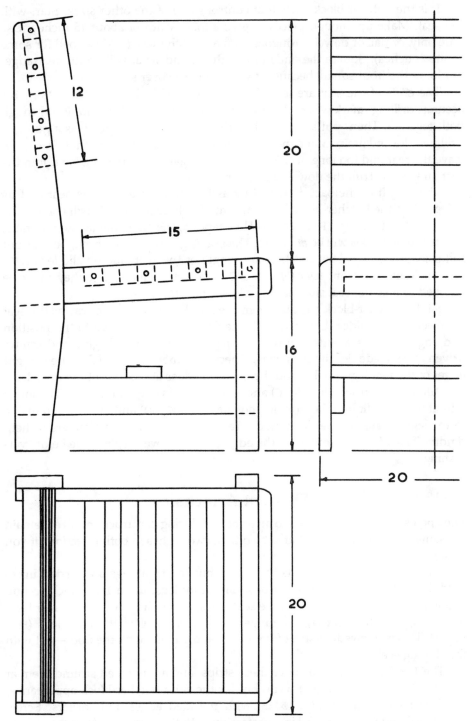

Fig. 12-15. *Sizes of the flat-seated, butcher-block chair.*

It is the butcher-block parts that control some of the other sizes. Start with the seat. Make up enough pieces to give a total width of about 15 inches. Use glue only, or nail or dowel through as you add each piece (as described for some of the benches). Square the ends to length. Round what will be the rear edge, but leave the front square because it will receive a cover strip.

The ends of the seat are joined to the sides with dowels (FIG. 12-16A). For accurate drilling, mark where the holes will come in the sides, and drill through both together. Then, put a side against the seat and use its holes as a guide to drill into the end grain. Make the front end of each side square with the seat, but leave the rear end too long at this stage. Cut it against the rear leg later. Join the seat and sides. Trim the dowel ends later.

The length of the back is the same as the distance across the seat and its sides. Make the butcher-block back, and mark where its dowels will come.

Make the back legs (FIG. 12-17A). They taper to the ends, but are kept parallel where the seat sides will be attached. The seat is given a sloped back. Set this out full size, so as to get the position and angle of the seat side on the legs (FIG. 12-17B). Make the front legs (FIG. 12-17C). They are square, but they must be notched to take the seat sides and the lower rails (FIG. 12-16B).

Fit the butcher-block back between the rear legs in the same way as the seat is doweled to its sides. Use your full-size setting out as a guide to the position and angle of the seat sides on the rear legs. Then, join with glue and screws driven from inside. Fit the front legs. Check that they are parallel to the straight edges of the rear legs. Well round the exposed edges at the tops of the front legs.

Add the seat front (FIG. 12-16C) and well round its edges and ends. The lower rails at the sides fit into the front leg notches (FIG. 12-16D) and are screwed inside to the legs parallel to the floor. Add a rail across between their centers to help rigidity. Take off the sharpness of the edges, and remove surplus glue before varnishing.

Flat-seat Armchair

The open seat can be converted to an armchair during construction. Sizes remain the same, or increase the seat area by one or two inches in both directions if you prefer.

The general design remains the same, but the front legs are carried up to hold the arms (FIG. 12-18). Instead of square front legs, use a 1-×-3-inch section that is screwed to the outsides of the seat sides, in the same way as the rear legs. At the tops of the front legs, arrange a 1-×-2-inch rail to the back legs (FIG. 12-18A). This is screwed outside of both legs, and parallel with the floor—not with the sloping seat.

The 1-×-3-inch arms go above these strips, and are notched around the rear legs. Curve the outline if you wish, but for the solid butcher-block appearance, they are better straight (FIG. 12-18B) with rounded edges and corners. Screw downward and into the back legs, preferably with the screw heads counterbored

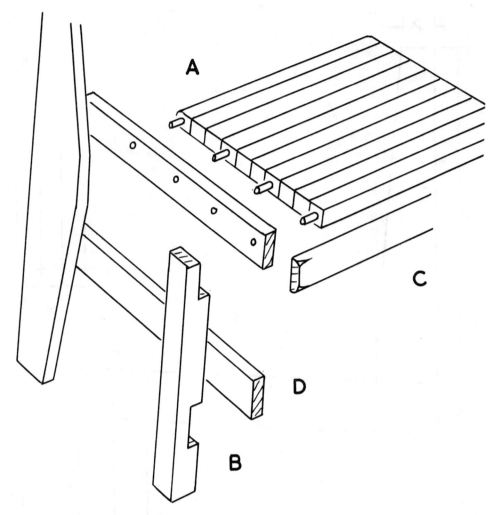

Fig. 12-16. Assembly details of the flat-seat chair.

and plugged. If you screw outward from the rear legs, the heads will not be very obvious.

Shaped-seat Chair

If a chair is to be comfortable for long use without padding, it needs some shaping. Ideally, there should be compound curvature in the set, but that is almost impossible to produce in wood without considerable careful work. The most important need is shaping from front to back. Arrange fairly easily with the butcher-block technique. Provide some curvature across the chair back, which is also fairly easy to make.

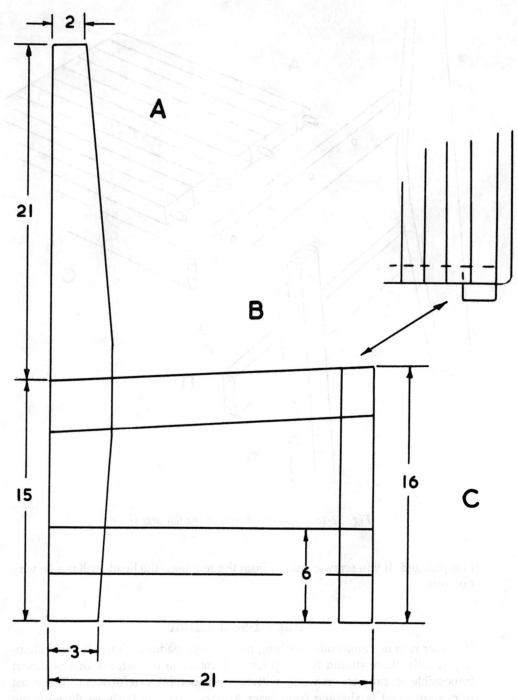

Fig. 12-17. Layout of a flat-seat chair.

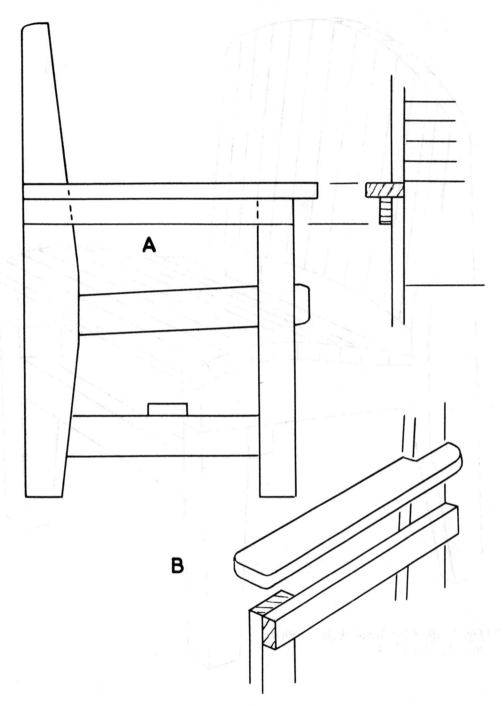

Fig. 12-18. *Adaption of the flat-seat chair to make an armchair.*

Fig. 12-19. A butcher-block chair with a shaped seat and back.

Materials List for
Shaped-seat Chair

2 legs	4	×35×1½
2 legs	3	×16×1½
2 sides	3	×20×1½
1 front rail	3	×20×1½
9 seats	1½×21×1	
12 backs	1½×16×1	
2 back supports from	6	×20×1

The chair shown in FIG 12-19 is intended to be rather more advanced than hammer-and-nail construction or even dowel construction. It is an example of cabinetwork taken outdoors. The finished chair can have uses in the house as well as outside (if it is given a good finish). If made of hardwoods—probably of mixed colors—and finished with clear varnish, it becomes a very attractive piece of furniture for use anywhere. The general drawing (FIG. 12-20) shows a chair of fairly roomy proportions. Sizes could be reduced slightly if it is to be used indoors with other smaller chairs. Outdoors, a large size will often be appreciated.

The rails that support the seat, slope back for economy in cutting the curve. Make a full-size outline drawing of a side view (FIG. 12-21A). From this, get the shape of a rail and mark the angles of the cuts and joints on it. Then, draw the curve of the top edge. Use the pattern of 1½-inch squares as a guide (FIG. 12-21B). Cut the curve on the two matching sides.

Mark out the front legs, so that you can cut the joints between them and the seat sides. They are best made with double tenons that are cut back about ½ inch from the front (FIG. 12-21C). They can go about 1¼ inches into the seat sides. Cut the mortises in the seat sides before cutting the wood to length, in order to reduce the risk of short grain breaking out.

The curving of the top edge reduces the rear end of the sides to about 2½ inches. Make a mortise and tenon joint there to the leg—with double tenons similar to those on the front legs—but there is no need to cut back from either edge. Cut the tenons on the sides; leave the matching mortises until later.

With the two sides prepared, now add the pieces that will make the seat. Because of the varying curve, their edges have to be planed to meet, as you fit each one in turn. This is not as difficult as you might think because one edge of each piece is always square in section. Start at the front, and work back. Take care to keep the assembly square. Although the joints will be glued, it helps in assembly to put one screw in the end of each piece as it is fitted. In the finished chair, the seat will look good with plugs over counterbored screw heads. At this stage, simply use thin, temporary screws. When the seat is fully assembled and the glue set, remove the screws; drill and counterbore the holes for larger screws and plugs.

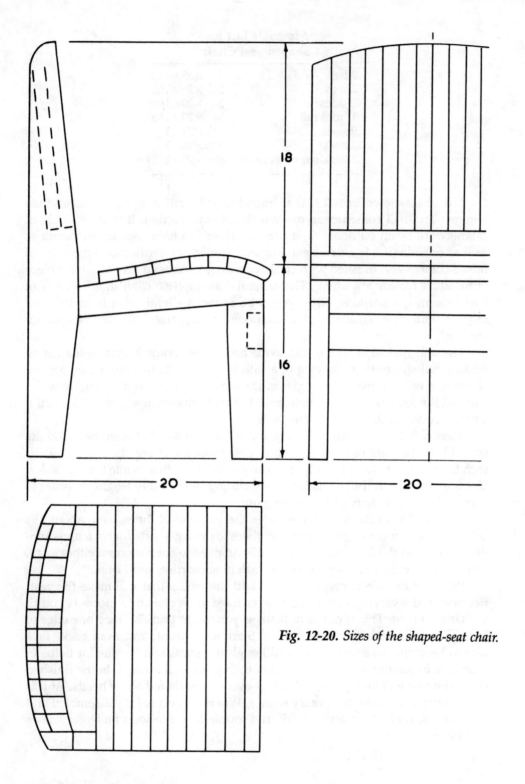

Fig. 12-20. Sizes of the shaped-seat chair.

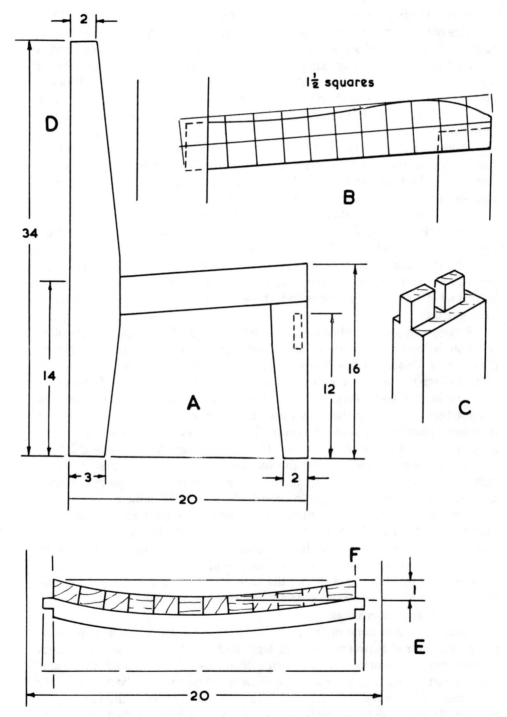

Fig. 12-21. Layout of the chair side and the curves of seat and back.

Start at the front with one piece having both edges square (FIG. 12-22A). Plane the edge of the next piece to fit against it closely. Leave its other edge square (FIG. 12-22B). Then, glue and screw it in place. Do the same with the next one, and so on, until you have made up enough for the seat. Later, plane and sand the top surface to a smooth curve, if you prefer. The series of narrow flats will not be noticed when sitting, and they help to give the butcher-block appearance. Level the outer ends of the strips and round the top edges. Well round the front edge of the seat.

Make the back legs (FIG. 12-21D). Cut the mortises for the seat sides, but leave preparation for the back until that is made up. The butcher-block back has to fit between the back legs—which will be the same distance apart as the sides of the seat—so use them as a gauge for the overall width.

In the finished chair, there are two curved pieces behind the back tenoned into the back legs (FIG. 12-21E). To get the curve of the butcher-block back true, these pieces are made too wide at first. They can be used as cradles in which to assemble the back. If made too narrow, they could buckle during assembly. They are shown about 6 inches wide, but that is not important. Mark on these pieces their final shapes and the tenons (which have to be cut after the strips have all been glued on).

Arrange one piece at what will be the bottom edge of the back, and the other far enough down to allow for its curved top edge. Then, put on the central strip (FIG. 12-22C). This has both edges square, and it must be square to the supports. Glue and screw it in the same way as the seat strips. Work outward from that; keep the bottom ends level. Plane the next pieces to match it, but leave their other edges square. Fit them in turn on opposite sides, so that the width increases symmetrically about the center. When you reach the outside, plane the edges to size and to the angle that will fit them between the legs (FIG. 12-21F).

Cut off the surplus wood from the supports at the back. Trim them to a neat curve, and round their exposed edges. Draw a curve over the tops of the strips and cut it. Make it resemble anything you like, but keep it symmetrical and about 2 inches lower at the sides than the center. Besides the tenons and glue between the back and the legs, include some dowels (FIG. 12-22D). Use the back to mark where mortises and dowel holes have to come on the legs. Shape the tops of the legs to follow on the curve of the back, and round the outer corners.

Complete the front legs. Make the front rail (FIG. 12-22E) that crosses far enough below the seat to avoid its joints and provide crosswise stiffness without interfering with a sitter's legs.

Assembly is best done in one process, instead of in two steps as with many chairs. Fit the rail between the front legs, and join them to the seat. Check squareness in the front view by measuring diagonals. Check the angle in the side view by comparing with your full-size drawing. Assemble the back to the rear legs—preferably pulling tight with bar clamps—and then bring the rear legs to the seat. As you close those joints, check that the rear edges of the back legs are parallel with the front edges of the front legs.

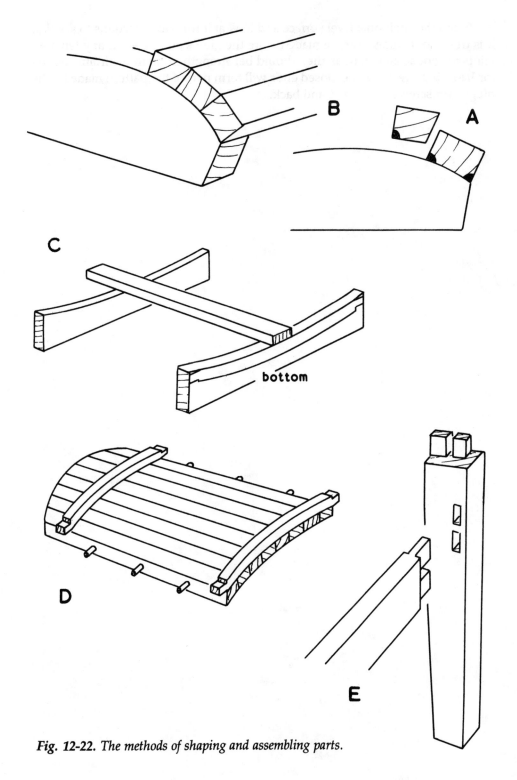

Fig. 12-22. The methods of shaping and assembling parts.

Stand the chair on a level surface and look at it from all directions to see that it is true. Adjustments can be made before the glue starts to set. If any tenoned joints are not as good a fit as they should be, strengthen them by drilling across for 1/4-inch dowels. Their exposed ends will form part of the pattern made by the plugs over screws in the seat and back.

13
Other items

A primary use of outdoor furniture is for seating, in its many forms: sitting upright to eat, lounging, or laying flat. Seats are closely followed by tables, which usually complement the seats and, in some cases, might be attached to them. There are many other woodworking projects that can be undertaken for use on the patio or deck, in the yard or about the garden. They can be regarded as supplementary furniture.

For children's needs, you can scale down adult furniture. Some of their requirements are for activity equipment, such as swings and playhouses. A climbing frame will have to take its place among other outdoor furniture. Similarly, a bird feeder has to fit in with other wooden items you make for the yard.

If you are a gardener, there will be many things you wish to make to help in your hobby or activity. You might want to display your plants, flowers and shrubs. Many of the things you make can be regarded as furniture. Besides helping in the garden, such things as plant containers can bring parts of the garden onto the deck or patio.

The examples described in this chapter might suggest other projects you can tackle to improve your outdoor facilities and enhance the land surrounding your home.

Trash Container

An attractive container for trash can be made by coopering (like a barrel). Fitting a large number of sides together to make something that comes close to being a circle (coopering) calls for skill and patience than might be justified for this use.

However, you can use a similar method with eight sides; an octagon comes close enough to the circular metal or plastic liner. Moreover, this shape doesn't leave any gaps large enough for anything but the tiniest things to fall through.

The container can be made parallel, or it can be given a slight taper. Two sides can be extended to be slotted as handles (FIG. 13-1). This gives an appearance reminiscent of an old-time milking pail.

The angles involved are the same, whatever size container you make. If you decide on a taper and keep it slight, the angles remain the same for all practical purposes. For a considerable flare, the angles planed to meet edges would be different. With eight equal sides, a setting out (FIG. 13-2A) shows the angle of each triangle at the center is 45 degrees (one-eighth of 360 degrees). Because the three angles in any triangle must total 180 degrees and the other two are the same, they are each $67\frac{1}{2}$ degrees (half of 135 degrees). That is the angle you have to make the edges of the panels (FIG. 13-2B).

An adjustable bevel will serve as a guide, if you will be planing by hand, or that is the angle to set the fence on a jointer. To make sure the outsides of the container come close, make the angles very slightly less by ignoring the $\frac{1}{2}$ degree. If there is any discrepancy, it comes inside, where it will not show.

Draw a circle of the outside size of your liner. Allow some clearance around it, and draw two crossing lines square to each other. When they cross the outer circumference, draw lines square to them, long enough to meet and form a

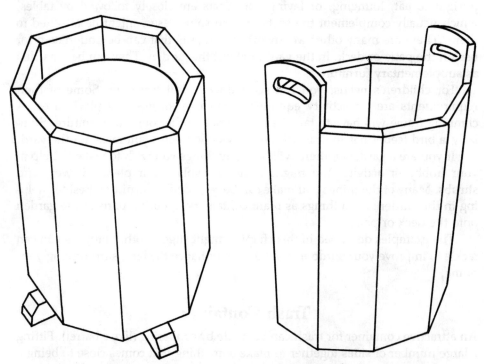

Fig. 13-1. Trash containers can be coopered around a metal or plastic liner.

square (FIG. 13-2C). Check that the four lengths are the same. Measure from the center to a corner; use this length to mark along each side from each corner (FIG. 13-2D). If you join these points, the lines make tangents to the circle; you now have eight equal sides (FIG. 13-2E) representing the inner surfaces of each stave (the coopering term). If you mark the thickness of the wood, that will give you the section of a stave (FIG. 13-2F). Prepare eight identical ones.

The thickness of wood has to be proportional to the overall sizes, but it should not be less than 3/4 of an inch. It could go up to twice that size for a large box.

For a tapered container, set out the top and bottom to get the widths of staves at these levels. They are made to this taper. Otherwise, the work is the same as

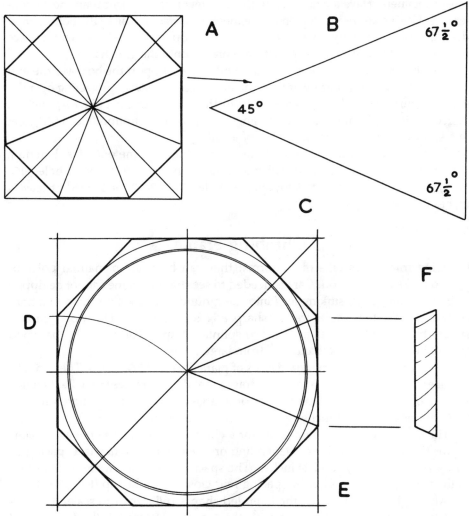

Fig. 13-2. *The shape of a trash container is set out geometrically to get the angles of the wood panels.*

for a parallel box. If you want to extend a pair of staves to make handles, remember to prepare them about 6 inches longer than the other six staves.

At the bottom, make an octagonal base to fit inside (FIG. 13-3A). Ideally, this will be a perfect fit. Avoid making it too large because the staves will not be drawn closely around it. A size marginally too small is better than being oversized. The bottom might rest on the ground, but it would be better to provide feet; four are sufficient (FIG. 13-3B). Do not carry them right across. Individual feet are better able to stand firmly on uneven ground.

In the barrelmaking tradition, the tops of the staves should be drawn together with a metal band. This can be a strip of any metal; aluminum is easy to work. Its width depends on the size of the box, but between 1 inch and 2 inches will suit most containers. Have a length ready that is a few inches longer than the circumference. Use a waterproof glue on all the meeting surfaces. Nail to the bottom, and draw the tops together with a rope, twisted as a "Spanish windlass," with a piece of scrap wood (FIG. 13-3C). Keep that pressure on until the glue has set.

Pencil around where the metal band will come. Support the box over the end of a stout board that is narrower than the inner face of a stave, projecting over the edge of your bench. Nail progressively to the staves. Use a pointed punch to pierce the metal; hammer it over the angles as you work around (FIG. 13-3D). Let one end overlap the other on the flat of a stave.

Plane the tops of the stave level, and round them on the outsides. Extend a pair of opposite staves as handles. For a smaller container, use a round hole (FIG. 13-3E). For a wider stave, make a shaped hole (FIG. 13-3F). You need at least 4 inches for a hand space.

Climbing Frame

Climbing frames can take many forms; they can be made of natural poles or planed and squared wood. Care is needed to see that the frame cannot be tipped or moved, usually by sinking legs into the ground or bracketing them to a hard surface. Check that there are no sharp edges or corners. The wood chosen should be a type that does not tend to splinter or split. For strength, the wood should be straight-grained and free from large knots.

Make the frame from standard sizes of planed wood (FIG. 13-4A). The sections you use will depend on the size of the frame, but do not use less than 2×2 inches for rails or 2×3 inches for the posts. For a large assembly, as illustrated in FIG. 13-4B, the posts are 2×4 inches and the rails are 2×3 inches.

The spacing of rails should allow for a child standing on one rail and reaching for the second one above. Depending on the child, this means a spacing of somewhere between 15 and 24 inches. The spacing does not have to be the same all the way up. Make it safer by spacing rails closer near the top (FIG. 13-4C).

Although you can set out the intended shapes full size or to scale, it is simplest to set up the four uprights with the top rail. Determine the locations of joints and rail lengths from that temporary assembly.

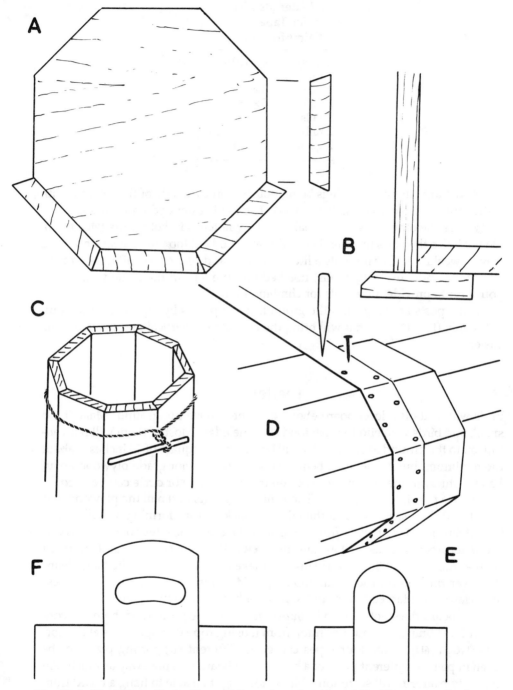

Fig. 13-3. *The bottom fits inside, and it can have feet (A and B). The top may be drawn together with rope and a metal band put around (C and D). Sides can be extended as handles (E and F).*

Materials List
for Tapered
Climbing Frame

4 legs	$4 \times 120 \times 2$
1 top	$4 \times 74 \times 2$
2 rails	$3 \times 74 \times 2$
2 rails	$3 \times 82 \times 2$
2 rails	$3 \times 90 \times 2$
2 rails	$3 \times 50 \times 2$
2 gussets	$7 \times 14 \times 1$

At the top, allow for the legs being notched on each side of the top rail, with a strengthening piece across (FIG. 13-5A). The rail is extended and rounded.

Where the other rails come, make shallow notches in both parts (FIG. 13-5B). Do not halve the parts together because that would cut too much away and could leave a weakness. Cut the rails a little too long, and plane level after assembly.

At the ends, use single rails, notched into the legs in the same way, unless you want to provide more rails for climbing there.

If the posts are to go into the ground, make points by tapering on the outsides only (FIG. 13-5C). That will bring the cuts almost vertical and make driving easier.

Feeders

Birds will feed off a level board about 48 inches above the ground. Make it too small, and birds will tend to push food over the edge. Most of them will not venture on to the ground to eat it and it will be wasted. A square of 15 inches is about the minimum, but 24 inches is better. This can be exterior grade plywood about $1/2$ inch thick. It does not have to be square; a rectangle or circle can be used.

Drive a post into the ground. Then cut its top level and nail the plywood to it (FIG. 13-6A). Use strips around the edges to make a rim, forming a shallow box (FIG. 13-6B). To prevent water from being absorbed into the edges of the plywood, use waterproof glue, as well as nails or screws. Put strips on top, and cut them short at the corners (FIG. 13-6C). This will make it easier to brush the table clean. Whatever rim you fit, round the top edges. Most birds perch on tree branches; their claws are adapted to a round surface rather than angular ones.

The board does not have to be supported from the ground. If there is a convenient tree branch, it could be hung from it using rope through holes at the corners (FIG. 13-6D). If the four ropes can go to different supporting places or be taken in pairs to different parts of a branch, the board will not sway as much. An unsteady platform will scare some birds. You might be able to hang a board from a projecting arm from a building or other nearby object. If so, sling a rope and hang the board from it.

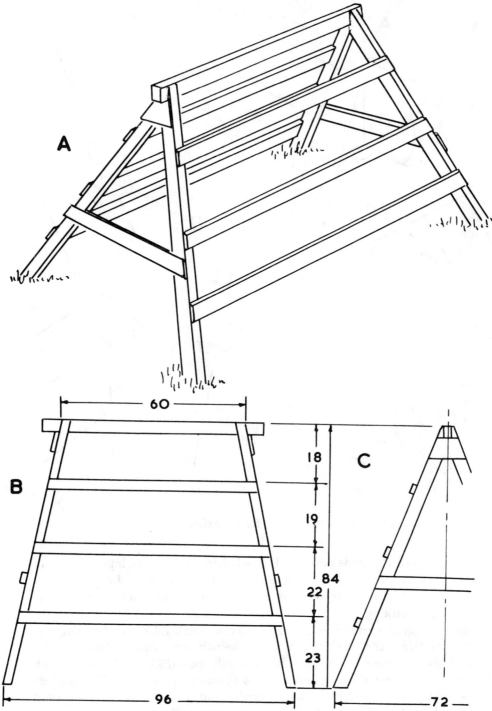

Fig. 13-4. *A climbing frame can be made from squared wood.*

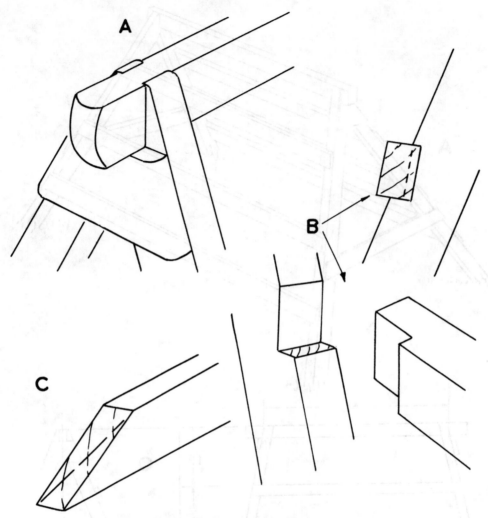

Fig. 13-5. Construction details of a climbing frame.

The feeder can be made portable. Instead of driving the post into the ground, it can have some sort of base. Then it can be lifted and moved easily. Take it under cover in bad weather, or move it to different parts of a lawn for convenience in grass cutting.

Any base should extend far enough to ensure stability. Crossed legs ought to extend about 18 inches each way under a 48-inch post with a 24-inch square feeder. Halve two pieces of the same section as the post (FIG. 13-7A). Then, attach the post with a screw through and brackets all around (FIG. 13-7B). The brackets can be solid blocks, or strips arranged further out (FIG. 13-7C). Nailing should provide all the strength needed, but you can cut joints if you want to show your skill. To allow for uneven ground, put feet under the ends (FIG. 13-7D).

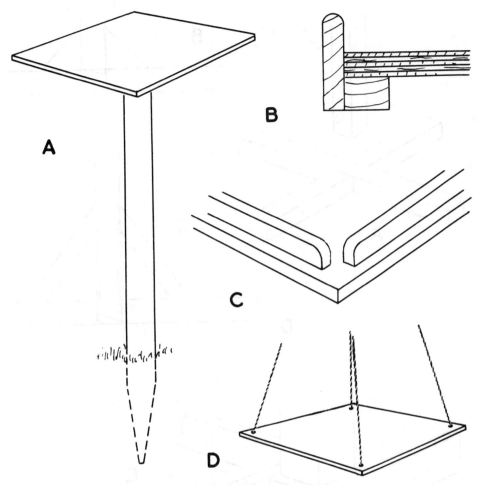

Fig. 13-6. Simple arrangements for feeding birds.

Another arrangement of feet is made from flat pieces on the sides of the square post (FIG. 13-7E). They can extend squarely, and either have feet attached or they might be given a slight slope (FIG. 13-7F), so that only the tips touch the ground and give support as far out as possible.

A round post could have similar feet to a square one, or you could provide three feet with the advantage of freedom from wobble. To equally space three leg positions on a cylinder, wrap a strip of paper around and push a spike through the overlap (FIG. 13-8A). Open the strip, and divide the distance between the spike holes into three (FIG. 13-8B). Wrap the paper around the post again and draw lines along it at the spacing on the paper (FIG. 13-8C).

Arrange feet with rustic pieces to match a natural pole by tapering their ends to fit holes. Do not join them in at the same level; otherwise, the holes will run into each other. Use pieces that are too long; then trim their ends to give level

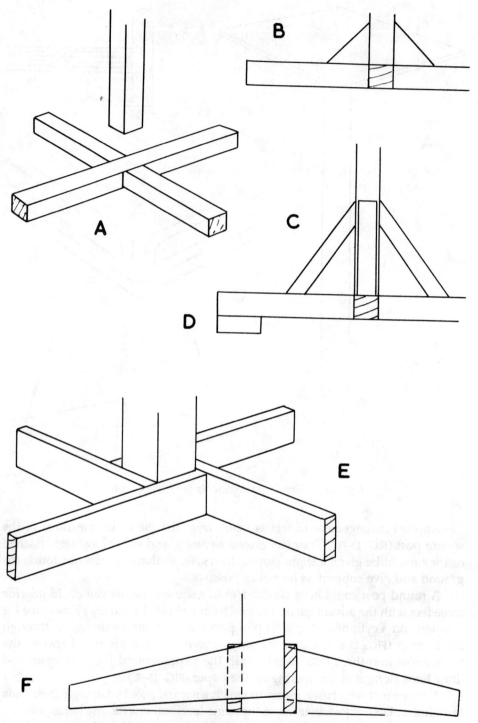

Fig. 13-7. Suggestions for feet to support bird tables.

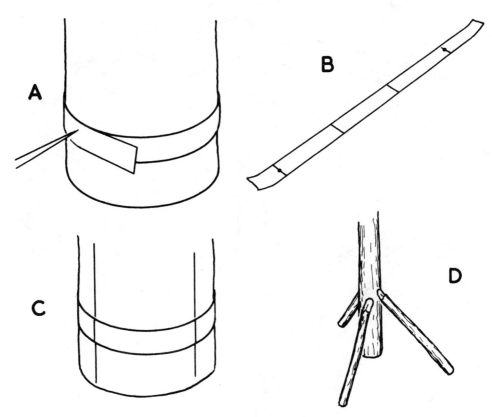

Fig. 13-8. Using a strip of paper to get three legs equally spaced around a post.

support after fitting (FIG. 13-8D). It does not matter if the slopes vary a little, but get a fairly even spread to the ends. The end of the post need not touch the ground.

Compost Bin

Although a place to make compost might not be strictly classed as furniture, to an enthusiastic gardener it is as important a piece of outdoor equipment as chairs and tables. This compost bin (FIG. 13-9A) fulfills the main requirements of making compost in keeping the contents together, but it is well ventilated and has an

Materials List for
Compost Bin

4 posts	$2^1/2 \times 28 \times 2^1/2$
16 strips	$^3/4 \times 35 \times 4^1/2$
8 strips	$1 \quad \times 40 \times 2$

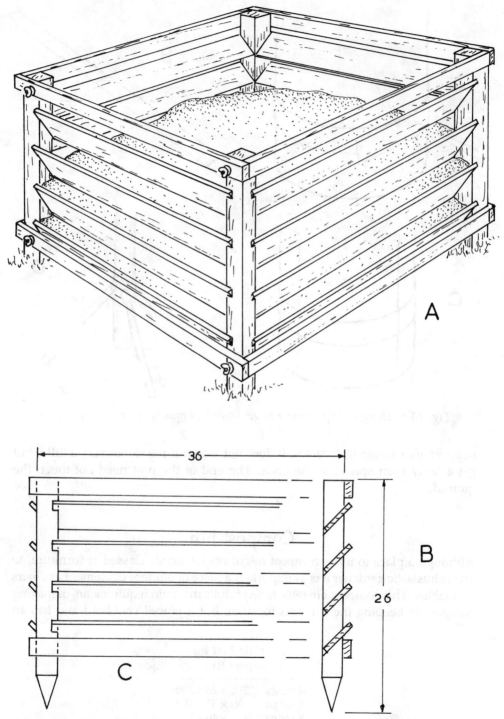

Fig. 13-9. *This compost bin has slatted sides and can be opened.*

acceptable appearance. You can throw in all the garden waste, such as grass cuttings, vegetable matter, fallen leaves and other suitable scraps, to rot down and be used to enrich your soil without much risk of making an untidy mess in the area.

The bin is rigid in use. The corners can be pushed into the ground to prevent movement. You can disassemble it to pack flat when out of use, or you can remove one side when you want to dig out the contents. If you make it square to the suggested sizes (FIG. 13-9B) the capacity is up to 17 cubic feet. However, you can use the same method of construction for a bin of different size, to suit your needs or fit into available space.

Use a durable hardwood for a long-lasting bin. The wood will be continually wet, so softwood should be protected by preservative, but use a non-toxic one so there is no risk of affecting the compost. The parts of the bin will stay cleaner if all wood is planed, but you could use wood with a sawn surface. If the bin is to be positioned on a hard surface, leave off the pointed ends to the corner posts.

Make four identical corner posts (FIG. 13-10A). Mark the grooves on two adjacent surfaces at 45 degrees (FIG. 13-10B). Cut the grooves 1/2 inch deep and with widths to allow the side strips to press in. Point the ends of the posts, if required.

The sixteen side strips (FIG. 13-10C) should match each other so they can be interchangeable. Cut back each end 1/2 inch (FIG. 13-10D) so its inner long edge will come level with the inside corner of a post. Cut the outer part to hook over the post edge (FIG. 13-10E). Two strips might interfere with each other where they meet, so cut off corners to provide clearance (FIG. 13-10F). Rounding outer edges and corners will reduce the risk of damage or splintering, if it is that sort of wood.

The bin is formed of two fully-assembled sides, joined by removable parts the other way. Make the two opposite fully-assembled sides. Glue the side strips into their slots and lock the assembly with outer pieces glued and nailed on at top (FIGS. 13-10G and 11A), and below the bottom diagonal strips (FIGS. 13-9C and 10H). Use waterproof glue in all joints. Check squareness by comparing diagonal measurements.

In the other direction, the sloping strips fit dry in their slots and are locked there with bolts through outer pieces. At the corners you could use 3/8-inch bolts through the posts (FIG. 13-11B). Choose carriage bolts; then the square necks will prevent a bolt falling out or turning. An alternative is to use hanger screws (FIG. 13-11C). To drive a hanger screw, drill an undersize hole, and lock two nuts together on the threaded part (FIG. 13-11D). Start the woodscrew end in the hole by a tap with a hammer, then tighten with a wrench on a nut. Finally, release the locked nuts. Have a large washer against the wood, and use a plain nut, or a wing nut on each bolt or hammer screw.

Arrange the outer strips that will fit on the bolt or screw ends with slots (FIG. 13-11E), so you can press the sloping strips tight in their slots and lock them by tightening the nuts. The slots need not be very long. Drill two holes against each other and cut away the wood between.

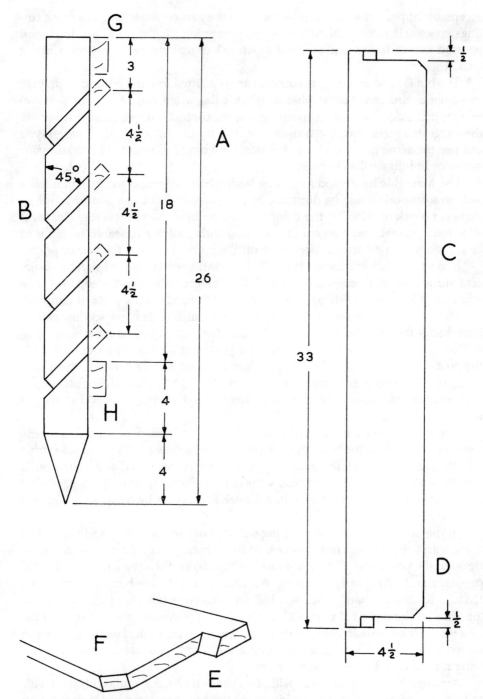

Fig. 13-10. Sizes of posts and slats of the compost bin.

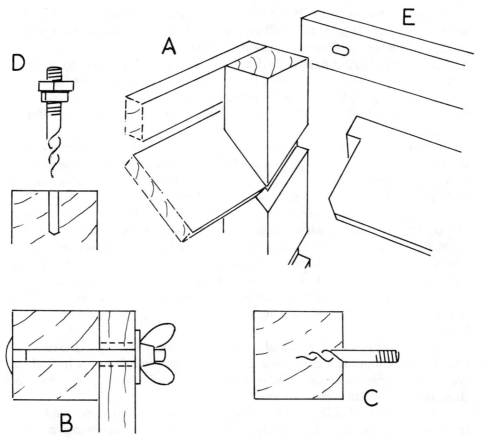

Fig. 13-11. Construction details of the compost bin.

Log Flower Trough

A hollowed piece of natural wood makes a decorative holder for growing flowers or plants. Several of them can be positioned alongside paths, or as borders for gardens. They have the advantage of being portable—if they are not too large—so you can rearrange a garden layout or lift the container on to a deck or other solid surface. You can also take a trough indoors, so that plants can be started early in the season and put outside when the weather gets better.

The main need is for a suitable log. Choose one with a reasonably straight grain, so that you can split it in two. If you can be certain of hitting where you aim, split the log with an ax. Otherwise, use a steel wedge and hammer. If the split follows a slightly wavy line, that can be ignored and treated as a decorative feature. Any large humps should be leveled off.

If you use the trough without legs, make a flat surface underneath parallel with the top (FIG. 13-12A). That will give you an easier hold when you start hollowing. If legs are to be added, make them later.

Hollowing does not have to be done with a great deal of precision, but get a sufficient amount of wood removed to allow plenty of soil to be put in. In cross section, the shape follows the outline (FIG. 13-12B). In the length, there will have to be a curve down (FIG. 13-12C) to leave more thickness at the end grain—for the sake of strength.

Drill into the wood to near the depths you expect to go. A penciled outline on the top will serve as a rough guide. The more holes you drill, the easier it will be to remove the waste. For most of the work, use the largest bit your electric drill will drive or your muscle power will suffice, (if you use a brace).

A large gouge, sharpened on the outside, is the best tool for hollowing (FIG. 13-12D). You can manage with chisels used with their bevels downward. In both cases, the tool goes where you direct it without the tendency to pull deeper; that goes with a tool used bevel upward. Do all chopping toward the center of the log, with the grain or diagonal to the grain. All cuts should slope down toward the center. A cut the other way would lift the grain, and start a split. Driving a chisel in line with the grain would have the same effect, but a gouge would be less troublesome.

Remove the waste in the central area first. Go almost as deep as the final hollow. Further chopping can be toward it. As you progress, you might find you want to go deeper than was drilled originally. Drill again; this requires less effort than more work with a chisel or gouge.

One problem is holding the log. If it is fairly large and you have made a flat underneath, its weight will be enough to hold it against the tool being hit with a mallet. It does not have to be on a bench. You might find it easier to work at a large log on the ground. You could even dig a hollow for it, so it will stay put as you work on it. If it is smaller, you might find an angle somewhere into which it can be put (FIG. 13-12E). Perhaps you could use a porch doorway, while you kneel or sit on a step to work.

Feet can be short lengths of natural wood, tapered to go into holes (FIG. 13-12F). You could use pieces across that are partly in grooves and partly shaped to the log (FIG. 13-12G).

Although anything planted in soil in the trough will need water, guard against too much water. Drill a few holes through the bottom. To prevent the soil from falling through, put stones over the holes. The stones should not fit so tightly that the water cannot get out.

Flower Boxes

Flowers and plants can be grown in pots, or they can be planted directly in boxes you make. Boxes in a garden allows you to alter the layout. They give you extra growing space because boxes can be put on decks, patios, or other hard surfaces.

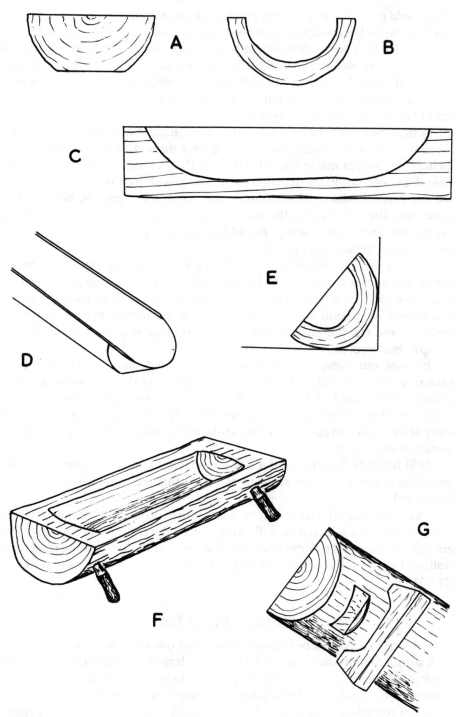

Fig. 13-12. Steps in making a log flower trough.

They could go on top of a wall for plants that can then hang down. Construction needs to be fairly substantial; you need enough soil for plants to grow in.

The size of a box is determined by available boards, or space needs. With plant pots, their size will control the inside measurements. If several pots are to be used, the length will then be a multiple of the width, and the depth has to suit the pots. Do not settle on too tight a fit. You need to be able to lift the pots; they are not always exactly the same size.

A plain box might be all you need. If the foliage is to hang all over the box, there is no point in making the box itself very decorative. For added strength, include the bottom inside the sides (FIG. 13-13A), so that the load on screws or nails does not come in the direction that tends to withdraw them. It is stronger at the end grain if sides overlap the ends (FIG. 13-13B). The greatest bursting loads come near the top. Even if the sides are nailed to the ends for most of their depth, use screws near the top. For added strength, put dowels across the ends for the screw threads to grip (FIG. 13-13C).

Often a plain, rectangular box is all that is needed, but tapers always look better than square corners so the box could be made to flare out toward the top. That is easy to arrange at the ends (FIG. 13-13D), but if you slope them out as well, you have a compound angle at the corners. If the flare is not much, you can ignore it and cut the parts square across. Another way is to leave the ends upright, but bevel extending sides (FIG. 13-13E).

In most situations, raise the box off the ground. Simply put strips across underneath (FIG. 13-13F). If the box is tall or tapers, let the feet extend a little for stability (FIG. 13-13G). A long box will need some intermediate feet. Achieve a similar effect by extending the ends downward (FIG. 13-13H). With a wide box, cut away at the center so support is only at the sides, and steadiness on an uneven surface is easier to get.

Drill holes in the bottom of a box for drainage even if the contents will be pots. Pots are best stood on strips of wood, so that their drainage holes are not obstructed.

Use waney-edged boards for box sides. If the waviness is not much, it could be upward as well as downward. Packings under the bottom will have to be high enough for the uneven edges to clear the ground. If the box is to be placed on a wall, its front could have a straight top. The waney edge could overlap the wall (FIG. 13-13J).

Single Plant Pot

A small tree in a pot can be featured alone or as one of many. Similarly, you can have shrubs that produce large or high foliage. It needs to be in a fairly large container to take care of the roots and the base has to be stable. It can be in a pot that is decorative in itself, but if a wooden container is used, the earth and roots can be put in something that has no beauty in itself (such as a cut-off oil drum or something similar). You could plant directly into the box, but most gardeners

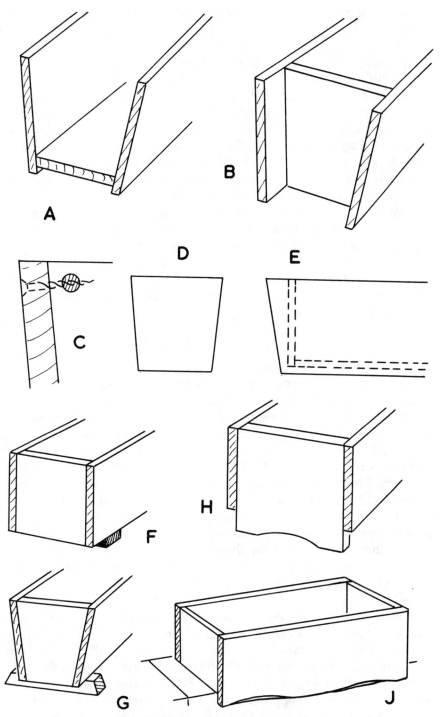

Fig. 13-13. *Construction of flower boxes.*

would prefer to have an inner container that could be lifted out. That would also make the wooden box longer lasting and more accessible for painting or maintenance.

Suitable containers could be made from slabs of sawn wood from a log (with or without a waney edge to the top). One way of making a plain box more interesting is to overlap the sides and cut them to uneven curves (FIG. 13-14A), so they look something like the waney edges along the grain. Such a box should be made with the bottom between the sides and ends above it. Then, put strips across as feet, usually projecting slightly. The strips protect the bottom from direct contact with the ground (FIG. 13-14B), and allow water that drains through holes in the bottom to flow away. Sizes depend on the container and the type of plant, but boxes about 18 inches each way are the sizes to consider for outdoor use.

Boxes do not have to be square or with vertical sides. Much depends on what has to be put inside. If there is a taper, 5 degrees from vertical should be enough (FIG. 13-14C), and the feet should extend far enough for stability.

One interesting variation has four identical sides. One end is cut square or to a slight taper; the other end is cut to irregular curves. They are put together to project in turn (FIG. 13-13D). The bottom should be fitted inside, given drain holes, and supported with feet.

Paneled Plant Pot

For a more formal display, such as a pair of small trees or flowering shrubs at the corners of a porch or deck, build the containers in a cabinetwork construction. Paint to fit in with the home frontage or the furniture on a deck.

The example shown in FIG. 13-15A has a stout framing with exterior plywood panels and a border at the top. The bottom is made from slats to allow drainage. Turned parts are shown at the corners, top and bottom. If you do not have a lathe and cannot buy suitable finials (decorative tops) and feet, the top border could be left plain. Square blocks could be fitted as feet rather than let the end grain of the corner posts rest on the ground and absorb moisture that might cause rot.

All of the frame parts are 2-inch square section. That will be undersize after planing, but it does not matter, as long as you allow for it in cutting joints. Plow grooves in all pieces to suit the plywood (FIG. 13-16A). This is shown as 1/2 inch thick, but it could be thinner. Two of the bottom rails must also be given rabbets to take the bottom slats (FIG. 13-16B). At this stage, have all the parts too long to allow for cutting joints.

Tenon the horizontal rails into the corner posts. Cut back the tenons to the bottoms of the plowed grooves (FIG. 13-16C). The mortises will cut away the grooves, and the meeting grooves will suit the plywood panels. At the top, the border will cover the joints. It does not matter if you make the joints open at the ends of the posts. The posts project below the bottom rails, so the mortises there are closed in any case. Make up two opposite sides. The plywood panels need not bottom in their grooves, providing they are glued in. Allowing some play in the fit of the plywood ensures the corner joints will pull tight.

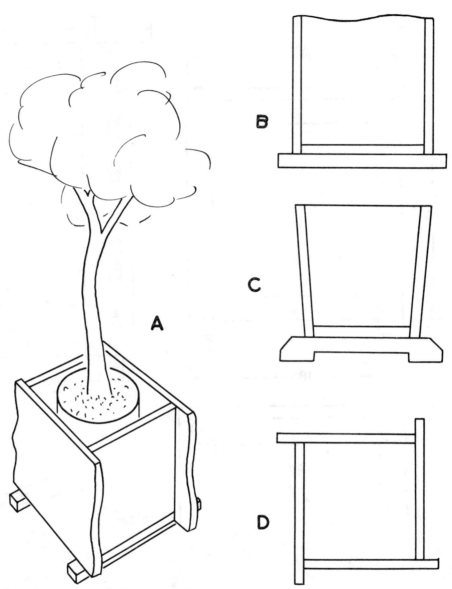

Fig. 13-14. *Construction of a single plant pot.*

Materials List for Paneled Plant Pot

4 posts	2×20×2
8 rails	2×18×2
4 borders	3×21×1
7 bottoms	2×18×1
Turned parts from	2×30×2
4 panels	16×16× 1/2 plywood

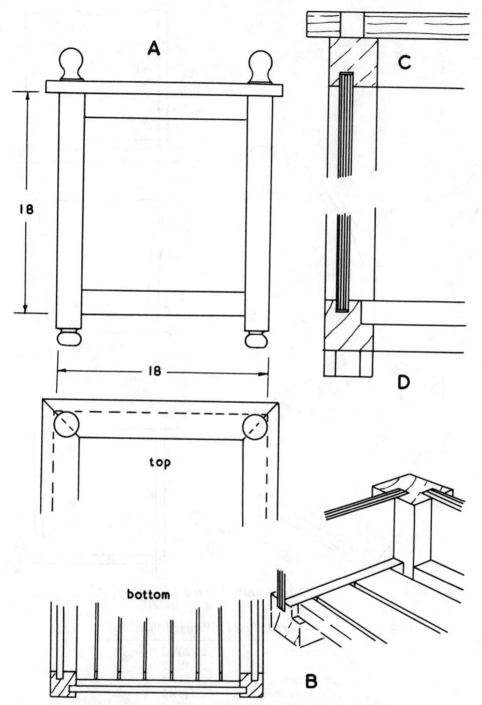

A

18

18

top

bottom

C

D

B

Fig. 13-15. Sizes and construction of a paneled plant pot.

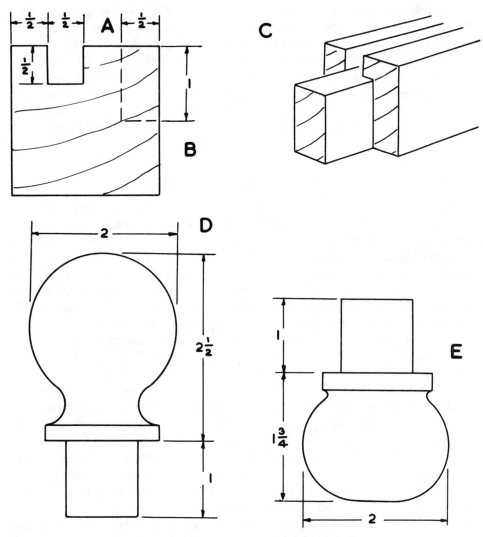

Fig. 13-16. Rails and turned parts of a paneled plant pot.

With the two sides squared and matching, add the parts the other way to complete the side assembly. For the bottom, space the slats to leave narrow gaps (FIG. 13-15B). The strips should be stiff enough. If you think there is risk of sagging, put another slat across the others underneath their centers.

Cut the pieces for the top border carefully, as they are prominent features. Make them level with the insides of the framing, round their outer edges, and cut the miters closely. Glue and nail, or screw the border on.

If you plan to use turned parts top and bottom, drill holes for the dowels on the finials and feet (FIGS. 13-15C and 13-15D). They need not go far into the wood;

1 inch will be enough. The holes could be 1 inch in diameter, but any convenient bit up to that size can be used. At the same time, drill a similar hole in a thin piece of scrap wood to use as a gauge when turning the dowels.

Use your own ideas for turning. Avoid points on the finials (FIG. 13-16D). Make the feet flat, or slightly hollow underneath (FIG. 13-16E). Although the rest of the construction can be softwood, it is better to make the turned parts of hardwood. Hardwood is easier to turn accurately and less liable to suffer damage in use.

This sort of container looks best painted. The color could match its surroundings, but otherwise white is always a safe choice.

Shiplap Plant Pot Holder

Common plant pots are usually functional rather than attractive in appearance, so they are better enclosed. You might not want to spend time making a jointed stand or box, particularly if you need a large number of holders. This plant pot holder (FIG. 13-17) is nailed together; it could be made of scraps from larger projects. The sizes suggested (FIG. 13-18) will take a pot up to 11 inches in diameter, but vary sizes to suit your needs. The height suits three shiplap boards 5 inches wide, but you can vary this considerably without affecting the method of construction. The holder is raised on feet, and there are drainage gaps in the bottom.

Use available wood of different sizes, but as described, the framing pieces are $1^1/2$ inches square and all other wood is $3/4$ inch thick. Sides could be parallel, but a slight taper improves appearance without affecting stability.

Keep the holder symmetrical by drawing the main outline of a side view (FIG. 13-18A) full-size on scrap plywood; use this as a base on which to assemble sides. Start by cutting the corner pieces slightly too long. Lay two on the drawing, and nail on the shiplap boards (FIG. 13-19A). Make the opposite side in the same way. Join the first two sides with boards the other way, overlapping the first boards. Check symmetry and see that the assembly is square at top and bottom. Trim overlapping board ends level, and hollow corners to match the shiplap section. Cut the top and bottom edges of the assembly level.

Put strips around the inside top and bottom (FIG. 13-19B) to fill the spaces between the corner strips. Make the bottom with pieces of almost any available width, but leave gaps (FIG. 13-18B) for drainage. These pieces will also hold the assembly square, so check the shape as you nail in the strips.

Materials List for
Shiplap Plant Pot Holder

4 corners	$1^1/2 \times 16 \times 1^1/2$
8 rails	$1^1/2 \times 14 \times 1^1/2$
12 shiplap boards	$3/4 \times 16 \times 5$
4 tops	$3/4 \times 18 \times 3$
4 feet	$3/4 \times 3 \times 3$

Fig. 13-17. This plant pot holder is made with shiplap boards.

Frame over the top with level strips inside, but projecting ³/₄ inch outside (FIG. 13-18C). Miter the corners (FIG. 13-19C). Put 3 inch, square feet under the corners, also projecting ³/₄ inch (FIG. 13-18D and E). Round all edges and corners; then finish with preservative or paint.

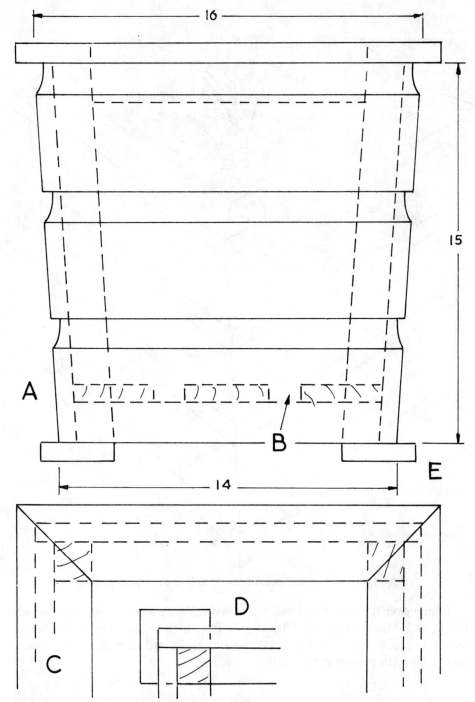

Fig. 13-18. Sizes of the shiplap plant pot holder.

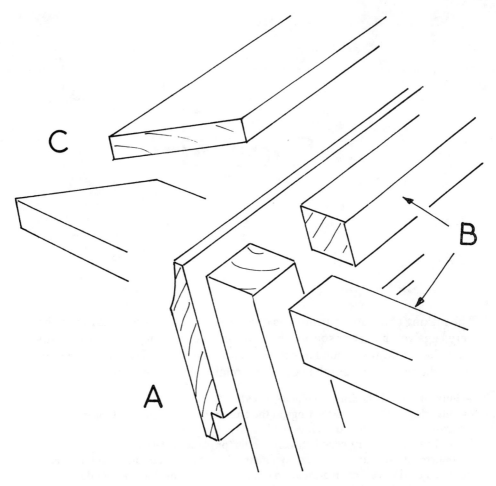

Fig. 13-19. Details at a corner of the shiplap plant pot holder.

Glossary

The making of outdoor furniture is only one branch of woodworking. It shares a very large vocabulary of special terms; a complete glossary of all such words that might be met would be too large for this book. These words are in use today, with the addition of a few obsolete ones that might be encountered.

Alburnum The botanical name of sapwood.

annular rings The concentric rings in the cross section of a tree that form the grain pattern. One ring is added each year.

arris The line or sharp edge between two flat or plane surfaces.

asymmetrical A shape that is not symmetrical or of balanced form about a centerline.

autumn growth Part of an annual ring in a tree. It is formed as the sap descends.

balk (baulk) A roughly squared block of lumber.

ballpeen (pein) hammer A hammer with one side of its head rounded like half a ball.

bamboo Cane sometimes used for furniture. It differs from ordinary wood, in that as it grows the new wood is formed on the inside of a tube.

barefaced tenon A tenon shouldered on one face only.

batten Any narrow strip of wood. A board fitted across other boards to join them (also called a cleat), cover a gap, or prevent warping.

bench stop A wood or metal projection on a bench top. Wood can be pressed against it to prevent movement under a plane or other tool.

bevel An angle or chamfer planed on an edge. Also the name of an adjustable tool used for marking and testing angles.

blind Not right through, such as a stopped hole for a dowel or a mortise for a short tenon.

bracket An angular piece used to strengthen or support a shelf or flap.

cast Twisting of a surface that should be flat.

chaise lounge Literally, a long chair, but more like a bed with an adjustable head board. Sometimes called a chaise longue.

chamfer An angle or bevel planed on an edge.

check A lengthwise separation of the grain in a piece of wood.

cleat Any small piece joining other parts together, but particularly a strip across other boards to hold them together and prevent warping.

clench nailing Using nails long enough to go right through so the projecting ends can be hammered over.

coniferous Cone-bearing. Most softwood trees are coniferous.

conversion The general term for cutting a log into boards and smaller sections of wood for use.

counterbore Drill a larger hole over a smaller one, so the head of a screw is drawn below the surface and it can be covered by a plug.

countersink Bevel the top of a hole, so a flat-headed screw can be driven level with the surface.

cross-lap joint Two pieces cut to fit into each other where they cross.

cup shake A crack that develops in the growing tree and follows the line of an annual ring.

dado joint A groove in wood, cut across the surface to support a shelf or other part.

dead pin A wedge. Sometimes a dowel.

deal Trade name for some soft woods, such as pine and fir, but now less commonly used. Can also mean a plank or board.

deciduous A leaf-shedding tree and the source of most hardwoods.

dovetail The fan-shaped piece that projects between pins in the other part of a dovetail joint. It is cut to resist pulling out.

dovetail nailing Driving nails so they slope slightly at opposite angles and resist the boards being pulled apart.

dowel A cylindrical piece of wood used as a peg when making joints.

draw bore or draw pin A peg or dowel across a mortise and tenon joint to pull the parts together.

ellipse The inclined transverse section across a cylinder. Often wrongly called oval, which is egg shaped.

fastenings (fasteners) Collective name for anything used for joining—such as nails and screws.

feather edge A wide, smooth bevel taking the edge of a board to a very thin line.

fillet A narrow strip of wood used to fill or support a part.

folding wedges Two similar wedges used overlapping each other in opposite directions so they provide pressure when driven.

foxiness The signs of the first onset of rot. It can be regarded as decoration.

foxtail wedging Wedges arranged in the end of a tenon, so it is spread when driven into a blind hole.

gauge A definition of size, such as the thickness of sheet metal or the diameters of wire or screws. Numbers are used in recognized systems.

grain The striped marks seen in wood due to the annual rings.

groove Any slot, cut in wood, such as a dado. Less commonly, a rabbet.

half-lap joint Two crossing pieces, notched into each other, usually to bring their surfaces level.

handed Made as a pair.

hardwood Wood from a deciduous tree. Usually, but not always, harder than softwoods.

haunch A short cut-back part of a tenon that joins another piece near its end.

heartwood The mature wood near the center of a tree.

housing joint Alternative name for a dado joint where a shelf fits into a groove in another part.

jointing The making of any joint, but particularly planing edges straight to make close-glued joints to make up a width.

kerf The slot made by a saw.

knot A flaw in wood due to where a branch left the trunk. A method of joining cords.

laminate Construct in layers with several pieces of wood glued together. Used particularly to make up curved parts. Plywood is laminated.

lap joint The general name for joints where one piece of wood is cut to overlap and fit into another.

laying out Setting out the details of design and construction, usually full size.

marking out Indicate cuts and positions on wood before cutting, shaping, and drilling.

medullary rays Radiating lines from the center of a log. These can be seen in some woods radially cut, but they are invisible in others. The markings are most prominent in oak.

miter (mitre) A joint where the meeting angle of the surfaces is divided or bisected, as in the corner of a picture frame.

molding (moulding) Decorative edge or border that can be a simple rounding or an intricate section of curves and quirks.

mortise (mortice) The rectangular socket cut to take a tenon.

mortise and tenon joint A method of joining the end of one piece of wood into the side of another. The tenon projects like a tongue on the end to fit into the mortise cut in the other piece.

needle-leaf trees Alternative name for cone-bearing trees that produce softwoods.

oil stain Wood coloring with the pigment dissolved in oil.

peck marks Penciled marks used to transfer points on one thing to another.

pedestal A supporting post. A central support for a table or a support at each of its ends.

pedestal table A table with a central support and spreading feet.

pegging Dowels or wooden pegs through joints.

piercing Decoration made by cutting through the wood. Similar to fretwork, but more robust.

pilot hole A small hole drilled as a guide for the drill point, before making a larger hole.

pintle A dowel or peg on which a part pivots. The name is taken from the pivot of a boat rudder.

plain sawn Boards cut across a log.

plywood Board made with veneers glued in laminations, with the grain of each layer square to the next.

quartered (quarter-sawn) Boards cut radially from a log to minimize warping and shrinking, or to show the medullary rays in oak and some other woods.

rabbet (rebate) Angular cut-out section at an edge, as in the back of a picture frame.

rail A horizontal member in framing.

rake Incline to the horizontal.

rod Strip of wood with distances of details of construction marked on it. Used for comparing parts instead of measuring with a rule.

run In a long length. Lumber quantity can be quoted as so many feet run.

sapwood The wood nearer the outside of a tree. Not as strong or durable as the heartwood in most trees.

sawbuck Crossed sawing trestle. The name can be applied to table legs crossed in a similar way.

seasoning Drying lumber to a controlled moisture content in preparation for use in constructional work.

segments Curved pieces of wood used to build up table rails and similar things in round work.

set To punch a nail below the surface. The tool for doing that. The bending of saw teeth in opposite directions to cut a kerf wider than the thickness of the saw metal.

setting out Laying out details, usually full size, of a piece of furniture or other construction.

shake A defect or crack in the growing tree that might not be apparent until it is cut into boards.

shot joint Planed edges glued together.

slat Narrow, thin wood.

softwood The wood from a coniferous, needle-leaf tree.

Spanish windlass A device using rope twisted with a lever to give a tightening effect.

splay To spread out.

spline A narrow strip of wood fitting into grooves. Commonly used to strengthen two meeting surfaces that are glued.

staple Two-ended nail forming a loop. Two-legged fastener driven by a special tool and used instead of tacks for attaching upholstery cloth.

star shake A defect in a growing tree, with cracks radiating from the center.

stiffnut A nut to fit on a bolt that incorporates a means of resisting loosening.

stile Vertical member in chair framing.

stopped tenon A tenon engaging with a mortise that is not cut through the wood. A stub tenon.

stretcher A lengthwise rail between the lower parts of a table or chair.

stub tenon Alternative name for a stopped tenon.

tack Small, tapered nail with a large head.

tang The tapered end of a tool, such as a file or chisel, to fit into its handle.

template (templet) Shaped pattern to draw around when marking out parts.

tenon The projecting tongue on the end of one piece of wood to fit into a mortise in another piece of wood.

tusk tenon A tenon that goes through its mortise and projects at the other side. There it can be secured with a wedge.

underbracing Arrangement of rails and stretchers to provide stiffness between the lower parts of a table or chair legs. Also called underframing.

varnish A near-transparent paintlike finish, once made from natural lacquers, but now usually synthetic.

waney edge The edge of a board that still has bark on it or is still showing the pattern of the outside of the tree.

warping Distortion of a board by twisting or curving because of unequal shrinkage as moisture dries out.

winding A board or assembly is said to be "in winding" when it is not flat and a twist can be seen when sighting from one end.

working drawing A drawing showing sizes—usually in elevations, plan and sections—from which measurements can be taken to make furniture. Not a pictorial view.

Index

Other Bestsellers of Related Interest

GARDENING FOR A GREENER PLANET: A Chemical-Free Approach—Jonathan Erickson

Control pests in your lawn and garden with these environmentally safe methods. Using a technique known as "integrated pest management," this book shows you how to protect food and foliage from destructive insects without contamination from toxins found in chemical pesticides. He explains, in easy-to-follow steps, the correct way to use natural methods such as beneficial insects and organisms, companion planting, minerals of soaps, and botanical insecticides in the war against garden-hungry bugs. 176 pages, 108 illustrations. Book No. 3801, $13.95 paperback, $21.95 hardcover

BRICKLAYING: A Homeowner's Illustrated Guide—Charles R. Self

In this handy do-it-yourself guide you'll learn the basics of bricklaying: how to create different pattern bonds, mix mortar, lay bricks to achieve the strongest structure, cut bricks, finish mortar joints, and estimate materials. You'll also find out how to mix, test, and pour concrete to create foundations and footings for your brickwork. With the step-by-step instructions and illustrations found here, you can build any project with little difficulty. 176 pages, 146 illustrations. Book No. 3878, $14.95 paperback, $24.95 hardcover.

CREATIVE GARDEN SETTINGS
—John D. Webersinn and G. Daniel Keen

Look at the ways you can landscape your property and turn your house into a panorama of outdoor creativity, at the same time increasing the value of your home. Whether you want to build a deck, a patio, a stone fence, or a trickling fountain—nothing is beyond your reach. Keen and Webersinn combine their skills to bring you a well-written guide to everything from building permits to outdoor lighting. 200 pages, 100 illustrations. Book No. 3936, $14.95 paperback, $24.95 hardcover

PSYCHED ON BIKES: The Bicycle Owner's Handbook—B. Andrew Renton

Select, ride, maintain, and repair your own bike. This guide covers all types of bikes—one speed, three speed, and derailleur—and is not brand, make, or speed specific. Plus, it offers valuable advice on what to look for when buying a bike and shows you how to get the best value for your money. 192 pages, 135 illustrations. Book No. 3668, $14.95 paperback only

MAKING SPACE: Remodeling for More Living Area—Ernie Bryant

After you've developed your remodeling plan, this book gives you the step-by-step instructions and diagrams you need to complete your project. You'll find easy-to-follow techniques for constructing space-enhancing attic, garage, basement, full-room, and porch/deck conversions. Plus, easy-to-understand instructions highlight all the important steps of construction, and lead you through the entire process. 248 pages, 262 illustrations. Book No. 3898, $12.95 paperback, $22.95 hardcover

CERAMIC TILE SETTING
—John P. Bridge, Photography by Robert A. Bedient

Discover how easy it can be to install your own ceramic tile floors, walls, and counters for a fraction of what you'd spend to hire a pro. From initial layout to floating and leveling, this easy-to-use guide contains all the information you need to start and finish a professional-looking project. Projects are arranged in order of difficulty and include step-by-step instructions. 244 pages, 165 illustrations. Book No. 4053, $14.95 paperback, $24.95 hardcover

Look for These and Other TAB Books at Your Local Bookstore

To Order Call Toll Free 1-800-822-8158

(in PA, AK, and Canada call 717-794-2191)

or write to TAB Books, Blue Ridge Summit, PA 17294-0840.

Title	Product No.	Quantity	Price

☐ Check or money order made payable to TAB Books

Charge my ☐ VISA ☐ MasterCard ☐ American Express

Acct. No. _____ Exp. _____

Signature: _____

Name: _____

Address: _____

City: _____

State: _____ Zip: _____

Subtotal $ _____

Postage and Handling
($3.00 in U.S., $5.00 outside U.S.) $ _____

Add applicable state and local
sales tax $ _____

TOTAL $ _____

TAB Books catalog free with purchase; otherwise send $1.00 in check or money order and receive $1.00 credit on your next purchase.

Orders outside U.S. must pay with international money in U.S. dollars

TAB Guarantee: If for any reason you are not satisfied with the book(s) you order, simply return it (them) within 15 days and receive a full refund. BC